THIS DIVID

Samanth Subramanian studied journalism at Pennsylvania State University. He has written for, among other publications, the *Guardian*, the *New Yorker*, the *New York Times*, *Mint*, the *Far Eastern Economic Review*, *Foreign Policy*, *New Republic*, *Foreign Affairs*, *The National* and *The Hindu*. His first book, *Following Fish: Travels Around the Indian Coast*, was published by Atlantic Books.

'There is only one word to describe this book: it's a masterpiece, a Book of the Year, even possibly the decade.'
Mani Shankar Aiyar, *India Today*

'Like Philip Gourevitch's account of the genocide in Rwanda, *We Wish to Inform You That Tomorrow We Will Be Killed With Our Families,* this is a superbly reported book.'
Rahul Jacob, *Business Standard*

'A tour de force. Written with journalistic prowess and integrity, the book succeeds in bringing the war uncomfortably close, so close you can smell the blood.'
Vaishna Roy, *The Hindu*

'This is narrative journalism at its most literary, diligently researched reportage presented with poetry and flair.'
Shehan Karunatilaka, *Mint*

'The best book on the subject and, what is more, a book different in kind from nearly all that have appeared this far.'
Shyam Tekwani, *Tehelka*

'The book is not just a journal of reportage but is also a meditation on memory ... Pick up *This Divided Island*; it'll be one of the best books you'll pick up this year.'
Aditya Sinha, *The Asian Age*

'Subramanian's *This Divided Island* is a welcome read, very different from any other book written on this terrible chapter of human struggle. Slow-cooked over a number of years, meticulously constructed and with a passion and sympathy for Sri Lanka and her people, this Tamil Indian writer illuminates the central dilemma established midway through the book, and around which all hinges: What did it take for an ordinary, peaceable Tamil to commit to violence?'
Gordon Weiss, former UN spokesperson in Sri Lanka, *Open*

'To integrate these interviews into a broader historical narrative as seamlessly as Subramanian has done is a rare achievement.'
Keshava Guha, *Scroll*

ഇ‌ဃ

Also by Samanth Subramanian

Following Fish: Travels around the Indian Coast

THIS
DIVIDED
ISLAND

STORIES FROM THE SRI LANKAN WAR

SAMANTH SUBRAMANIAN

ATLANTIC BOOKS

London

First published in hardback in India in 2014 by Penguin Books India.

First published in trade paperback in Great Britain in 2015 by Atlantic Books, an imprint of
Atlantic Books Ltd.

2 3 4 5 6 7 8 9

A CIP catalogue record for this book is available from the British Library.

Trade Paperback ISBN: 978-0-85789-595-0
EBook ISBN: 978-0-85789-596-7
Paperback ISBN: 978-0-85789-597-4

Typeset in Sabon Roman by Servis Filmsetting Ltd, Stockport, Cheshire

Printed and bound by CPI Group (UK) Ltd, Croydon, CR0 4YY
Atlantic Books
An Imprint of Atlantic Books Ltd
Ormond House
26–27 Boswell Street
London
WC1N 3JZ

www.atlantic-books.co.uk

For Sanjaya,
who, like his namesake in the Mahabharata,
opened up the world to his unseeing friend

I wish I could persuade you to regard death
as casually as we do over here. In the heat of it
you expect it, you are expecting it, you are not surprised
by anything anymore . . .

—Jorie Graham,
'Spoken from the Hedgerows'

PREFACE

In May 2009, when the civil war ended in Sri Lanka, the world sat up and took note. Wars rarely end in such punishing victories these days, and all things considered, perhaps that is a blessing. In its crusade to section off an independent state for Sri Lanka's Tamil-speaking minority, a rebel force of guerrillas—the Tigers—found itself squeezed into the north-east corner of the island, hiding behind hundreds of thousands of Tamil civilians on the run. Here the Sri Lankan army, wise to its advantage, rained shells from the sky, wiping out the Tigers but also uncaringly, or even deliberately, slaying thousands of civilians. The United Nations thought more than 40,000 non-combatants must have died in this way—more than 40,000 women, children and men routed from their homes, trapped on the front, baking in the early summer heat, huddling in tarpaulin-covered bunkers, praying for survival. The shells pulverized trees and gouged out the earth. As a pebble does in a tin box, the carnage reverberated particularly loudly within this small island, this knot of rock just off the coast of India.

For a while, the sheer misery and tragedy of these events swamped any ability to think about the full arc of the war. Interrupted only by a couple of short, patchy ceasefires, Sri Lanka fought the Tigers for the better part of three decades. Unwatched by most of the world, the war raged and raged, feeding itself some strange fuel that lent it such durability; it must be among the longest continuous wars since the beginning of the twentieth century, if not the very longest.

It is curious to locate the proximate cause of a war in something as noble as a desire for education. When Sri Lanka broke free of British rule in 1948, the seats in its universities were occupied to disproportionately high levels by the minority Tamils, who through quirks of colonial history spoke better English and were better educated than the majority Sinhalese. The Tamils then went on, after university, to fill the civil service, the country's most reliable provider of employment at the time. To the country's Sinhalese who suddenly found themselves empowered with a vote, and therefore to the government, this state of affairs appeared too lopsided and unfair to continue.

When laws and quotas were enacted to protect the interests of the Sinhalese, the Tamils felt they were being discriminated against. The frictions between the two communities erupted repeatedly into ghastly riots; in the worst of them, the Black July riot in 1983, roughly 3,000 people were killed, many of them burned alive. Tamil houses and shops were looted and burned, and 150,000 Tamils were rendered homeless. When a clutch of Tamil militant groups had begun to emerge in the 1970s, to agitate for a free Tamil state, they found only a trickle of willing recruits; after Black July, though, they were flooded by young men and women wanting to fight, and none more so than the Tigers.

Starting as a ragtag outfit carrying out the odd guerrilla attack, the Tigers grew into a fearsome terrorist organization. They ran arms and drugs, pulled in funds from a Tamil diaspora scattered across the planet, killed thousands of civilians, assassinated presidents and prime ministers, and perfected the art of the suicide bomber. They kept their own people, the Tamils, in line by intimidation and murder. In their full pomp, the Tigers controlled vast wedges of territory in the north and east of Sri Lanka, where flat, hot, sandy coasts meld gradually into jungle. Here they ran their own country in all but name, collecting taxes and policing the streets and adjudicating disputes. But the Sri Lankan state was always just outside the door, impatient to snatch back its land, working itself up into a state of angry nationalism. Buddhism, the religion of most Sinhalese, developed a vocal right wing; its monks entered politics, pressed for a more merciless war, and dreamed of a purely Buddhist island.

The vicious turbulence of these social changes, and of the war itself, made it easy to forget that, underneath it all, there were Sri Lankans trying to lead regular lives: earning a living, sending their children to school, writing novels, playing cricket, making lunch. The very word 'regular' was, in such a lengthy and ferocious war, bent almost unrecognizably out of shape. A regular day came to involve keeping your children from being conscripted by the Tigers or being wary about buses that might have bombs planted within them. It came to involve messy loyalties and scarred psychologies, and being sucked into the fighting in unexpected and devastating ways. The longer the war wore on, the more it transmuted the substance of life, into something simultaneously strange and revealing. I went to Sri Lanka to discover what became of life before, during and after the decades of war, and to find out what the conflict had done to the country's soul.

CONTENTS

Timeline   xv

The Terror   1

The North   91

The Faith   179

Endgames   233

Acknowledgements   319

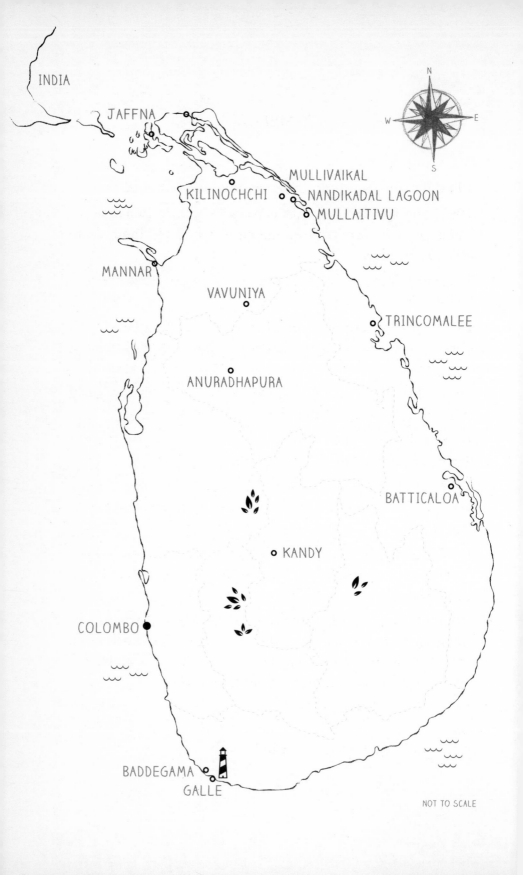

INDIA

JAFFNA

MULLIVAIKAL
KILINOCHCHI   NANDIKADAL LAGOON
MULLAITIVU

MANNAR

VAVUNIYA

TRINCOMALEE

ANURADHAPURA

BATTICALOA

KANDY

COLOMBO

BADDEGAMA
GALLE

NOT TO SCALE

TIMELINE

1948: Ceylon gains independence from Great Britain.

1956: The Sinhala Only Act is passed, making Sinhalese the language of governance and failing to recognize Tamil as an official language.

1958: Anti-Tamil riots break out. An estimated three hundred Tamils across the island are killed.

1971: The government implements the standardization policy, setting higher benchmarks for Tamil students to enter universities.

1972: Ceylon is renamed Sri Lanka, and Buddhism is given 'the foremost place' among the country's religions.

1975: Velupillai Prabhakaran, 21 years old, assassinates the mayor of Jaffna, Alfred Duraiappah.

1976: Prabhakaran creates the Liberation Tigers of Tamil Eelam (LTTE), a successor to his earlier group, the Tamil New Tigers.

1977: Following the general elections, a fresh wave of anti-Tamil riots breaks out. Around three hundred Tamils are slaughtered.

1983: A Tiger ambush of an army convoy in Jaffna triggers the worst anti-Tamil riots yet. Although numbers are unclear, up to three thousand Tamils may have been killed. The ambush is often considered the beginning of the civil war.

1987–90: Indian Peace Keeping Forces swarm across the north and the east, trying without success to eliminate the Tigers. When they retreat, the Tigers hold Jaffna.

1991: In retribution for sending in peacekeeping forces, the Tigers assassinate the former Indian prime minister Rajiv Gandhi.

1993: The Tigers are held responsible for the assassination of the Sri Lankan president Ranasinghe Premadasa.

1995: After a brief truce, the Tigers lose control of Jaffna.

2002: Norway brokers a ceasefire between the Tigers and the government.

2004: The Tigers, having pulled out of peace talks the previous year, go on the offensive to regain the east, signalling a return to hostilities. That December, a tsunami kills 30,000 Sri Lankans.

2005: Mahinda Rajapaksa becomes president of Sri Lanka.

2006: The beginning of the fourth—and last—phase of the civil war.

2007: The government announces that it has cleared eastern Sri Lanka of Tigers.

January 2009: The army captures Kilinochchi, which has served for a decade as the Tigers' capital.

February 2009: Concern mounts over the welfare of civilians trapped in the battle zone.

May 2009: The government announces a victory over the Tigers, even as it shrugs off accusations of bombing civilians. Prabhakaran is killed on the final day of fighting.

2010: Rajapaksa wins re-election to the presidency.

2011: The United Nations releases a report accusing the Sri Lankan army of war crimes. The report estimates that forty thousand civilians may have died in the final months of the civil war.

THE TERROR

1

WE HAD LEFT Colombo too early for me to remain awake on the drive up into hill country. Just past 5 a.m., the streets glowed of sodium-lit emptiness, and Uncle W.'s hatchback skimmed eastwards in silence. It was late August, and there should have been damp, blacker-than-black patches on the tarmac, but there weren't. The rains had been meagre this season, and the days stayed bright and dry. At this hour of the morning, cool air gusted through my open window, and I fell asleep even before we hit the suburbs. I remember that drive in the way we remember the images thrown off by a slide carousel: skittering frames of green banana-tree groves and a pink sky, of MAK Lubricant billboards and little Buddhist shrines, of kiosks selling cream soda and mobile phone recharges, of earthenware shops with pots hanging from the rafters, of papayas and pumpkins displayed in neat cairns on truck tailgates, and of the road's shoulder dropping suddenly away into the valley below and then catching up with us again a few hundred metres later.

Next to me, Uncle W. hunched his bulk over the steering wheel, his eyes devouring the road, the head of the gearstick engulfed within his mammoth left hand. He was a friend's father; this was why, in honest South Asian fashion, I called him 'Uncle.' Uncle W. was a Tamil and a Hindu—minority folded upon minority—and he had lived nearly all his life in Colombo. He used to import and sell prawn feed until the 1990s, when an epidemic of white-spot disease raced through the country's prawn farms, shutting many of them down and driving him entirely out of business. He sold his bungalow in tony Colombo 3, paid back 40 million rupees in loans, and picked himself up again. Now he imported alloy wheels from China: lightweight car wheels crafted in far more exciting designs than the humdrum defaults installed by car manufacturers in their factories. 'Alloy wheels for cars,' he once told me, 'are like lipstick for women.' His voice was so bass that it bordered on the ursine.

Uncle W.'s shipments of alloy wheels rolled in from China once every two months, which left him plenty of time to pursue a line of volunteer work: organizing some of the activities of the Hindu Swayamsevak Sangh (HSS), a group seeking to protect Hinduism from any perceived threat to its existence in Sri Lanka. Given the country's tangled demographics, the HSS could discern such threats to Hindus—all Tamil-speaking—from virtually any direction it chose: from Sinhalese-speaking Buddhists, the country's majority, or from the Christians who speak both Tamil and Sinhalese, or even from the population of Tamil-speaking Muslims, who are considered neither Tamil by the Tamils nor Sinhalese by the Sinhalese, and who therefore dwell in a curious ethnic interstice of their own. The HSS is an earnest but spindly body, its few thousand members acutely aware of their minority status and thus contenting themselves with good works and mild proselytization. 'One fine morning, they'll wake up and find out we've gotten big,' Uncle W. promised. It sounded grand and ominous, but he fell instantly back to earth. 'And then I suppose they'll find a way to shut us down.'

Outside Kandy, we stopped at a *kade* for breakfast: cold string hoppers made of rice, served from behind a glass-fronted display cabinet. Then we drove on. Uncle W. skirted around Kandy and climbed further into the hills, past rubber plantations and small, bashful villages that revealed themselves as the sun dissolved the last of the morning mist. Near the village of Kandenuwara, we slowed down, searching for the local school. Uncle W. didn't know where precisely this was, so he thrust his head and shoulders out of his window to get directions from passers-by: women returning from the market, or men on bicycles pedalling so languorously that their wheels seemed to be rotating through molasses.

We arrived into the midst of some confusion. The HSS had rented this school—and three other schools, in nearby towns—for the full duration of this Saturday, to conduct camps for children. Its volunteers had materialized early to arrange chairs in neat rows and to install, upon the pecan walls of a long classroom, portraits of Hindu deities and of other especial Hindu luminaries. But then the local police had descended upon the school and had commandeered the classroom for a hastily convened citizens' meeting. There were already a few dozen people present when we entered, and more streamed in. The conversations around me seemed to sweat with alarm.

'What's going on?' I asked Ganesh, one of the HSS workers, a young, burly man who had been shifting furniture all morning.

Ganesh replied: 'This must be about the Grease Yakas.'

For weeks, the Grease Yakas had mesmerized Sri Lanka, occupying the front page of every newspaper and the heart of every conversation. There weren't *actually* any supernatural devils—any *yakas*—daubing themselves with grease and attacking women in the countryside at night. They had to be men, and yet that invited only further bewilderment. Which men were these? Why did these attacks occur in predominantly Tamil areas—in the north near Jaffna, or the east, or in lonely patches of hill country? Had the Grease Yakas really affixed metal springs to the soles of their shoes, to enable them to leap over bushes and stiles? Did slathering your body with axle grease truly make you more slippery, harder to hold in a tussle? Most crucially: If they were only men dressed up as greased devils, why had none of them ever been caught?

Fresh theories broke water every day. Officials of the state blamed a Marxist party that had twice, decades before, armed itself and risen against the government. (It was unclear, though, if the Marxists were being accused of *being* the Grease Yakas or of merely fabricating the tales of their antics.) Simultaneously, army officers and policemen denied that there were any greased beings out there at all. In the *Sunday Leader*, a newspaper that had published many eyewitness accounts and even an identikit sketch of a Grease Yaka, a police inspector flatly discounted the stories on the basis that 'grease is harmful to the skin and will result in blocked pores and skin diseases.' He sounded like a cosmetician. Some of the villagers, incredulous but nonetheless frightened, suspected that the Grease Yakas were agents of the state's security apparatus. The hysteria was designed, they thought, only as an excuse to fortify the army's presence in the north and the east. Some Tamils thought that the Grease Yakas were Muslims; some Muslims thought that the Grease Yakas were Tamils.

Round and round the conjecture went, a whirligig of dread and suspicion and naked distrust. The civil war had ended a couple of years earlier, after three decades of murderous fighting; the Liberation Tigers of Tamil Eelam, guerrillas who had sought an independent state for the country's Tamils, had been defeated. But Sri Lanka still felt tense, and the peace was already curdling into something sour and unhealthy. Old fears continued to throb; old ghosts transmuted into new ones.

Ganesh and I sat in on the citizens' meeting, perching on tiny chairs designed for smaller bottoms. He passed me a sign-up sheet, on which I absently scratched my name. Presently the meeting came to order. Three senior police officers, their uniforms rich with braids and badges, sat on plastic chairs, next to a microphone on a stand. The microphone was utterly redundant: the classroom was dead quiet, and the translator— the man the Tamil villagers really needed to hear—was unamplified. The translator summoned up the first police officer, who welcomed the assembly and told them how glad he was that they could all make it. Then he introduced his boss, the town's police chief, and got out of the way.

On display in this fashion, before the microphone, the police chief resembled a boy in a school's theatrical production. He didn't know what to do with his hands, so he first twisted them around each other and then gave them his cap to hold. He fumbled his lines: forgetting that he needed to be translated, he set off at a furious gallop in Sinhalese, while next to him, the translator's eyes grew wide with panic. This was not the plan. Only after a minute or perhaps two did the police chief pause long enough for his words to be rendered into Tamil, but after that he settled down, and the remainder of his speech was dispensed sentence by sentence. 'Basically, I wish to tell you all that there is no such thing as the Grease Yaka,' he said, before slipping into a little abstract music about communities living happily together. He advised his audience not to resort to killing anybody based on mere suspicion. 'I know my people. I know my people are intelligent, and I urge them to treat all this as a lie. There's no need to regard the police or the army with any doubt. We are your protectors. Don't be fooled by these speculations.' His people absorbed this advice without a flicker of emotion.

More speeches followed. A local community organizer in a cream-coloured T-shirt, a skein of coloured talismans tied around his right wrist, harangued his fellow Kandenuwarans in Tamil. They were being unnecessarily scared, he said. 'We're all going back home at 5.30 in the evening and locking our doors. The other day, I went to visit a friend at 7. I knocked on the door, and I could see him at the window, drawing the curtain back to see if I was a Grease Yaka!' This anecdote drew some reluctant titters. 'There's no rule that we're allowed to beat people up before handing them over to the police,' he went on, 'and you know this well. So why would we want to do that? Don't do that.' It was midway between a whining plea and a sturdy call to common sense.

Another policeman appeared, rangy and curly haired. It was only when he delivered his piece in uninterrupted Sinhalese, in the interest of time, that I realized what a token gesture the translator's presence was, the gesture of a country that had just ended a war born out of linguistic grudges. Of *course* they all knew Sinhalese, and Ganesh confirmed this, because how would they get by otherwise? For my benefit, he whispered a translation of this final speech, his breath hot and raspy in my ear.

'One rumour says the Grease Yaka is bald, one says he has long hair, one says he's tall, one says he jumps a lot, one says he has an oiled body. But they're all just rumours. Show me one person who has really seen a Grease Yaka,' the policeman declared. He raked the room with a glare, waiting for somebody to respond to his challenge. 'For 30 years, the Tigers were there. But now they're gone and there's a void, and this is why these rumours will find ground.' Meanwhile, the police chief leaned back in his chair and took photographs, on his mobile phone, of his colleague in mid-speech, and of an audience rigid with attentive silence. They hadn't gathered here just for information on the Grease Yakas; they were also trying to figure out how much they could trust the police to keep them safe.

Uncle W.'s Hinduism camp, anticlimactic after discussions of such dramatic moment, was an amalgam of insecurity, sincerity and blustery chauvinism. First Ganesh led 28 boys in some tuneless Tamil singalongs. Then Uncle W. spoke for many minutes, elaborating upon the grandeur of the Hindu faith. My attention started to wander, and I gazed out of the open windows. The sun was higher now, and the green hills steamed in the distance. After nightfall, I thought, these forests must turn menacing and dark. Perhaps it was easier to believe in demons then—or to believe in inexplicable evil, at any rate.

Towards the end of his speech, Uncle W. exhorted the boys not to fall into the embrace of any other religion. 'All this while, we Hindus haven't cared enough to stop each other from getting converted. Now we should watch out for this. And we have so much support. If the Hindus in this country have a problem, the Hindus living in 50 other countries are ready to help.'

At this point, I was reminded of something he had told me a week earlier, across a table in his alloy-wheel warehouse. We had been drinking tea, and he had been discursive about the war. 'The problem with the Tigers was that they fought their war based on language,' he had said. 'That was a mistake, because language isn't a unifying enough force. These struggles are better organized around religion.' In the morning, Kandenuwara's adults had been soothed and comforted; that same afternoon, their sons were being told that a low-grade fever of wariness was not wholly out of place.

All Sri Lanka was wary; this was a country perpetually steeling itself for bad news. The war had made it this way: the agonizing longevity of the fighting; the Tigers' sneaky guerrilla tactics; the manner in which the army had finished the war, rampaging through Tigers and Tamil civilians without distinction; the government's excesses in the two years since its victory. In such an inflamed atmosphere, rumour prompted quick violence and tragic consequences.

Up the coast from Colombo, in Puttalam, a mob accused the

police of protecting the Grease Yakas and lynched—or beat to death, or hacked into pieces, depending on the newspaper you believed—a traffic constable. Elsewhere, villagers formed vigilante committees, but the army, reflexively hostile to any aggregation of Tamils under any circumstances, waded into these committees and disbanded them by force. I read about some of these incidents in grim, exact reports issued by a small watchdog group in Colombo. In the north, in Thottaveli, army jeeps thundered towards a small crowd of Tamils assembled near a church, and '20 officers got down from the vehicle and started beating the people. Women and children were also in the crowd and were attacked.' Later in that same church, the report offered by way of black comedy, the army called a meeting, where a brigadier 'ordered the people to apologize for attacking the military and for breaching the peace.' Further east, 11 Tamil men were arrested, and two of them were beaten. 'The officers dragged me up and asked: "Will you hit the police?" one of these men said. 'When I tried to tell them that I did not hit the police, they asked me to shut up . . . When he hit my ears, I felt an electric shock pass through my body.'

Sri Lanka was a country pretending that it had been suddenly scrubbed clean of violence. But it wasn't, of course. By some fundamental law governing the conservation of violence, it was now erupting outside the battlefield, in strange and unpredictable ways. It reminded me of a case of pox, the toxins coursing below the skin, pushing up boils and pustules that begged to be fingered and picked apart.

After a delayed lunch, Uncle W. and I and three others squeezed into Ganesh's geriatric Nissan van, with its squeaky seat springs and its windshield decal of a crucifix with the legend: 'My presence shall go with thee.' ('I bought the van from a pastor here,' Ganesh explained, embarrassed, 'and I still haven't gotten around to peeling that sticker off.') We drove half an hour to a school in Rattota, where another camp was puttering too slowly to a close. Two hours' worth of activity remained in the day's programme, but they had only half an hour left on the clock. Twenty-five girls were standing in rows in front of a fluttering saffron flag planted in a flowerpot, singing prayers in ragged unison. Our arrival precipitated a short break for tea, during which the girls' instructors—three women, not even out of their twenties, from villages near Rattota—joined us in a classroom. It was inevitable: within five minutes, we were talking about the Grease Yaka.

Night fell suddenly in these parts, like a tent collapsing upon unsuspecting campers. By the time the girls regrouped in another classroom to listen to Uncle W.—who told them that Guglielmo Marconi had swiped a Hindu scientist's notes about shortwave communication when they were both travelling on the same ship, but that they should nevertheless write 'Marconi' if they were asked who invented the radio in their exams—all of the schoolhouse's lights needed to be turned on. The hills around us were consumed by the gloom, and Rattota grew enormously quiet. It was barely 7 p.m.

Outside the classroom, even as Uncle W. was winding down his lecture, a worried conversation was taking place between the three women, Ganesh and his colleagues. The girls and their instructors needed to get home, but nobody wanted to travel in the dark. Ganesh, his smile now flickering and its wattage definitely dimmed, proposed that they might all call their parents and then stay in the school for the night.

'I thought you didn't believe in the Grease Yaka, Ganesh,' I teased.

'I don't! I don't!' Ganesh replied. 'But look, there's no point taking chances.' Much of Rattota's population was Muslim and relations between the Muslims and the Hindus were not good. He never outlined what he thought the Muslims might do to these young women walking or riding the bus home. 'And then there's always the army. It's just better to be safe.'

An azan burst from a nearby mosque, calling the faithful to the final prayer of the day. It reminded Ganesh of a joke about an ancient contest of power between Allah and the Hindu god Anjaneya. 'They tell this joke a lot here,' he said. 'Allah won the toss, and he hit Anjaneya first. His blow was so powerful that Anjaneya disappeared, and he didn't return for 55 minutes. There were five minutes left to go in the fight, and everybody who was watching thought Allah had won. Then Anjaneya came back, and he just tapped Allah lightly on the chest. And the Muslims have been looking for him five times daily ever since.'

The joke received only broken laughter. The azan wailed on. Within our tight circle, the conversation pulsed with nervousness and fear. Above Sri Lanka, the skies brooded and faded to black.

2

IN CONVERSATIONS ABOUT politics in Sri Lanka, and therefore in conversations about the war and the peace, rumour forms the chief currency. Everybody appears to have their own particular runnels of information, flowing from indistinct sources. Even the newspapers, rather than investigating rumours, just transmit them onwards through columns of political gossip. But in the absence of definitive fact, a certain measure of knowledge can be gleaned from the outskirts of hearsay. Perhaps, like real currency, rumour even keeps things liquid, because it does not always require you to commit to an opinion or to modify your views. During the war, this must have been a useful quality.

On buses and trains, in tea shops and on verandas, in Colombo and Jaffna and a dozen other places, the rumour mill never stopped churning. The momentous and the trivial were relayed with equal urgency. The Grease Yaka was just one man on the move, criss-crossing the country on his well-lubricated tour of terror. A former president, now long dead, used to insist on being bathed by virgins. The Tigers were rearming. Gillian Anderson, the actress from *The X-Files*, had bought a house just outside Colombo but was now reconsidering her decision because she felt the country was too unsafe. The government was repopulating the north and the east by moving thousands of Sinhalese families up from the south, settling them on farmland snatched from the Tamils. One of the president's brothers had installed a tank full of sharks on his lawn. In the north, the army was abducting Tamils at random. In the north, the army was *not* abducting Tamils at random. The opposition was being paid off to lie low. Funds stashed overseas by the Tigers were being siphoned back into the country, and so the fighting would soon begin again.

When I had newly moved to Sri Lanka, in the gummy summer of 2011, this flood of rumour was disorienting: there was too much information and, at the same time, there was not enough. I learned, over months, to sieve what I heard, just as I learned to subconsciously note the precise moment when an innocuous chat broke away into a discussion of the war. It rarely took long, and that was not surprising. The Sri Lankans I met had lived most of their lives watching their country at war with itself. In Jaffna or in Batticaloa—the north and the east, which the Tigers had wanted to peel away from the rest of Sri Lanka—it was an abject impossibility to meet anybody who had not lost a friend or a relative in the *prachanai*. (The Tamil word translates into 'the problem,' which always reminded me of the Troubles, the Irish term for their own three decades of conflict.) In Colombo too, where the Tigers had executed countless attacks on civilians and politicians, and where security policy was made, the war hovered above every conversation, waiting to insinuate itself at the most slender of opportunities. The change of topic could happen imperceptibly, or it could happen abruptly.

'India?' somebody would ask me in Jaffna. 'Where are you from, in India?'

'I live in New Delhi,' I'd reply.

'But you speak Tamil.'

'Yes, my family is from Tamil Nadu. I'm Tamil too. I grew up in Madras.'

'Madras. I know Madras. I've been there. I went away to

Madras to live with an aunt when the fighting got very bad around here. That was in 1987.'

And then we would be off.

It never required much to begin a conversation in Sri Lanka. The very air was primed for it. In a country so full of uncertainty, all life, and all death, was rehearsed through conversation. It was a form of art, well honed and practised with skill. Just as much information was solicited as given. Threads of thought spun out into fractals. Conversations became explorations, really, shifting and moving and pushing gently at the boundaries of their authors' knowledge. Time, never in a hurry in Sri Lanka anyway, slowed down even further.

My friend Sanjaya was one of the masters of this art. He was a big man in every way—tall and broad and nearly bald, and then with a personality that was even larger than his physical frame. Sanjaya was an intermittent journalist, having studied briefly in Madras. He would work producing news documentaries for a few weeks, nose diligently applied to grindstone; then his pace would slacken, and he would play video games and watch movies for a couple of months. It was impossible not to like him. He was curious about everything, and he told yarns tall and magnificent, embellishing on the run and possessing such a fondness for the absurd that he giggled as if he were hearing the tale and not narrating it. When he laughed, his eyes narrowed into letterbox slits, he quivered noiselessly, and his shoulders heaved. His mirth was tectonic.

When I moved to Colombo, I first stayed with Sanjaya, in his family's house on the outskirts of the city. We had several friends in common, but Sanjaya was also a popular point of first contact for journalists arriving in Sri Lanka. It was, I think, because of his eternal willingness to sit and swap stories, to examine all Sri Lanka and even all creation over a single bottle of beer. Journalists yearn for people like Sanjaya.

'Come, we'll go to Machang?' he'd say, so we'd set out for the pub, which was owned by a brewing company and served its beer in tall plastic towers with a core of ice. A dour fug of smoke hung always in its rooms, and Sanjaya added to it with frequent, well-relished cigarettes. Around us, young men in tight T-shirts inhaled their beer and ate hot buttered cuttlefish and played pool.

'So I met this guy in Mullaitivu, right?' Deep drag. 'He got 25,000 rupees because he was a refugee, and he's set up a local cinema with it! He has a 25-inch television and a DVD player and a generator and 30 or 40 chopsocky movies from the 1980s.' Silent laughter. Deep drag. 'And during the day, he charges mobile phones on his generator. This is his living.' Deep drag. 'I wonder what the other refugees do with the money they get.'

This was how Sri Lanka sucked me in deeper and deeper: by discussing itself incessantly. The more I listened to Sanjaya, and then to others, the more the country and the history of its war revealed itself to me. A bigger, clearer picture always dangled just out of reach, around the corner of another conversation or two. Sanjaya made me realize that all I wanted to do was to wander around the island and talk about the one subject that everybody wanted to talk about. The war loomed too close to hand and too enormous for my senses to grasp it properly, like a wall that spread away to infinity in every direction. But in conversations, I heard stories of individuals—fantastic or tragic or melancholic or even happy stories, stories that had human proportions, and that could be multiplied in my head to gain a larger truth.

It was like this when I had first visited Sri Lanka too, with a friend in 2004, for a week's holiday. A ceasefire was officially in force, but the Tigers and the army still attacked each other with regularity, as if they were keeping themselves in practice for the eventual return to open warfare. The streets of Colombo teemed with metal barriers and security checks; we were advised to carry our passports wherever we went. Once, in a trishaw, we asked our driver if the fortified white building we had just passed was Temple Trees, the prime minister's residence. He half-swivelled around and rolled a suspicious eye over us, wondering why we wanted to know.

We stayed at the Grand Oriental Hotel, near the harbour. It was once magnificent, we could see, but it had acquired that distinct shabbiness that comes to a building too deeply entrenched in the past. The ceilings were too low, and the dark-wood fixtures swallowed light, creating unsavoury corners and an atmosphere of grime. The breakfast room looked down upon the harbour, and here every morning we ate string hoppers, watched container ships come in to berth, and read in the newspapers about the slow evaporation of the ceasefire.

On our second night there, after my friend had gone to bed, I was still restless, and I went down into a club in the hotel's basement, looking for a drink. I sat at one end of the neon-lit room; at the other end was a man sitting amidst three women on a couch. Unrecognizable music poured through tinny speakers. There was no one else around. It was the most profoundly depressing club I had ever visited.

After 15 minutes, the man loped over and sat on the next chair. He never once glanced around at me; he gazed steadily at the women and asked, in English: 'Which one of them would you like?'

I explained that I wasn't in the market. He shrugged affably and continued to sit beside me, both of us sipping our drinks. Then a question struck him. 'Are you a tourist?'

I was, I said.

He nodded very rapidly, seven or eight times in a row. 'So

what do you think?' he asked. 'Will the ceasefire hold?' It had been a smooth, easy transition, from the subject of prostitution to the subject of the war. I sat on for another half hour, talking politics with a pimp.

We travelled a little on that trip, down the coast to the beach in Bentota and then up to Kandy to see the Temple of the Tooth, which holds, somewhere out of sight, one of the Buddha's canines. The hulking apparatus of a country in wartime—the endless security checks; the soldiers milling around, caressing their machine guns; the reports and rumours of violence—lost its novelty within that single week. It gave me pause when I realized this. If the extraordinary was so quick to become the ordinary, what must the routine business of life have been like for those trapped in the very heart of the war?

In its most hackneyed perception, the island of Sri Lanka is shaped like a teardrop. But it also looks like the cross section of a hand grenade, with the tapering Jaffna peninsula, up north, forming the top of its safety clip. Or perhaps this resemblance exists entirely in my fancy. I cannot remember a time when I could think about Sri Lanka without thinking immediately about its war. By the time I was able to understand the contents of Indian newspapers, the conflict was already a decade old and grinding through one of its bloodiest, most complicated phases. From Tamil Nadu, where I did much of my growing up, the nearest Sri Lankan sandbar lies just 29 kilometres away; the ties of politics and language bind Sri Lanka close to Tamil Nadu, like a tugboat to an ocean liner.

So it never surprised us when news from Sri Lanka made bigger headlines than news from distant New Delhi; in fact, that seemed only appropriate, living as we did in Madras, the capital of Tamil Nadu but also of the world's community of Tamils. The war became a constant acquaintance. It proceeded without relent as I grew older, finished school, obtained my university degrees, fell in and out of love, changed jobs, moved countries. Its constancy amazed me. Sometimes it even ripped gashes directly into the fabric of our daily lives. Once, on an overnight train from Hyderabad to Madras, my mother and I awoke with a start at 2 a.m. to find that we'd halted, unscheduled, at a tiny station. Outside our window, the platform swarmed so busily with people that it might have been noon; jumbled conversation filtered into our carriage.

'What's going on?' my mother asked a passer-by.

Somebody had just assassinated Rajiv Gandhi, the former prime minister who had, in the late 1980s, sent peacekeepers into Sri Lanka and earned himself the enmity of the Tigers. Late the previous night, he had been campaigning in a small town just outside Madras, and he had allowed a toothy, bespectacled woman with flowers in her hair to garland him. Then, as she bent down to touch his feet as a mark of respect, she flipped a switch on her suicide vest.

I wondered about this woman—about the sort of village she came from, why she had joined the Tigers, how she had accepted the need to blow herself up. Then I wondered about the stories of other people—the displaced, the bereaved, the chauvinist, the young—that were being drowned out by din of the fighting. I grew curious about the island that was producing these stories, and that remained pitched into war for decade after decade. We all live now in societies inured to violence, but the violence of a full-fledged war is unique in its refusal to hide, in how openly it declares its intent to harm other men and women. I wondered how a country transformed when such violence started to feel routine instead of rare—or even whether it could ever feel routine—and how people tried to reclaim and lead an ordinary life out of all this extraordinariness.

Beginning around 2004, I started to visit Sri Lanka on

brief trips, on holidays or to report travel articles, taking the 50-minute flight from Madras to Colombo; later still, I met and wrote about some of the 100,000-odd Sri Lankan Tamil refugees in Tamil Nadu, people who had streamed out of their country and across the Palk Strait into India ever since the early 1980s. On the day the war finally ended, in May 2009, I sat in a newsroom in New Delhi, unable to look away from the images flashing on television. By this time, reports had leaked out of Sri Lanka about the steep toll of the war's last months, and about the army's uncaring shelling of Tamil civilians as well as Tiger militants. The United Nations would conclude that 40,000 civilians had been killed in the army's push to wipe out the Tigers. The television showed snatches of these battlegrounds, on the coast in the north-east. The land looked as if it had been crumpled by some giant hand: the vegetation flattened, the earth clawed out, the water turbid.

With the end of the war, a rare window opened up—for reconciliation, but also for people to talk about their lives as they had been unable to for almost thirty years, and for a different history to be stitched out of these stories. Two years later, in 2011, I arrived in Sri Lanka in the spirit of a forensics gumshoe visiting an arson site, to examine the ashes and guess at how the fire caught and spread so cataclysmically, but also to see if any embers remained to ignite the blaze all over again.

3

AFTER A WEEK at Sanjaya's house, through some blissful luck, I found myself an apartment on a hushed cul-de-sac off Park Road, on the first floor of a bungalow that presented to the world only high walls frosted with barbed wire and a heavy rolling gate painted a Tiffany blue. The bungalow sat on the perimeter of a large municipal cricket ground, around which I thought I might run for exercise. In all my months in Colombo, I never lapped that cricket ground once.

By trishaw, the Tamil quarter of Wellawatte was 10 minutes away in one direction; in the opposite direction, at approximately the same distance, lay the Galle Face, a strip of promenade that adhered to the shore of the Indian Ocean. I was so close to the coast that, in my living room with the windows flung open, I could smell rain even when the clouds were still out at sea. There were grocery stores and restaurants around the corner and a hospital, should I need it, down the road. It was a lovely place to live—and yet, when I told Sanjaya about it, he cackled with glee and said: 'Ah, that's right near Douglas's house!'

Douglas Devananda was one of the bizarre characters that the war had helped create, and it was incredible that he had even survived long enough to temporarily become my neighbour. He had eluded death so often and so theatrically that the story of his life seemed to really require the services of a medieval balladeer to do it justice. Douglas—always called

Douglas, never Devananda—had been a young Tamil leading a militant group that rivalled the Tigers. After being arrested several times in Sri Lanka and India, he made a seamless transition into politics, hitching himself to mainstream Sinhalese-dominated parties, criticizing the Tigers, and running government ministries, his newfound wealth and power making up amply for being known as a Tamil turncoat.

The Tigers tried to assassinate Douglas 11 times, and they failed with astonishing consistency. In 1998, for instance, Douglas walked out of the hospital in mere days after a visit to the Kalutara prison, when Tiger inmates set upon him and shredded his torso with shivs. He emerged unhurt—but his secretary died—after a Tiger suicide bomber blew herself up in 2007, on the premises of the Ministry of Social Services and Social Welfare, where he worked as minister. His most swashbuckling escapade came one evening in 1995, when Tigers stormed his Park Road house, lobbed hand grenades at his security guards, and raced up to his first-floor office. Douglas, the tale goes, pulled a pistol out of a desk drawer, shot out the lights in his office, and used the darkness to leap off his balcony and then vault the gate on to the road.

'I talked to the security guard at that house once,' Sanjaya told me, by now rocking with giggles and enjoying my round-eyed amazement. 'He said Douglas's sarong got caught on the gate as he jumped over it. Then the Tigers jumped the gate too. So Douglas is running down the street in his underwear and firing his gun back over his shoulders, trying to pick off the guys who are chasing him.'

This frantic clash of gunslingers was the first thing that Sanjaya recalled when he thought about the quiet pocket of the city where I had decided to stay.

Colombo never stopped feeling layered in this manner. It wore over all else a mantle of bluff charm. Its people were laid-back and so convivial that, to someone from a harder and more inhibited country, they seemed to live within winking distance of hedonism. Its houses were large, its boulevards leafy, its arrack bottomless and its pace leisurely. Even its weather abetted the city's relaxed disposition: the day's few hours of peak heat, when the sun bronzed the nape of your neck, gave way reliably to evening sea breezes, the air fresh and seasoned with salt. But then, in abrupt ways, the veneer would peel away just a little, and I would get a glimpse of the hidden warts and scars, the anxieties and tensions. This made Colombo constantly surprising and utterly disconcerting, a very easy city to settle into but a difficult one to get to know.

One evening, I went for a ride around the city with Indi Samarajiwa, a young blogger who had grown up in the United States and Canada and had then moved to Sri Lanka, a country his parents had left decades ago. I waited for him at the Independence Memorial Hall, a rectangular pavilion modelled on the royal audience chamber of the Kandyan kings, guarded by magnificent stone lions with arched tails, and watched over by a statue of Don Senanayake, the first prime minister. Friezes of scenes from Sri Lanka's Buddhist history ran around the pavilion's interiors, just below the ceiling and above the stubby stone pillars that propped up the roof. The country's official Buddhist flag flapped atop a pole just outside the hall. It had been planted by President Mahinda Rajapaksa during the Buddhist festival of Wesak in 2010, one year after the war ended. The flag's installation was a celebration of a second independence, but it was also a loud signal of majoritarianism—an affirmation of Sri Lanka's Sinhalese Buddhist core and its triumph in the war.

It had begun to pour by the time Indi arrived to pick me up: spheroid, obese drops of rain that popped and burst as they landed on the windshield. Indi, a year younger than me, had hair buzzed close to his head, a lightly sprouted beard, and large eyes that shone in the gloom inside the car. 'I should show you some of the city,' he said, and then he queued up a batch of Led Zeppelin songs, adjusted his rear-view mirror, and drove off.

The Independence Memorial Hall, Indi said, had been attacked by a terrorist in 1995, a man who had sold coconuts from a cart for three years before he strapped a bomb on to the cart and trundled it down here. This building now, this is the Cinnamon Gardens police station. It's a lovely building, but I hadn't even seen it properly until last year, because they had protective walls all around it. That's the case with a lot of buildings in Colombo actually, no? The prime minister's house, for instance, you couldn't have seen that either, during the war, because of the walls. Ah, right here, this spot, this is where a trishaw with a bomb in it hit the Pakistani ambassador's convoy—at least, I think it was the Pakistani ambassador's convoy—because Pakistan was giving military aid to the Sri Lankan government. Okay, this is an area called Slave Island. You see that hotel, the Nippon Hotel? A bomb blew up a bus next to it, around lunchtime. On this side, this is the Beira Lake, and now we're passing the building where all the tax records are kept. A light aircraft, on a Tiger bombing run, crashed into it a few years ago, although it was probably aiming for another target. Was that the bombing that nobody paid attention to because everybody was watching the cricket World Cup final? I can't remember. And this is the Central Bank building. You must have heard of this place, no? The Tigers bombed it in 1996. They drove a truck of explosives through its gate. This is awful traffic. But Pettah is the old part of the city, and it's always crowded like this. The riots in 1983 were particularly bad in Pettah. Shops were burned down, people murdered, that kind of thing. This road we're on, it goes to a suburb called Maradana. On this spot, on Armour Street, the Tigers killed President Premadasa. A suicide bomber blew him up in 1993. See, now we're driving by the naval headquarters. Four or five years ago, if you were in a car on this road, you'd be stopped again and again so that the police could check your ID. It still feels strange to drive through without hitting any checkpoints at all. On the waterfront, around this area, the army held an exhibition last year, of stuff they captured from the Tigers, even the ammo they used, that kind of thing. I have photos of some of it back home. Remind me later. I'll show them to you.

After 90 minutes, just as the Led Zeppelin set was nearly spent, Indi pulled up to my house and promised gaily that we'd meet again soon for a beer. The rain was whipping Colombo hard, soaking me as I fumbled with the slick lock of the rolling gate. I sprinted across the yard and up into the apartment. Then I sat in the living room, with the lights still off, dripping on to the tiles and listening to the wind careen over the damaged city outside the door.

Colombo is named for its harbour. The etymology runs to the ancient Sinhalese for either 'the port on the river Kelani' or to 'the port with the mango trees,' but either way, the harbour is crucial. It is almost perfectly U-shaped, formed by the main coastline and a crooked finger of land that seems to beckon travellers from across the seas. The harbour first drew Roman, Chinese and Arab traders, then Indian Muslims—'Moors,' as Sri Lankans call them—who settled in Colombo, and finally the conquering successions of the Portuguese, Dutch and British empires. The empires have withered, but the harbour holds, bristling with derricks and ships with yawning holds, the docks stacked neatly with multicoloured containers, looking like building blocks in the play pen of an outsized but organized child.

The cultural force that has most deeply imprinted Colombo and Sri Lanka, however, arrived on the wings of neither commerce nor colonialism. Nine months after Siddhartha

Gautama became the Buddha, local legend has it that he came to Sri Lanka for the first time and chose it as a haven for his religion. The Buddha visited twice more, launching himself upwards from India and landing in Sri Lanka, and travelling around the country with colossal bounds. So smitten was he with this island that, when he was on the brink of nirvana, he is thought to have told his disciple Sakka: 'My faith will be established in Lanka.' Later, three centuries before the birth of Christ, the Indian king Ashoka dispatched his son Mahinda to spread Buddhism in Sri Lanka, sending with him a sapling from the tree under which the Buddha attained enlightenment. 'Go to convert Lanka,' the god Indra is said to have urged Mahinda. 'It has been foretold by the Buddha. We gods will help you there.' Indra kept his word. Seven out of ten Sri Lankans are Buddhists, and even though Christianity, Hinduism and Islam are all present and vibrant, the state considers itself officially and unabashedly Buddhist.

The Buddha is everywhere in Colombo: in the name of Bauddhaloka Mawatha, the arterial avenue that begins a block from the ocean and hustles through the city's heart; in the cream or white pagodas that emerge abruptly out of clusters of other buildings; in decals pasted on trishaw windshields; on banners and flex billboards, alongside the images of prominent, shaven-headed monks; on artefacts distributed throughout the vitrines of the national museum; in tiny neighbourhood shrines; or even by himself on road corners, seated cross-legged in sculpture, his amused, heavy-lidded eyes surveying the people he has entrusted with his message.

The Isipathanaramaya Temple stood halfway around the circumference of the cricket ground near my house, its loudspeakers positioned perfectly to flood my bathroom with Buddhist chants every morning. Each panel on the head-high outer wall of the temple complex was carved with the Wheel of Life and two deer, recalling the deer park in the old Indian town of Isipathana where the Buddha preached his first sermon. The temple was next to an intersection that was always clogged with grinding, belching minivans, but a limpid silence surrounded me as soon as I passed through the temple's gate into its brick-floored courtyard. Near a modest, bell-shaped pagoda, a Bodhi tree thrust into the sky, its lower branches festooned with Buddhist flags or with talismanic strips of cloth knotted into place by pilgrims. Whatever time of day I visited, I would see at least one old woman— her feet ritually bare, her sari as white and unadorned as the pagoda—sitting in the Bodhi's green-black shade, her lips fluttering in prayer. Inside the temple were the titanic, saffron-robed Buddhas: one reclining on its side and another seated, both surrounded by a swarm of frescoes. These Buddhas had no trace of the beatific peace that some other statues wore; instead, they looked brawny and purposeful, and the seated Buddha positively glowered at the raggedy offerings of flowers by his feet.

The Sinhalese like to think of their Buddhism as muscular. Their faith had seeded and nourished itself in Sri Lanka, and it had proven hardy enough to thrive here, even as it crumbled under the weight of Hinduism in India, the land of its birth. A politician from a Sinhalese nationalist party once described to me the Sri Lankan state's relationship with Buddhism 'as equal to that between the Vatican and Catholicism, or between Saudi Arabia and Islam. Actually, it's superior to those, because our record is much older than either of these two countries.' Sinhalese Buddhism is a coiled and wary creature, its reflex always to be aggressive in defence. Since 2006, when the Sri Lankan government had started winning the war, and after its victory in 2009, this ready Buddhist aggression had fused with military triumphalism. There were signposts to this odd and disquieting mixture all over Colombo, if only you knew where to look.

One lazy day, reluctant to work and itching to get out of
the house, I called Mahesh, a friend who worked at a non-
profit nearby and whose beard reminded me of the beards
of bees that carneys wore in old photographs. Mahesh had
once been a doctoral student in sociology, and he had decided
that he wanted to write a dissertation on 'Urban Buddhism,'
on how Buddhism constantly reworked the city, often to
its detriment. 'I had been watching the changes around me,
taking photographs, burning them on to CDs, and so I wrote
up this proposal for my PhD,' he said. First the university
senate asked him to change the title and the text, because
they weren't too crazy about the phrase 'Urban Buddhism.'
After he rewrote the proposal, the senate told his adviser:
'This isn't a proper topic. Ask him to change it to something
else.' Mahesh dropped out of his PhD program, but he never
stopped noting and mulling over the shifting cityscape around
him.

We took a trishaw ride that day. It was early afternoon,
a time when schools were letting out and when Colombo's
roads were routinely engorged with minivans full of children,
all baking cheerfully in the sun. For many minutes on end,
we would sit in one place, crunched in on all sides by these
minivans. A break would appear, and our trishaw would
stagger forward with gasps, like an old man who had not used
his legs in weeks. Then the walls would close back around us.
Mahesh, who possessed the patience of a mountain, gazed out
of the trishaw and pointed out things I should see. He laughed
often, as if reminding himself of the absurdity of these things
helped to shrink the dismay he really felt.

This sort of bus, for instance, Mahesh said, indicating a
particularly noxious specimen stranded in traffic next to us:
'These buses began to appear right after the war ended.' A
long poster on the bus's flank bore the name and photograph
of the Sri Lankan president, an image of a pink flower, and a

slogan in Sinhalese: 'This is the kingdom of Gautama Buddha.' New roadside shrines to the Buddha were emerging all over the city, Mahesh said, as were new clusters of loudspeakers to broadcast Buddhist chants. Once, when our trishaw had idled for a quarter of an hour in the same knot of traffic, Mahesh pulled me out and steered me to a pedestal on the shoulder of the road. On it, a framed photograph of Gangodawila Soma Thero, a right-wing monk who had died in 2003, stood within a glass case, alongside flowers and an extinguished oil lamp. 'This whole practice of worshipping the monks themselves, rather than the Buddha—this was never done before,' Mahesh said. 'I have only started to see it this commonly over the last five or six years.'

We stopped briefly at the Devram Maha Viharaya temple, so that our trishaw driver could go pick his daughter up from school and return to us. The temple had been built on land donated by the parents of a lieutenant colonel in the army who had died in the war. It was larger and richer than any other temple that I had yet seen in Colombo, sprawling through many shrines and pavilions, all of them prominently annotated with the names of sponsors. Dozens of eight-foot-tall slabs of granite, sombre as tombstones, had been planted upright at points around the temple complex, serially inscribed with the text of the Tripitaka, the Buddhist scriptures.

Inside one of the shrines, a fresco had been funded by the parents of soldiers who had died during the war. It showed the Buddha, radiant with civilization, seated in the middle of a forest and keeping at bay, through his sheer Buddha-ness, a host of confused, dark-skinned savages. The savages were Tamils, it was quite clear. The Buddha, the personification of love and kindness, had found people to hate.

Outside the shrine, Mahesh and I stopped in front of a glass ziggurat that had been erected in 2010 to hold 2600 Buddha statues, one for each year that had passed since the birth of Siddhartha Gautama. Many of the Buddhas were golden skinned and pointy headed, and they winked fiercely in the sun. We stood there, hypnotized by the drama of the light, until somebody from the temple came up to us. 'Would you want to sponsor one of those granite slabs?' he asked in Sinhalese.

Mahesh turned. 'Uh, no. No, we're just here to visit.'

It would only cost us 250,000 rupees for a slab, the temple official said. A couple of tens short of 2000 dollars.

'No, that's all right. We don't have that kind of money,' Mahesh replied. He grinned, and the official smiled back, each complicit in the lie that had just been constructed.

In another, older temple in the suburb of Bellanwila, we squatted at the threshold of the main hall of the Buddha and watched visitors trickle into a pair of small auxiliary shrines that were dedicated to Hindu deities. These Hindu shrines had been, for centuries, routine components of Buddhist temple complexes, but the clergy's new conservatism—led in part, until he died, by Soma Thero—wanted to strip them away, so that the temples would be precincts of pristine Buddhism. 'The Hindu gods are so popular,' Mahesh said. 'You're allowed to ask them for things—for jobs or for money. You can't ask these things of the Buddha.'

When we were halfway home, Mahesh suddenly instructed the trishaw to pull over, and he urged me to dash with him across the heaving road, on to a traffic island formed by the confluence of three avenues. A stone quartet of lions sat watch upon the four corners of a cubic base, guarding a carved, totem-like pillar that rose out of their midst. At the top of the pillar was the grey disc of the Buddha's Wheel of Life. Mahesh translated for me the Pali quotation etched into a plaque on the base: *Sukho Buddhanam Uppado*— 'Joyful is the birth of the Buddhas.' Except that the pillar was not a monument to the Buddha but to President

Mahinda Rajapaksa—the second Mahinda, as it were, the one who had saved Buddhism by winning the war, long after the first Mahinda had brought the faith into Sri Lanka. The war ingested everything whole, bent everything to its service: religion and politics, history and geography, fact and mythology. As on the island of Sri Lanka, so on this traffic island four paces long: the war loomed always above us.

4

SOMEWHERE IN A book, I had seen a photograph that haunted me, and when I arrived in Sri Lanka, I dug around online and discovered it again. It dates from July 1983, and it shows a reed-thin Tamil man, stripped naked by a mob, sitting on a stone plinth at a bus stop in a Colombo suburb, his head held in his hands and his body whipcord-tight with despair. It is late at night. His tormentors stand around him smiling; the broadest grin belongs to a youth in spectacles, a white shirt, slacks and rubber slippers, who is mugging for the camera as he dances a little two-step in front of his victim. Minus the naked man, the photo might just be a group of friends fooling around, shooting the breeze, waiting for a bus. Every time I looked at it, I felt a hollow shock in the pit of my stomach at the casual cheer with which this brutality is being enacted.

These were the riots. But first there was the ambush.

The date traditionally fitted to the start of the civil war is 23 July 1983, when the Tigers killed 13 soldiers in an army patrol in Jaffna. For nearly a week thereafter, in what came to be known as the Black July riots, Sinhalese mobs visited retribution upon Tamils across the south of the country, killing more than three thousand men, women and children, unhindered—and sometimes even abetted—by the police. Cars were stopped on the road and, if they were found to contain Tamils, burned without hesitation. Property was looted. Even before the practice grew notorious in

South Africa's race riots, Tamils were pulled out of their homes and necklaced: their torso inserted into a rubber tyre which was then set on fire.

At their best behaviour, soldiers and policemen watched the violence helplessly; at their worst, they conspired in it. In Nuwara Eliya, witnesses recounted in a book called *The Broken Palmyra*, a mob 'laid a ring of petrol around a Tamil shop which was then burnt. They were supported in this by the army who supplied them with gallons of petrol . . . Tamil people who walked the streets were beaten by soldiers . . . Shops which had not been burnt by the mob were set fire to by the army. Around noon, Nuwara Eliya was like a sea of flames.' Hundreds of Tamil families had to be sheltered by their Sinhalese friends and neighbours; thousands more simply abandoned their houses and fled north towards Jaffna.

The riots were brought under control, but the violence never truly ceased thereafter. It was as if, after many tugs at its starter cord, a motor had finally roared into unstoppable life. The Tigers had ambushed and killed government and army personnel ever since their formation in 1976. There had also been Sinhalese–Tamil riots before—in 1956, 1958, 1977 and 1981, during the last of which Uncle W.'s father-in-law and every other Tamil in Pelmadulla vacated their town in a frenzied hurry. ('My father-in-law was the only one who went back, and for a long time, he was the only Tamil living there,' Uncle W. told me. 'They didn't touch him in the 1983 riots though. Sinhala anger is like that. It's like a flicker.') But through it all, a tenuous peace had been maintained, until it snapped in 1983.

Discontent can fan its own flames, bring itself to a boil. One narrative of Sri Lankan history has always portrayed the country's Tamils as foreigners who had come to the island, in peace or during invasions, from kingdoms in south India. In the late 19th century and over the first half of the 20th, these frictions found renewed purpose, as Sinhalese grumbles grew about the disproportionately large number of Tamils studying in universities and working in the civil service. Through a quirk of colonial character, the British had set up few schools in the country's south, compelling Sinhalese children to earn their education in the local language; in the north, though, generations of Tamil students attended schools established by American missionaries, growing fluent in English, the language of pedagogy and administration. Through no doing of their own, the Tamils found themselves unfairly advantaged.

The schisms between the country's various ethnicities started to dilate—coaxed in no modest measure by the British, who had already divided and ruled India with such efficiency. Novel ways were discovered to emphasize differences—communal representation in electoral bodies, for instance—and even to define identity, to dice finer and finer the peoples contained within this small island.

In old census reports, I found a hint of how British administrators had vivisected Sri Lanka in the early 20th century. In 1901, when Tamils constituted just over a quarter of the country's population of three and a half million, the census classified people into seven categories—Europeans; Burghers; Sinhalese; Tamils; Moors, referring to Muslims of south Indian origin; Malays; and the indigenous Veddahs of eastern and south-eastern Sri Lanka.

A mere 10 years later, the matrix had exploded. By ethnicity, a Sri Lankan in 1911 could identify himself in any one of 10 ways, and then again in any one of 11 ways by religious denomination—a multiplicative tumult of identity. Slender distinctions were now officially recognized. A Sinhalese could be a low-country Sinhalese or a Kandyan Sinhalese; a Tamil could be a Ceylon Tamil or an Indian Tamil, depending on how recently his family had settled in Sri Lanka; a Christian could be a Roman Catholic, Presbyterian, Wesleyan, Methodist, Baptist, Congregationalist or a Salvationist, or he could belong to the Church of England or 'Other Sects.' Assembling legislatures based on such muddled ethnic loyalties helped the British by disrupting solidarity and nationalism because, as Governor William Manning once wrote to his secretary of state in London, 'no single community can impose its will upon the other communities.'

After Sri Lanka won its independence in 1948, the demands of Sinhalese nationalists found real purchase. For some decades, Tamil plantation workers were stripped of the right to vote, on the grounds that their ancestors had migrated so recently to the country from India—only a hundred-odd years ago, a mere teaspoonful of time—that they weren't really Sri Lankan. In 1956, Parliament passed an act declaring Sinhalese to be the sole official language of Sri Lanka. A compromise, with the puzzling name of 'Sinhala Only, Tamil Also,' was built into the act two years later, but it did nothing to bring Tamil on a par with Sinhalese. It only conceded that some schools could teach in Tamil, that Tamils could take exams in their language to enter—but not subsequently progress through—the ranks of the civil service, and that official documents in the north and the east could be written in Tamil.

In 1971, universities started to demand higher admission marks of Tamil students than of Sinhalese—a 'standardization' policy that was modified, not long after, to introduce quotas for each district. These were both forms of affirmative action—and, to the Tamils, outright discrimination—that proved remarkably effective. In 1969, when Tamils comprised around 20 per cent of the population, they formed 50 per cent of the student body in Sri Lanka's medical colleges and 48 per cent in its engineering colleges; by 1983, those numbers had dropped to 22 per cent and 28 per cent. A new constitution in 1972 gave Buddhism 'the foremost place' amongst Sri Lanka's religions and notified the state of its duty 'to protect and foster Buddhism.'

Over and over, through the 1970s, Sri Lanka found ways to tell its Tamils that their status in their country was subject to change. It was during this period that Tamil political parties decided to press for full sovereignty rather than regional autonomy. During this period also, new militant groups in Jaffna, like the Tigers, decided that a sovereign Tamil state—an Eelam—could never be wheedled out by political procedure and that it was far better demanded from behind the comforting stock of a gun.

The riots of 1983 notwithstanding, as I picked my way through Sri Lankan history, I always dated the real commencement of hostilities to 27 July 1975. That morning, as he did every Sunday, Alfred Duraiappah, the mayor of Jaffna, drove with two friends to the Varadaraja Perumal Temple in his white Peugeot. Duraiappah, a man of patrician looks and unflagging industry, had always been a popular politician. But a dense, hot head of anger had built against him for an incident that had happened under his administration the previous year, when a Sinhalese officer and 40 anti-riot policemen had tried to disperse a crowd that had gathered to listen, late one evening, to a talk by a scholar of Tamil. Amidst clouds of tear gas, seven people were electrocuted when overhead power lines were dislodged and swung into the melee. It was not difficult, for Tamil nationalists, to stuff this tragedy with symbolic meaning, to convert it into an attack on Tamil itself.

At the temple, where Duraiappah got out of his car, four young men—boys, really—stood waiting. I like to believe the account in which they greeted him, in chorus, with 'Vanakkam, aiyya'—'Good morning, sir'—a final moment of civility before the shooting began. One of Duraiappah's companions later remembered a short youth shivering as he aimed his pistol at the mayor. This was Velupillai Prabhakaran in his Gavrilo Princip moment, his assassination of a representative of a state he did not wish to belong to, his inauguration of a war. Unlike Princip, Prabhakaran remained the protagonist of his conflict: he created the Tigers in 1976, and the curtain on the civil war fell only with his death on 18 May 2009, cornered and shot up by the army in a lagoon in north-eastern Sri Lanka.

After Prabhakaran killed Duraiappah, he went on the lam, eventually finding his way to the house of a friend, Raghavan, in Punnalaikattuvan, a village in the north of the Jaffna peninsula. Quite taken with Prabhakaran, Raghavan stashed him for a while in his grandmother's house, across the road, until the manhunt went off the boil. A few years later, Prabhakaran founded the Tigers, and Raghavan was among the handful of restless young men who were the first recruits. When I met him, Raghavan alone, among Prabhakaran's first comrades, was still alive.

I found Raghavan in a roundabout, fortune-favoured way, having been introduced first to his partner, Nirmala. When I met her in Jaffna, Nirmala, a short woman of feisty spirit, was in her late fifties. Her hair was still mostly black, but a streak of white had started at her forehead and was creeping backwards like a slow flame; over the next two years, I would see the white methodically consume the rest of her hair. She lived with Raghavan and their children in England, but she had come to Jaffna for a long visit, spending her time going to the courthouse every day to settle a land dispute for her father. Her skin, accustomed by now to the polite English weather, had reacted badly to the sun. Her cheeks and forehead were mottled badly by a rash, and she scratched with absent fury at the nape of her neck, which peeped out above the collar of a white shirt. Watching her, I felt a sympathetic itch on my own skin.

As a teacher in Jaffna during the 1970s, Nirmala had been a strident advocate of the Eelam cause and an enthusiastic member of the Tigers. For these reasons, she became, in 1982, the first woman to be arrested under Sri Lanka's antiterrorism laws; she spent 22 months in prison before the Tigers, in a night-time jailbreak lifted straight out of the cinema, sprang her and smuggled her out of the country. She had lived overseas ever after: first, briefly, in south India, where the Tigers sheltered her, and then, souring on the Tigers' love of violence and fearing the whiplash of their wrath, in London, where she was granted asylum.

Raghavan and Nirmala fell in love in India, where he too was being hidden by the Tigers, out of the reach of Sri Lankan law. When she left for London in 1986, he followed her four months later, also having wearied of the Tigers' readiness to devour their own. Eventually, he went to university and became a case worker at a law firm that specialized in immigration. 'When he came to England, he had no skills. He had been a guerrilla for 10 years!' Nirmala told me. 'After I became pregnant with our first child, he had to run a petrol station so that we could make ends meet.'

Raghavan was a ropy man, his leanness softened in recent years by the arrival of a slight paunch. His jaw was encased in a smattering of salt-and-pepper beard; he was one of those men who looked like they sprouted stubble five minutes after a clean shave. He was, I would discover in due time, an easy-going man, but his eyes behind their spectacles were so perpetually heavy and his speech so frugal that he seemed to have shut the world away from himself quite effectively. His limbs moved languidly and methodically, as if they were underwater, and his voice was gravelly and cool, stripped of any ardour. It would have been very difficult to imagine him as a Tiger—as somebody passionate enough about a cause to be willing to go into battle for it—were it not for the immense air of wariness that hung about him. In fact, without the intercession of Nirmala, with whom I had become great friends, I suspect Raghavan might never have agreed to talk to me.

On the day that Nirmala brought him to meet me for the first time, Raghavan had just flown in from London. In a coffee shop in Colombo, he slumped peaceably in his chair, his legs furled under the table, volunteering only wry smiles to the conversation as Nirmala and I caught up. He might have skipped out in an hour, I realized later, except that the heavens opened up with supreme ferocity. The coffee shop, designed to be as open to the elements as possible without actually being outdoors, wrapped around a long, unroofed courtyard, and here the rain pounded thunderously into the flagstones. The spray soaked the back of my shirt. We were trapped there for nearly five hours. And so, working his steady way through many cups of tea, Raghavan came slowly alive and began to talk about himself.

5

HE WAS 15 years old, and still in school in Punnalaikattuvan, when the government implemented the standardization policy in universities. It was 1971. 'Even before that, there was some talk of a separate Tamil state, but that was only by a few individuals. Not many people were interested.' His parents were teachers, and they had scant interest in politics. 'But standardization—ah!' He almost smacked his lips. 'That was the start of something, the start of a political awareness. There was a procession in 1972, I remember, against the policy. Thousands of students must have taken part. I was one of them.'

The 1972 constitution also riled him up, he said, but then he confessed sheepishly that he had really only read the full text of the constitution much later—well after he left the Tigers, in fact. 'Back then, I only learned about it from news reports. But you know, there was talk about it everywhere. Buses were being burned. Black flags were flying in protest. There was no escaping it.'

Raghavan joined these agitations with vigour. In the dead of night, along with a couple of friends, he would steal out of home and make his way to the village's biggest crossroads. They would tie their black flags to a length of string, fasten the other end of the string to a stone, lob the stone over an electricity line running above their heads, and thus hoist their flags. They would appropriate cans of Solignum, a black wood-preservative that was daubed upon palmyra-thatch roofs to protect them, and paint anti-government slogans in untidy letters on the village's walls.

'Once, in 1973 or 1974, the education minister, Badi-ud-din'—Badi-ud-din Mahmud, an architect of the standardization policy, and therefore to Jaffna a man of unspeakable villainy— 'was making a visit. My father was teaching in the village school, and the principals of all the schools in the area had been asked to decorate their schools for the visit. After all this decoration was done, at night, I went down to my father's school and wrote: "Go home, Badi-ud-din" on a wall. I think he suspected it was me. He was very angry.'

Across Sri Lanka, in the early 1970s, ferment was in plentiful supply. Quite unconnected to the Tamil nationalist movement, the Marxists staged an insurrection in April 1971, preparing bombs in factories, attacking police stations with home-made guns and Molotov cocktails, and even briefly seizing two substantial towns that later needed to be liberated by the army. A state of emergency fell upon the country, curfews stretched from dusk till dawn, and security forces commenced summary executions.

Thousands died; later, Sri Lanka could only debate how many thousands, precisely. A thousand only? Fifty thousand? A French journalist wrote that he saw corpses floating in Colombo's Kelaniya River, 'with hundreds of motionless onlookers . . . The police, who had killed them, let the bodies float downstream in order to terrorise the population.' Where there were no convenient rivers, the security forces turned to the soil. Young men, on the merest suspicion of being Marxists, were requested at gunpoint to dig their own graves before occupying them. These dirty secrets festered under Sri Lanka's topmost layer of skin. Every so often, a mass grave burst forth, like a pustule, revealing a little of the infection in the body.

This was all in the south of Sri Lanka; in the north, the Tamils' sense of aggrievement sparked and flared. Samuel Chelvanayakam, a beloved Tamil politician of near-Gandhian rectitude, resigned his parliamentary seat in October 1972, saying that he despaired now of a negotiated solution to Sri Lanka's linguistic frictions. On a road not far from his village of Valvettithurai, on the Jaffna coast, a young Velupillai Prabhakaran and his comrades stopped a state transport bus, ordered its passengers to disembark, bathed the bus with diesel from its own tank, and set it on fire. The very being of Sri Lanka was racked with self-doubt and pain.

Raghavan did not find it easy to explain how, exactly, he went from being one of Jaffna's juvenile delinquents to being a Tiger. The transit, in his memory, was organic and inevitable, as if there were only one kind of political education to be had by a young man in Jaffna at the time and only one consequence of such an education. He'd go to the Jaffna Library and read nationalist papers like *Viduthalai*—Freedom—and then he would pick apart their contents with two friends from his village. Through a neighbour, he met Jeeva, a thin, soft-spoken man who had once tried to assassinate a Tamil member of Parliament for the sin of voting for the 1972 constitution.

Two other militants—from the Tamil New Tigers, a group formed by Prabhakaran in 1972—were also hiding out in Punnalaikattuvan around this time. Raghavan remembered Chetty in particular. 'My job was to take him from one hideout to another on my bicycle, using a different route on each occasion,' he said. Chetty kept a Smith & Wesson revolver upon him at all times. 'I was thrilled when I saw it, because back then, in Jaffna, you didn't see too many firearms.'

A strange problem of sartorial etiquette presented itself here. Chetty wanted to stuff the gun into the waistband of his trousers, where it could be hidden from view by the panels of a long shirt. But good Jaffna boys always tucked their shirts primly into their pants; to fail to do this would look so slovenly that it would attract dangerous attention. 'Finally, he decided to wear only sarongs, because that way he could leave his shirt hanging out. He wore a belt around the sarong and stuck the gun in there,' Raghavan said. 'Much later, the sarong became our trademark of sorts. We'd practise pulling our shirt quickly out of the way and drawing the gun.' Raghavan laughed hard at this memory, at the sheer triviality of their problems during these early days.

Chetty never allowed Raghavan to handle his gun, much less fire it, so Raghavan saved up the money he earned from tutoring students and bought a second-hand .32, from a local thug, for 400 rupees. He thought the Tamil New Tigers would accept him into their ranks if he had his own gun. 'So I went to them with the pistol and told them I wanted to join the group. Chetty asked me for the pistol and didn't give it back.' Chetty, who at 26 was a full 10 years older than Raghavan, told him: 'You're too young. We'll recruit you later. Now you should just study.' Later, Raghavan learned, Chetty held up a cooperative store with his .32.

Chetty's career in militancy was a short one. 'He started living the high life,' Raghavan said, with rasping scorn. 'He was spending money all over the place. He bought a car—an Austin A40. Finally, he was arrested.' But before he was caught, one afternoon in late 1974, Chetty introduced Raghavan to Prabhakaran, fresh from a self-imposed sabbatical from militancy and eager to discover violent new ways of winning Tamils their sovereign Eelam.

When Raghavan first met him, Prabhakaran was a slight young man, his bushy moustache and rotundity still a long way in the future. The others called him *thambi*, 'little brother.' 'He was only two years older than me, but he had already done so much,' Raghavan said. 'He had become a wanted man in 1972. He had fled to India for a while and had just returned.' In Raghavan's voice, there remained a trace of a bright affection for those days. It was almost infectious. Suddenly I could see it too: the glamour of the ideological life lived just outside the law, the impossible romance of a fraternity of young men out to change their world.

Prabhakaran impressed Raghavan. 'He was very, very friendly. He had real charisma. He was a little bit of a dreamer, but he could also be organized and practical.' Even though he was just 20 years old, Prabhakaran was already thinking and behaving like a seasoned revolutionary, his life taking on the superfluidity that would help preserve him until 2009. He remained forever on the move, staying a few nights at one supporter's house before moving on to the next. He wore nondescript clothes: half-sleeved shirts and sarongs. On his bicycle, as he roamed through the Jaffna peninsula, he avoided the main roads, where he might run into police patrols. He stayed away from government institutions entirely; even when he was stricken by jaundice, he refused to consult a doctor at a state-run hospital, preferring to recover slowly and alone. He painstakingly destroyed every single photograph of himself, so that policemen, even as they kept their eyes skinned for him, could only work with a dated image from an old school identification card. He rooted around tirelessly for funds, aware of the movement's need for money. 'Once he sent me all the way by bicycle to his village, Valvettithurai, to get some money from a sympathizer,' Raghavan said. 'So I went all that way for this guy's savings, which he had kept in a piggy bank. It turned out to be 10 rupees.'

Prabhakaran was also adept at persuading other young men to follow him, kneading their minds until they too lusted after an independent Eelam, precisely as he would do with legions of new Tigers for decades thereafter. 'We were all convinced that his way was the only way,' Raghavan said.

'Although, of course, now that I can look back on it, it's true that we were all feeling adventurous, and because of our age and immaturity, we were fascinated by the violence.' I was startled, for a moment, by the admission; then I wondered if it offered him the safest way out, and if it was better to own up to foolhardiness than a fondness for terrorism.

The militants had noted with gloom that the democratic methods of the Tamil parties were foundering. Before every election, these parties, stunted and weak, would barter with the larger Sinhalese parties, promising them the Tamil vote in exchange for more rights. Once the election had been won, the Tamil parties would be jilted and the pre-poll agreements ignored. 'The whole process was just never transparent,' Raghavan said. 'So for my part, I was only interested in an armed struggle.'

After the assassination of Duraiappah, Prabhakaran kept his head down for months, using Raghavan's grandmother's home as his chief hideout until April 1976. 'At the time, I was tutoring O-Level students for pocket money. Prabhakaran was short, and he looked younger than his age, so I told my grandmother he was one of my students who needed a place to stay for a while.' Raghavan paused, and then he wheezed and laughed. 'You know, now that I think about it, I lied not because I was afraid of the police but because I was afraid of my parents. I was afraid of what they'd say.' Prabhakaran's solitary public appearance in that period was dramatic: he led a group of armed cohorts, including Raghavan, into a local branch of the People's Bank and, after a mere five minutes, left with cash and jewellery worth 700,000 rupees. In May, Prabhakaran renamed the Tamil New Tigers as the Liberation Tigers of Tamil Eelam, and he gifted his guerrilla outfit with its new logo: a tiger in mid-roar, its forepaws resting on the stocks of two crossed rifles and its head ringed by a halo made up of .33 bullets.

A few weeks later, he moved the Tigers—numbering perhaps 20—into the Vanni, the Tamil-dominated region immediately south of the Jaffna peninsula, its thick forests offering the sort of cover that Jaffna's flat, open land never could. Near the town of Vavuniya, in a 40-acre farm called Poonthottam, or Flower Garden, Prabhakaran established his first training camp. The farm, owned by an acquaintance of Prabhakaran's, came with ordered vegetable patches and paddy fields, little tokens of rural peace. But immediately to the rear loomed the Vanni's jungle, eternally prepared to swallow the Tigers, to permit them to conduct their war from within its recesses, and to hide them from the world.

For a small country, Sri Lanka possesses an astonishing variety of terrain. Its navel is in Kandy, the former royal capital up in the hills, where the last of the Sri Lankan kings succumbed to the advance of the British Empire in 1815. Practically the entire coastline in the country's west, south and east is comprised of beach, miles and miles of it, so that from the air the island appears to be wearing a hemline made out of faded yellow ribbon. A circuit of the country would run a little over a thousand kilometres; Marco Polo, who likely never visited 'Zeilan' but wrote about it with pronounced authority, thought that the island must have been larger in ancient times, but 'the northern gales, which blow with prodigious violence, have in a manner corroded the mountains, so that they have in some parts fallen and sunk in the sea, and the island, from that cause, no longer retains its original size.' Perhaps travellers had told him that Sri Lanka somehow felt like a bigger country—older, more complicated—than it really was. I felt that frequently.

To the north and south of Kandy lie great tracts of warm, wet forest, broken by an occasional roll of hills. Driving up through the Vanni, the forest gives discreet way to scrubland

and then to the low coastal ground of Mannar and of
Jaffna, where the land has been planed so flat that it feels
indistinguishable from the sea, and where the sky hangs
similarly flat overhead, like a sheet of beaten blue metal.
The land feels gentler in the south, its lines softer and more
voluptuous, and its colours lush and warm. In the north, the
sun and the sea seem to have carved everything up, leaving
little that is forgiving or tender.

Everywhere I travelled, I was asked where I was from. I had
thought, at the beginning, that I could pass for a Sri Lankan
until I started to speak, and I played a game with myself,
trying to delay that moment of revelation as long as possible.
But there must have been something ineffably foreign about
me. Without having spoken a sentence, I was treated as a
stranger.

In the years after the war, for a visitor to Sri Lanka to
be both Indian and Tamil was to evoke distrust from every
quarter. The Tamils detested the Indian government for not
doing more to halt the carnage of the war's last weeks, and it
was difficult to fault this view. The Sinhalese loathed India for
covertly training and arming the Tigers in the 1980s, and they
considered India's Tamils to be meddlers who supported the
Eelam cause, and it was difficult to fault these views too. I was
a bloodless victim of my country's disastrous foreign policy,
and I had to learn very quickly to strike the appropriate note
of apology.

Just as it became important to disentangle my identity from
my work, it became important also to separate, like yolk from
white, the Tigers from the grievances of the Tamils. 'I don't
condone the Tigers' use of murder,' I would frequently clarify,
and I meant it. How could I not, when the Tigers showed
such an endless genius for brutality? They ambushed soldiers
and assassinated politicians, but they also killed monks and
pilgrims in the majestic Buddhist shrine of Anuradhapura,

shot up Sinhalese women and children across the country, and blew up airplanes and trains. They scattered mines across the land like farmers broadcasting seeds, so lavishly that demining work was still in progress in 2013, four years after the war ended; finishing the job will take until 2020. The Tigers planted bombs on buses and in other public places in Colombo and elsewhere, so that a mother sending her son off to school in the morning could never be quite sure that he would return whole in the afternoon.

Even stubborn little acts of nobility were rewarded with violence. In 1992, the Tigers stopped a bus full of Muslims, Sinhalese and a lone Tamil named Rajakulendran. The Tigers gave Rajakulendran the chance to get down from the bus and thus be spared, but he refused, remaining on the bus with the other passengers. The Tigers dragged him out of the bus and killed him first. Then they shot up the bus and its passengers.

Every account of the Tigers, or of the war, that I read inevitably became a catalogue of such murder, reminding me of Indi Samarajiwa, of his idea of introducing his city to me through the pain it had borne. For a long time, I struggled to understand the reason for this catalogue approach: Surely the power of a litany—even of horror—diminished with length? Then, one day, I caught myself identifying some town not in terms of its geography, or its vegetation, or its people, but by a Tiger massacre that had occurred there 20 years previously. The catalogue had wormed its way into my mind and replaced my mental map of the island. There was now no other Sri Lanka for me but the Sri Lanka of its war.

The history of the Tigers' struggle for Eelam is less a succession of political manoeuvres than a parade of slaughter, and they had no reservations about slaying their own. Tamil families in Tiger-controlled areas were forced to contribute one of their offspring to the movement; the Tigers promised they would extract just the single sacrifice per household, but when the war went awry, they came back for more. They recruited boys and girls, turned them into ill-prepared combatants, and hurried them to their deaths. They expected fighters to sling cyanide capsules around their necks, to be bitten and swallowed if the threat of capture was ever at hand. They stuffed men and women into suicide vests and commanded them to blow themselves up. They constructed human shields out of Tamil civilians, placing them in the line of artillery fire. They punished betrayal, as they perceived it in their warped universe, with ready death. A friend's husband, Neelan Tiruchelvam, a moderate Tamil member of Parliament, was assassinated one morning in 1999. He had been urging Prabhakaran to accept compromises that could end the war, but for a Tamil to even suggest a negotiation on Eelam was treachery, so a Tiger in a checked blue shirt sidled up to Tiruchelvam's Nissan sedan and set off a bomb.

This was the outfit that Prabhakaran built, cast in his own image of cruelty.

His father was an administrative officer working for the government, a job of considerable prestige in 1954, when Prabhakaran was born. They lived in Valvettithurai, a fishing village in the north of Jaffna. On his father's side, his family had been far wealthier in the 19th century, owning land across the coast, functioning as trustees of local temples, and even funding the construction of a new Shiva temple in 1867. But much of this fortune had eroded by the mid-20th century, and Prabhakaran's father needed his employment. When the government made it mandatory for civil servants to speak and write Sinhalese, he learned the language obediently.

The temptation to read into Prabhakaran's childhood signs of his capacity for violence is overwhelming; there must have been early indicators, we think, so that we can assure ourselves that we will now recognize them in another child, in another place and time. Some of his biographers discuss his fondness for catapults and air rifles, with which he picked off squirrels and chameleons; his hobby of brewing explosives, using chemicals swiped from the school's chemistry lab; his desire to learn karate. I once met a man from Valvettithurai who had gone to school with Prabhakaran's older brother, and whose cousin had married Prabhakaran's sister. He remembered the young Prabhakaran as an odd, inscrutable boy. 'I'd pass their house on Aalady Lane every day when I was bicycling to school, and if Prabhakaran was there, I'd give him a ride on my pillion, since I knew his brother,' he said. 'Once, when he was 11 years old, I had given a ride to another boy who had asked for one. We passed Prabhakaran's house, and he was standing outside, waiting for me. When I was going past him, he yanked the other boy right off the moving bicycle. Even then, he was a possessive sort of fellow.'

He remembered also that Prabhakaran would come over to borrow books on the short-lived Tamil secessionist movement in India. 'He was always interested in that stuff. He was younger than me, but he would still want to come and talk politics with me, though I had no interest in it at the time.' Prabhakaran had come under the sway of a tutor who supported Tamil nationalism, but he also nourished these early seedlings of ideology with the material of life around him. His father spoke of ethnic discrimination in the civil services. University students grew disaffected. The story of a Hindu priest who had been caught and burned alive by a Sinhalese mob somewhere near Colombo during the riots of 1958 rankled mightily. 'The widespread feeling was: "When a priest like him was burnt alive, why did we not have the capability to hit back?" he told an interviewer in 1986. "That was one atrocity that made people think deeply." Prabhakaran salted away these incidents into an account of grievances. When he turned 18, he set fire to a state transport bus, and embarked upon his chosen path.

In photographs, Prabhakaran is a squat, fleshy man of several chins; people who had met him told me that he was even shorter and fatter in person, and that he spoke in a thin voice that seemed entirely wrong for the leader of a mighty band of rebels. The moustache was nearly always there, a thick shrub of black across his upper lip, arcing downwards just as his jowls arced upwards. Most of the time, he wore jungle camouflage, green-and-brown streaks patterned to resemble a tiger's hide. The uniform clung to his belly like the skin upon a watermelon.

To protect the Tigers, Prabhakaran thought, it was necessary above all to protect himself, and perhaps he was not wholly wrong about this. He was driven by paranoia: sleeping in a different place every few nights, appearing in public rarely, forever weighing the loyalty of his men. He wanted his commanders to remain celibate and unmarried for the good of the movement. Watching a movie once—*Operation Daybreak*, in which the Nazis break a Czech dissident by threatening his wife and children—Prabhakaran turned to Raghavan and whispered: 'This is why I insisted that family life is not suitable for the cause.' Being a husband or a father was trivial, although Prabhakaran himself was both. No sacrifice was too great for Eelam—and since he considered himself the personification of Eelam, no sacrifice was too great for him.

The greatest of such sacrifices was life itself, of course, and Prabhakaran demanded this without hesitation. As a corollary, he persuaded himself that this also allowed him to take lives as he saw fit. He killed Tigers who disagreed with him, and he ordered killed Tamils who resisted him, Sinhalese civilians, and politicians. No one was off limits: not pacifists, not women or children, not the weak.

One afternoon, Nirmala and I were sitting in the canteen of the Jaffna Library, talking about nothing in particular over cold bottles of orange barley water. The lunch service had just ended, and the tin trays of the buffet were being cleared away with teeth-jarring clatter. Nirmala looked about her and said: 'You know who gave the library the funds to build this canteen?'

It was a man she would only call Sathish, a member of another Tamil militant group who had escaped to London in the late 1980s and done well for himself. Back in 1986 or 1987, during the peak of the turf war between the various Tamil factions, Sathish and a colleague had fallen into the hands of the Tigers. 'They played Russian roulette with his life, basically,' Nirmala told me. A coin would be tossed, the pair was informed. If it landed up heads, one of them would die; tails, and the other would die. 'Sathish survived, and the other guy was shot,' Nirmala said.

Ten years, I calculated to myself. That was how long it had taken for the Tigers to go from killing out of perceived necessity to killing for sport. It seemed like an abominably short time for the decay of a movement—unless the movement had been ridden with rot from the very beginning.

6

DURING MY FIRST months in Colombo, if I ever found myself at a
loose end on a weekday morning, I walked down to the shiny,
modern Lanka Hospitals building that stood at the other end
of Park Road. Except for a couple of hours in the afternoon,
the street was mostly silent, the tarmac spotted with patterns
of shade and sun. To get to the hospital, I passed a pizza place,
a small supermarket and a large playing field. The sidewalk
rippled up and down, unevenly built.

In a lower floor of the hospital, Chelliah Thurairaja
practised radiology every morning, peering inside his patients
for signals of damage. He was a Tamil who had retired as a
major general from the Sri Lankan army in 1998. I instantly
found this peculiar—not just the notion of a Tamil in the
army, although that was rare enough, but also the idea of a
Tamil who had ordered Sinhalese soldiers into battle against
guerrillas who claimed to be fighting for his own community.
As it turned out, Dr Thurairaja was the former director of
the Army Medical Services, accustomed more to saving lives
than taking them. But even his elevation to the rank of major
general intrigued me: it tousled the narrative, so beloved of
Tamil separatists, that the civil war began partly because
Sri Lankan Tamils were never allowed to rise in the
government's institutions.

'Come over, come over,' Dr Thurairaja would tell me when
I called him at 8 a.m. 'Today is likely to be a slow day. We'll

sit and have a chat.' So, a couple of hours later, I would go to the hospital, wend my way through its sunny, buzzing lobby, and knock on the door of his consulting room, across the corridor from the X-ray department. 'Ah, sit, sit. I'm just finishing this up,' he'd say.

But then, over the rest of the morning, doctors would pop in for consultations, the relatives of patients would linger to milk every last drop of hope out of his prognoses, nurses would come by to drop off X-rays, and new patients would arrive, their brows threaded with pain and worry. In these instances, I would shrink into the corner of the room, embarrassed about trying to filch the doctor's time away from these matters of life and death. Dr Thurairaja, for his part, would be profusely contrite when he rose to leave at half past noon. 'We talked for only 20 minutes today, no?' he'd say. 'So sorry, Samanth. It gets rushed sometimes. But come again tomorrow? Call me again in the morning. We'll have a nice chat.' Several mornings passed in this way.

The first time I met him, Dr Thurairaja was shuffling down the corridor in a baseball cap, blue trackpants, and a yellow polo-neck T-shirt that was unbuttoned just enough to reveal a gold chain and a surgery scar over his breastbone. I surmised that he might be a patient; in fact, he was returning from a session at the gym, and he was the most able-bodied 76-year-old I had ever seen. ('I was born in 1935. I never let people know my age, for a long time,' he once told me. 'I even coached my kids, when they were young, to tell people a lower age—lower by about 20 years.') He was an imposing man even at this age, with a broad, domed forehead, breadbasket hands, and a tall frame diminished only by a slight stoop; in an old photograph I found of him in service, the half-sleeves of his uniform shirt clung so tightly to his biceps that they might have been bandages taped into place. 'I used to play a lot of sport when I was young—badminton with the neighbours' boys, that sort of thing,' Dr Thurairaja said. Only after I knew him better and discovered his knack for genial understatement did I think of asking other people about his sporting career. It emerged that he had represented Sri Lanka in basketball, golf and badminton, boxed and played rugby and cricket at Colombo's Royal College, and won a gold medal in golf at the World Masters Games in 2002.

In his consulting room, Dr Thurairaja needed to nearly fold himself in half to bend and write on his low desk. He would extract X-rays from Department of Radiology envelopes and read them with practised speed, the violet light from the X-ray light box dawning upon his forehead like a strange sun upon a new world. He would then scribble his analysis, in spidery notation, on to strips of paper and hand these over to a nurse to type into Microsoft Word documents. Through long custom, the nurse had learned to read his scrawls, but even she had to ask, on occasion, what an especially illegible phrase said. 'Sebaceous cyst, ma, sebaceous cyst,' he would reply, for example, before turning back to our conversation or to his patient. He had an attentive but unsentimental bedside manner, and I saw the smile slip from his face only once. A patient's father had worked himself into an agitation over the condition of his daughter, exclaiming: 'One day you'll just call us and say, "Please come and take away the body. She's dead."' Dr Thurairaja seemed genuinely hurt, and he reached out, squeezed the father's knee, and murmured: 'Now, now, don't say that.' Then, with his pleasant grin hitched back into place, he continued to explain what treatment the man's daughter would get.

Dr Thurairaja's parents belonged to old Jaffna families. His father, a clerk in the civil service of British Ceylon, was transferred to Colombo, and after he retired, he managed a cooperative store. The family settled in Wellawatte. When I asked Dr Thurairaja how many brothers and sisters he had, he had to pause and tot them up on his fingers. 'We were six boys and three girls in total. I was the last but one.' His father spoke Tamil, Sinhalese and English with great flair; after his retirement, he even served as an arbitrator for labour tribunals, the proceedings of which were conducted mostly in Sinhalese.

On the other hand, Dr Thurairaja, enrolled in the English-medium Royal College and conversing in Tamil at home, spoke only some fractured Sinhalese and could read none at all. The year he joined medical school, in 1956, the Sinhala Only Act came into force, requiring all government employees to conduct official business exclusively in Sinhalese. Even the act's amended version, passed two years later, prescribed a degree of knowledge of spoken and written Sinhalese in order to be promoted.

Among the educated Tamils of Jaffna, who abided by the saying: 'Even if you're only keeping chickens, make sure you keep those chickens for the government', this barrier to government work sowed consternation and anger. A Jaffna writer named S. Pathmanathan—or So. Pa., in the popular Tamil contraction—was one of the recruits in the very first clerical service batch to be affected by the new law, and he once described to me how effectively it ossified his career. So. Pa. wrote, and still writes, pristine English and Tamil, but he had grown up in Jaffna and so he had to scramble to meet the strictures of the Sinhala Only Act. 'Politically, those of us who had decided to learn Sinhalese were considered traitors by the Tamil trade union,' he said. 'But some of the Tamils who had entered the civil service before us had refused, on principle, to learn Sinhalese, and I saw their careers stagnate before my eyes.'

So. Pa. attended Sinhalese classes organized within his department, and two other evenings a week, he paid for additional tuitions outside. Somehow he passed two exams, but then he reached a stage where he needed an O-Level knowledge of Sinhalese to be promoted, and in this he found himself competing with his Sinhalese colleagues. 'I mean, Sinhalese was their mother tongue! It was a losing battle,' he said. So in 1962, when So. Pa. was eligible to become a Class 2 clerk, he wasn't allowed to take the promotion exam because his Sinhalese was judged to be too clumsy. He pleaded his case through the clerical service union. 'All we asked was: We'll learn Sinhalese, but allow us to sit these promotion tests in English, since that was the medium in which we originally qualified for the clerical service. We were denied that chance. I think that was the straw that broke my back.' Deciding that there was little to be gained by complaining further, he quit the clerical service and became a teacher, so that he could be deputed to government schools in Tamil districts, postings that needed no proficiency in Sinhalese. 'You know, look, I had nothing against the Sinhalese,' he said. 'But I thought this policy was just plain discriminatory.'

Dr Thurairaja went similarly through the wringer. After he completed his medical degree in 1961, he joined the army, mostly so that he could continue to play sports. As a doctor in government service, he could have been sent to any state-run hospital in the country, including in towns that lacked anything resembling a basketball court or a boxing ring. As an army doctor in peacetime, though, he would always be stationed in Colombo or in one of two other large bases. 'And it wasn't as if there were any restrictions on Tamils joining the army,' he said. 'There were many of them—not just officers, but in every rank.'

Like So. Pa. Dr Thurairaja was forced to study written Sinhalese on his own time if he wanted to be promoted; unlike So. Pa., he chose to rationalize away this obligation. 'The way I looked at it was that the people who refused to learn Sinhalese were just penalizing themselves, no?' he explained, his declarations softened, as always, by that questioning lilt at the end. 'And I'd actually tell my Tamil friends who didn't want to learn the language, I'd say: Look, if you went to France and wanted to be promoted, you'd study French, wouldn't you?' He believed so fully in this analogy that he repeated it, tweaked very slightly, during another conversation: 'If young Tamils come to me for advice even today, I tell them to learn Sinhalese. If you go to Japan, after all, you can't get by without Japanese. You don't even expect to, no?'

How odd, I thought to myself, to have to equate the inevitable constraint of a foreign land with one imposed upon him in his own country. But it seemed to me, at first, as if Dr Thurairaja had never thought very much about his Tamilness at all; or if he had, he hid it well, behind his loose smile and shambling speech. When Colombo was stricken by the riots of 1983, he was on medical duty 24x7, allowed to go home only to eat dinner, even as his sister's house in Wellawatte was plunged into a bonfire by a Sinhalese mob. His family, he said, had to make the careful distinction, to their friends, that he was a doctor rather than a soldier.

'I didn't sympathize with the Tigers, nor was I against them. For any of these political issues, I don't put my head to it. It ends up troubling you inside,' he said. 'I simply thought: We're being attacked by the Tigers. And even if I went personally to Jaffna, they would have attacked me. They wouldn't have waited to see if I was Sinhalese or Tamil. And in a way, this was just like being a sportsman. Your team is your team. That's who you play for, no?'

But nothing in this war could be reduced to the simple binary terms of sport. Gradually, as Dr Thurairaja grew accustomed to me, I spotted glimpses of the trials of his situation. He told me about how the proportion of Tamils in the army declined as the war progressed, from around 20 or 30 per cent in the 1970s to practically nothing in the 1990s;

when he retired in 1998, Dr Thurairaja was quite likely the only Tamil officer still serving in the army. 'The Tamils were reluctant to join the military, of course,' he said, 'but also, there was a freeze on hiring Tamils, although nobody said this outright.' Tamil officers found it difficult to receive routine promotions. One of his corporals, a Tamil, stagnated for years in his rank. 'I had to speak up and say: If he isn't promoted, I'll have to hand in my own resignation.'

It even happened with Dr Thurairaja himself. 'I got the sense that they were delaying some of my promotions. So I'd come right out and ask them: "Is it because of the T factor?"' And here, in the re-enactment of his thundering question, he threw out his impressive arm, ending in a finger that pointed accusingly at the blackguards who were denying him his due. 'Then they'd back off. That was one way to tackle it.'

Another day, another wait outside radiology. An old man hobbled to and fro along the corridor, leaning on a cane, wincing with every step. I felt certain he was a patient, until an even older man emerged from the X-ray room in a wheelchair, his foot swaddled in snow-white plaster. The hobbler slowly pushed the wheelchair down the corridor and finally out of sight.

'Will you come to my golf club this evening?' Dr Thurairaja asked as he swept out of his clinic and past me, his hands busy with a confusion of jacket, car keys, satchel and cap. 'We'll have so much more time there. No interruptions!'

But that dolorous evening, I was late, stuck for an eternity in a traffic jam in the rain. 'This is bad luck, no?' Dr Thurairaja said when I finally reached. 'I have to leave. But come, I'll drop you to a trishaw on the main road.' He pulled his Kia SUV out of the parking lot, and we promptly plunged right back into the snarl of stalled cars.

Engelbert Humperdinck appeared on the radio, singing

Quando, quando, quando. Dr Thurairaja drummed his fingers on the steering wheel. 'Where have you been travelling?' he asked.

I told him about a recent trip to the Vanni, to the villages that had been shelled without compunction by the army in the waning stages of the war. He said nothing in response. The silence grew so oppressive that I felt compelled to break into Dr Thurairaja's thoughts. Had he become disillusioned with the Sri Lankan army now? I asked.

Not with the army, he said, not exactly. Perhaps with the politicians. 'But human rights violations definitely happened during the last days of the war. In all that shelling, they were trying to wipe out the next generation of Tamils. There's a racist tendency, even now, that is characteristic of a majority community. It's as if the Sinhala mentality is geared to wipe out Tamils. Even when I was treating Sinhalese patients down south, they would say: "We need to bomb them all." I'd get annoyed, but I'd say nothing.'

His anger dimmed briefly into reason—'Of course, you can't judge the whole community by some people who make such statements, no?'—before flaring up again. He recalled a police-led massacre of students in a school, in which the policemen were ultimately exonerated. 'What message does that send? All this shows that, in any country, the majority community can act without fear of retribution. They can do anything.'

Whenever he discussed the army, a degree of circumspection crept into Dr Thurairaja's manner—understandably, because he was still fond of his days in uniform, still playing golf with other retired officers, still living in Sri Lanka under the watchful gaze of a government that brooked no criticism of its soldiers. But there was something else: He spoke with apologetic pain, as if he was maligning his mother, as if he couldn't bring himself to believe the things his mother was said to have done, even as he suspected that they might all be true.

The truth was, and is, heavily contested territory. In its thirst to end the war, the Sri Lankan army certainly killed Tamil civilians; it would have been impossible not to when the front moved through Tamil towns and villages, and when the civilian population became—whether inevitably or by Prabhakaran's design—a human shield for the Tigers. Rather than cross into army-held ground, the Tamils of the Vanni preferred to follow the Tigers as they were beaten back towards the sea. In turn, Prabhakaran chose to remain hidden within his people, believing that he could plead for their safety if he ever needed to parley for a ceasefire.

But how many civilians died, and how were they killed? The government reckoned nine thousand; the United Nations calculated at least forty thousand, and probably more. The highest estimate I heard was seventy-five thousand, nearly as many fatalities as had accumulated in the previous 25 years of the war. Did the government block off the Vanni to journalists and aid agencies so that it could scorch the earth without fear of being held accountable? Were designated no-fire zone bombarded with heavy artillery? Were non-combatants and Tiger foot soldiers killed extrajudicially, as a Channel 4 documentary alleged? Were they arranged in a row, blindfolded and naked, and shot in the back of the head, so that they keeled over in a jumble of thin legs and arms, looking more like matchsticks than men? Did the army deliberately send shells whistling and spinning into a hospital, prompting an eyewitness to send Gordon Weiss, a United Nations spokesman in Colombo, a text message reading: 'Women and kids wards shelled. God, no words. Still counting the dead bodies'?

Or were we instead to trust the August 2010 testimony of Gotabhaya Rajapaksa, the president's brother and the country's defence secretary, to the Lessons Learnt and Reconciliation Commission, the testimony that ran in a vertiginous, near-continuous block of text for 17 pages and that included the assurance:

> *So you can see from the very beginning there was a very clear military planning parallel to the military plan we had a plan for humanitarian assistance whether it is for the no fire zone, the policy level, the zero civilian casualties, restrictions on use of heavy weapons, the training of soldiers, all these were done to prevent civilian casualties. Of course in a situation like a military campaign like this and with an equally strong terrorist group fighting and when they were using civilians as human shields to protect them there could be cases of civilian casualties.*

The Commission chose to trust Rajapaksa. In a 388-page report issued in November 2011, based on more than a thousand oral testimonies and five thousand written submissions, the Commission admitted that 'considerable civilian casualties had in fact occurred during the final phase of the conflict,' but that these were caused by crossfire, the Tigers' killing of their own civilians, their 'refusal to let the hostages get out of harm's way,' and—in a phrase of fine ambiguity—'the dynamics of the conflict situation.' The Commission heard no representations, the report said, 'that the Security Forces deliberately targeted civilians.'

These conclusions changed so few minds that they may as well have been whispered into a gale. Into the store of ammunition maintained by the regime's critics, the Commission's report deposited some extra rounds; in the opposite camp, it added a redundant rafter or two to the loyalists' support of the government. But the report did nothing to allay the uncertainties experienced by the people living in the middle of these two extremes. It did not convince them that their government was guilty of war crimes, so that they might unreservedly condemn it, or that no war crimes were committed, so that they might bask in the relief of a fair victory. Instead, they were trapped in the misery of not knowing what to believe—about their government, about their own indirect complicity in their government's actions, or about the moral cost of their hard-won peace.

One evening, back at the Colombo Golf Club, we were wading through bread-and-butter pudding, and Dr Thurairaja was again dancing, with his usual adagio delicacy, around the question of being a Tamil in the army. 'You know,' he said, 'you're in the wrong place for this, really.'

'What do you mean?' I asked.

'What you should do is go to Canada. Many of the Tamils who quit the army migrated there, no? The sort of things I'm telling you so guardedly, they'll be able to tell you with much more freedom.'

'Who would I talk to there?'

'There's a man called Sivagnanam, who lives in Toronto now. I knew him. He used to be a radiographer in the army until he got frustrated and quit. You should go track him down and talk to him.'

7

I WENT TO Canada in the middle of an iced-over February, many months later, armed only with a few contacts. From the air, Toronto looked dispiriting, as if the cold had emptied it and shut it down. I stayed miles out of the city, on a university campus, a 40-minute bus ride away from one extreme stop on one limb of the metro. Everything seemed daunting: the cold, the unfamiliarity, the distances. I spent the first two days in a funk, fighting jet lag and reading in the dining commons, where it was warm and bright.

I never found Sivagnanam the radiographer, but somebody at a local Tamil association gave me a phone number for Ravi Paramanathan, a retired major who had been living in Toronto for nearly two decades. Ravi sounded huffy when I called him one afternoon, but he explained that he was outdoors, on a hike. I had gotten lucky; even though it was the middle of the week, he had the day off.

'Take the subway out to McCowan this evening and call me, and I'll come pick you up,' he said. In the train, brown faces gradually replaced white and black; east Toronto, and the suburb of Scarborough in particular, was the nucleus of Toronto's Sri Lankan Tamil diaspora, a transplanted Wellawatte with temples and Tamil DVD parlours and strip-mall cafes selling hoppers and fish curry. Outside the McCowan station, I stood with my hands under my armpits, my knees knocking together from the piercing wind, until a pale chocolate Hummer pulled up inches from my toes. 'You're the writer? Get in.'

Like his car, Ravi seemed very emphatically to belong to the military. His hair was cropped close to his head, and his powerful frame was constructed around a javelin-straight back. Even his moustache appeared martial, tempered not at all by the soul patch sitting atop his chin. He steered his Hummer through the suburbs as if he was driving a tank, expecting lesser vehicles to scurry out of his way. As I thawed gratefully in the passenger seat, he appraised me out of the corner of his eye.

'You're meeting Tamils from the army?' he asked. I admitted that I was, and that I wanted to see the war from their unusual, and unexamined, perspective.

'Who else have you met?'

I mentioned Dr Thurairaja.

'Thurairaja? The major general? Isn't he dead?'

'What?' I exclaimed, my voice squeaky in alarm. It had been a couple of months since I had last met him, but surely that grand, fit man could not have died in that time. 'No, no. At least, I don't think so.'

'Maybe I'm mistaken,' Ravi said.

He had relaxed visibly at the mention of a familiar name. 'I used to know some others. There is one man, Kanagarajah, in the infantry in 1984. His mother is Sinhalese, so he took her name. He died in a grenade explosion.' He frowned to pull more names out of his memory. 'There is a guy called Mark, a Christian Tamil from Batticaloa. Did he become a general? I can't remember. When he joined, he didn't know a word of Sinhalese. Then, after a while, he didn't talk a word of Tamil. He just left his Tamil identity behind.' He eyed me again. 'Do you speak Tamil?'

'I do, yes.'

'Do you read it?'

'Very haltingly,' I confessed. In a corner of my mind, I wondered if I was being vetted in some way for trustworthiness.

Ravi became more genial and expansive once we were in his home. He brought me a mug of tea, settled me on to his sectional sofa, and introduced me to his son, who was a student at the University of Toronto. His son was on the verge of leaving the house, but after listening gravely to my explanation for why I had come to see his father, he dashed upstairs and returned with an iPod Touch. He flicked to a voice recorder app and set the device down on the coffee table. 'He never discusses this stuff with us,' he told me. 'I really want to know what he says.'

We talked for seven straight hours, or maybe more, and my fingers finally cramped from writing. They struggled to hold the pen, and the words on the pages of my notebook began running drunkenly into each other. Ravi spoke in large circles, digressing again and again, strewing information all along the way, but always unerringly returning to where he began, like a woodsman finding his way home after dark. He also had the curious habit of describing the past in the present tense, which lent his stories a vivid and unsettling immediacy.

'My father is in the army,' he'd say, 'because he's interested in nursing. It isn't an unusual thing, because there are a lot of Tamils in the army at the time. Those days, the army's strength is what, 2000, something like that? One of my uncles too, he is a sergeant major in an armoured corps regiment.'

I struggled, at first, to arrange these facts into a chronology. Did he mean his uncle was, as of date, a serving sergeant major? It took me a while to work out that everything that Ravi could tell me about his experiences in Sri Lanka was necessarily of the past. He had not been home since he immigrated to Canada 18 years ago. 'Going back now will bring back too many memories, and it will hurt too much,' he told me. His departure had sealed Sri Lanka permanently into a chamber of his personal history.

When I met him, Ravi worked as a correctional officer with a maximum-security prison in Toronto, a job he got some years after he came to Canada. He arrived here in a state of philosophical disrepair. His love for the army had been wounded, he held conflicted feelings about the Tigers, and he wasn't sure where he was wanted. Being a Tamil in the army, he said, was like being a bat. 'Because the bat is a mammal, he goes and talks to the other mammals, and they say: "No, no, you're a bird. Get out of here." Then he goes to the birds, and they say: "No, no, you're a mammal, you don't lay eggs. Get out of here."' Ravi was pleased with this allegory, and he described it so fluently that he must have thought it up years earlier. 'That's the situation of a bat. That's the kind of situation I was in.'

The unmaking of Ravi's sense of belonging was the making of his political education. Perhaps this is always the case. Before 1990 or thereabouts, Ravi had kept only casual tabs on the ideologies driving the war. He seemed almost to pride himself on his blithe ignorance of politics; over and over, he told me: 'I have no clue about politics at this stage.' When the Tigers first began to battle for the Tamil state, Ravi deemed them obnoxious. 'If you want to demand something, you negotiate, you talk, you go about it in a peaceful process. There's no way you take up arms and kill my friends and then ask for what you want.'

Then the edges of his own life sliced through his bubble. He heard Sinhalese soldiers talking with genuine worry about the *akhanda Demala rajya*, the project of a greater Tamil nation that would stretch from south India through Sri Lanka into Malaysia. 'The Sinhalese have this delusion: that the Tamils are going to take over our country, they're going to destroy it, and we have to protect Buddhism and the Sinhalese people from these evil Tamil people who came from India, who don't even belong here, that kind of thing.' When his promotions didn't come through on time, he said, he had a moment of sharp understanding. 'I said to myself: "Okay, now I know why the Tamils are pissed." You land a job in the government, but if you don't know the language, get out.' Even as he became 'a token Tamil officer,' he heard cascading stories about soldiers murdering and raping Tamils in conflict zones.

But the Tamil separatists were not Ravi's team either; he couldn't even look at the blood-red flag of the Tigers without feeling itchy and uncomfortable. The militants were no kinder than the worst of the army's soldiers, even to other Tamils, and whenever he was in Jaffna his pulse would run jagged out of fear.

Late one night, when he was travelling back from the north to Colombo, his bus was halted at the border so that two rifle-toting militants could rob its passengers of their cash and watches. 'One man is wearing pants, and the other is in a sarong. I remember the face. Even now I could tell you.' If Ravi had not had the presence of mind to stuff his army ID into a gash in his seat cushion, he is certain, they would have executed him without pause.

He had already seen, first-hand, how brutal and cavalier the militants' licks of violence could be. In the late 1980s—and Ravi, as ever, was not wholly sure of the year—he had travelled to the port town of Kankesanthurai, in the Jaffna peninsula, to visit his brother-in-law. 'We are waiting for the bus, and opposite us is another bus stand, and I can see a house and a shop next to it. So these guys come, and they are inquiring about a guy, and they pull him out of the shop and shoot him. Tan, tan. He falls. Tan, tan. Four shots.' The body of the man, so recently vital, now lay frozen on the ground. Two militants dispersed the crowd, and two others took away the body. Within minutes, no traces remained of this swift erasure of a life.

When Ravi was nine years old, in 1970, his family moved from Jaffna to a cantonment town named Panagoda, Sri Lanka's largest military base, 20 kilometres out of Colombo. From his family's quarters, Ravi had to walk 15 minutes to catch a bus to school, and he frequently heard soldiers talking Tamil around him, the Hindus among them additionally distinguished by a ritual streak of white ash drawn across their foreheads.

'But my sister and I don't understand Sinhalese,' he said. 'We are standing in the bus, listening to all these people talk, with open mouths'—and here his mouth made a stricken O—'and we aren't getting it at all.'

His parents had to be summoned to school so that his Sinhalese teacher could complain to them about his dire lack of progress. 'Then, finally, I see one of my friends holding a Sinhalese comic book, and I love comics, so I start reading it, forcing myself, just because I'm so enthusiastic to know the story. There is this Sinhalese cartoon newspaper that I buy every Friday, and I love this newspaper, so I read this, and that's how I learn Sinhalese.'

In his boyhood, Ravi first sensed rancour against Tamils during the ethnic riots of 1977. The riots burned for a week, and his school stayed closed for another ten days. His family was safe on the Panagoda military base; it was only on his first bus ride back to school that he saw the charred hulls of Tamil restaurants and cinema theatres, and the defaced Tamil signboards. One section of his school had been damaged by fire as well. 'There's a whole lot of furniture missing. Then we find out that the furniture had turned up in a Sinhalese school nearby.'

A week or two after the riots, when classes had started up again, a gas canister exploded in the chemistry lab, and plumes of black smoke drifted over the school. 'Mrs Rasaiah, my class teacher, comes running into our room, shouting, "Run, run,

run!" Everybody is panicking, imagining that somebody has thrown a bomb into the school. We are on the first floor, and one of my friends doesn't want to risk using the stairs, because there's where the smoke is coming from. So he jumps right down, and he breaks his arm. We were all thinking that we'd be cut into pieces or burned alive. Those are the sorts of crazy ideas going through your head.'

After he completed school, Ravi worked part-time jobs at a couple of hotels and as a night usher at the Rio theatre, making 40 rupees a month. He was trying not to follow his father into the army, but when no other options presented themselves, he applied in 1981 and went through a physical. One of his friends knew a local member of Parliament, a Sinhalese hardliner, on whose recommendation he could enter the army as a commissioned officer. 'I go into his office, and I'm standing there, and I remember him saying—and he's not even looking at me, he's looking at the secretary—he says: "Shouldn't he be going to see Mr Thondaman instead of me?"' Savumiamoorthy Thondaman was a prominent Tamil politician, and although Ravi had heard of him, the jibe missed its mark. 'I don't have any clue at this time about politics. So I am a little confused. He laughs, then he signs the letter and gives it to me, and he says: "You're not going to come back and shoot me, are you?" I know it is supposed to be a joke, so I also laugh.'

Ravi had paid no attention to the first quivers of trouble in the north. The Tigers were still small-time operators, ambushing an army lorry here, stealing a few guns there, or pulling off the killing of an occasional policeman or two. During Ravi's 18 months of training, somebody from the army's intelligence unit came to speak to these nascent officers.

'You don't have to worry about what you hear on the news,' Ravi remembered being assured. 'It's not a big thing.

They have some arms and they try to shoot people, but they aren't going to do any harm. We can beat them soon.' But of the 31 people in Ravi's batch, only 19 remained at the end of the training course, and I wondered if the dropouts had perhaps been the sharp ones and had bolted at the growing prospect of real fighting. After his training, Ravi became a second lieutenant in the ordnance unit, back in Panagoda, tasked with managing materiel and compiling receipts.

Around midnight on July 23 1983, Ravi and other second lieutenants sat in a bus in Panagoda, snoozing lightly, waiting to be driven to Ampara, in Sri Lanka's eastern rump, for an additional round of training. The sergeant had gone to procure some radio equipment, and he was away an unusually long time: first 10 minutes, then 20, then half an hour, then more. 'When he comes into the bus, he says: "Gentlemen, I have some bad news," and I think: "Oh, we're not going for training after all."' The sergeant told his colleagues about the Tigers' ambush of the army convoy in Jaffna, and about the 13 soldiers who had died; he read out the names of the slain 13, including that of the sole officer in the group.

'And I am in shock, because just two weeks ago, I was having drinks with him,' Ravi said. 'He was in army HQ and I had gone there for a visit. We met there and we were having a drink and a singsong, and we had a good time. Then he went that way and I came here. And then he got killed.'

Nobody on the bus spoke, Ravi said, all the way to Ampara. 'I am not expecting a riot. But we know what is coming. This is serious. I'm expecting: Okay, now we are going after these guys. The blood is boiling. When we train together, we aren't looking at each other as Sinhalese or Burgher or whatever. We're soldiers. We're army. We're buddies.'

In Ampara, the officers lived and trained for three months in near-perfect isolation, in quarters in the middle of the jungle. Weapons apart, the most advanced piece of technology that

Ravi possessed was a mosquito-repellent coil, and he would often wake up at night to see elephants ambling past his window. Too rarely, a visitor from a nearby army camp would drop in to the classroom and supply updates; one major solemnly told them: 'The country is burning.' Horrifying riot stories filtered into the jungle, where they were pounced upon and dissected by news-starved officers. Ravi remembered one, from Diyatalawa, a garrison town in Sri Lanka's highlands. A Tamil doctor and his family, well known to the locals, had been threatened in the thick of the riots, so they called for police assistance. When they were being driven to safety in a police jeep, a mob stopped them. 'Apparently the police inspector is given some sort of signal, because he allows these people to drag the doctor out and chop him up, right in front of his family.'

Ravi and the other Tamil officers in Ampara were offered transport back to their families, to check on them and make sure they were safe. It seemed to Ravi that all the Tamil officers from Panagoda and Colombo—all the ones he knew, certainly—had been dispatched to the Ampara training course as the riots spread. 'David is there. Patrick is there. I am there. Mahindan is there. Kanagaraj, I think, is there. Only two people are not there: Chandrakumar, from the engineers' corps, and Kadirgamanathan, from work services.'

He paused here, as if he was allowing this roll call to flare into significance for the very first time. The silence seemed to invite a question, so I asked it.

'But it was just a coincidence, right? That all these Tamil officers were in one place?'

Ravi picked at his trackpants with stubby fingers, divesting them of imaginary lint. He wasn't even looking at me; peering this deeply into the past had robbed his eyes of their focus, glazed them with a film of remembrance. 'I don't know,' he said. 'That's what I want to believe. But after coming here, to Canada, now I have a lot of questions. I learn a lot about things happening around the world, and my mind is going: 'How the hell was it possible?"

He chose not to return to Panagoda to see his parents—partly because he was sure they would be safe on the army base, but also because he had heard, from other officers who had just returned to Ampara, of the dismal business of the world outside.

'One guy is going to Wellawatte, to check on his brother, and his brother's house has been burned down. On the way to Colombo, they see people still burning and half-burned bodies, they see upturned cars and mobs still attacking at random, with the police just standing there, doing nothing.' His friends, Ravi said, could do nothing. 'They can only wave to the police and continue on their way, because if there are a hundred thousand people, or even a hundred people, and you have one pistol, you can go shoot one person, and even that isn't easy.'

In the immediate vicinity of the officers' training camp, Ampara remained relatively peaceful in July 1983. But after the riots ended, and when the war was swelling into its toxic fullness, Ampara became the stage for a free-for-all. Tamils went missing. Soldiers in trucks took potshots at bicyclists. 'One guy makes the kill, and then the truck will stop, and the others will run and strip the bicyclist of his watch and his money and so on.' A colleague told Ravi of a raid in which he had participated. 'The Tigers are making propaganda at the time, and they build temporary huts in remote villages, they take TVs there, and they show people training videos. And as a kid, you've never seen a TV, so you go running there to sit and watch, right?' The solitary Tiger guarding the entrance of such a hut had been silenced, and then the raiding party had stood outside the hut and riddled it with gunfire. 'They didn't know they are kids, you see. It is in the middle of the night. And my friend is sad that he had participated, but who can you blame in this?'

Gradually, inevitably, the stories flocked closer home. Some weeks after the riot, when Ravi had visited an Ampara photo studio to collect his prints, he spotted by accident a developed pack awaiting its owner, a member of a unit in which one of his friends served. In the pack was a photo of a fallen man, around 35 or 40 years old, half his head blown off by a shotgun, and a copy of the Tamil newspaper *Veerakesari* fluttering on the ground beside him. Ravi never mentioned the photograph to his friend. 'And then, much later I learned that in subsequent batches of that same training I went to, in Ampara, people were told: "You have to learn how to kill a guy. So pick a Tamil and kill him."'

Behind the Ampara training camp lay a quarry that Ravi had visited as a boy, when his father had been working in the area. 'I remember climbing through there, and I see an elephant, one lonely elephant, running up the hill. That's why I remember that place very well.' He hesitated for some seconds, unsure of how exactly to proceed. 'Look, I was told this first-hand, and I will protect this officer by all means. But you're the first person I'm telling this to, outside of my family.' The quarry had been dug in a locality called Nonivana Pahana, which translated into Eternal Lamp; in this quarry, the officer had told Ravi, soldiers had burned the bodies of civilians they had killed.

'Almost on a weekly basis, they randomly take the truck and go round up villagers, boys and men, herd them, and shoot them. This happened, I don't know, in the late 1980s, I think. And there is no one to question the soldiers.' The officer had served in Ampara for years, had even married into a family living in the area, and he was anguished by what he was being asked to do. 'He told me: "I can't handle it. I can't watch this. But this is happening."'

In Ravi's house, perfectly suburban, with its two cars in the garage and its open-plan kitchen, the lights had come on, and his wife, Selvy, had joined us in the living room, sitting silently to one side. I hadn't noticed; in fact, I hadn't even shifted position, for fear of puncturing Ravi's confessional spell. These stories spilled out of him so fast that there was no time to process them, to absorb their import, to even wonder if they might not all be wholly accurate.

Later, sifting through the literature about the war, I would constantly watch for references to these specific incidents in Ampara. I didn't find them—which wasn't surprising, because so much about this war remains undocumented and untold. But I often thought of Ravi's quarry. In my imagination of it, the setting is some amalgam of Ravi's childhood and the murderous years of the 1980s. The elephant runs up and down the quarry's sides as bodies burn in the Eternal Lamp. The land around the quarry is flat and chalky and desolate, and the fire has consumed every living being except the distressed elephant.

At some point, Ravi brought out his photographs: slim, old-fashioned albums with ringed spines, in which the prints sat between flimsy cellophane veils and dimpled white plastic. Many of them were of him in uniform, incandescent with pride, looking straight into the camera. In one photo, Ravi has just become a young officer, and he stands flanked by his parents and his two sisters, his rectangular belt buckle glowing gold against the dark material of his outfit. In another, Ravi and his fellow trainees kick back in a cramped room, all of them in shorts and T-shirts, many of them laughing lustily; I got the distinct impression that a clutch of liquor bottles had been judiciously left out of the frame. In a third, Ravi, older and now moustached, wears a beret and green camouflage, and he poses in his army quarters with his left foot jauntily perched on a low wooden table. His right arm is slung by his side, with its thumb hooked into his pocket. Behind him, on the wall, are posters of cars—not sports cars, curiously enough, but sedans and station wagons and hatchbacks. It is difficult to be sure, but on the table, next to Ravi's polished shoe, there seems to be a pile of just-read comic books. The effect is that of a soldier who has triumphantly conquered a little boy's bedroom.

In 1983, and for a couple of years after that, Ravi still loved being in the army. He was forever at pains, during our conversation, to point out that the army's excesses were perpetrated by rogue officers, or at the bidding of politicians. He didn't believe that every officer was a racist; most of them, in fact, were decent men. Perhaps, he reasoned, some of them caved in to peer pressure. 'Maybe they have to do it, or they have to let this happen, because if you don't, the soldiers are going to look down upon you and say: "He's a pussy, man. He can't even kill a person." That kind of talk.'

Slowly, though, the war stripped away from Ravi the strong sense of fraternity he felt in the army. The word *Demala*, Sinhalese for 'Tamil', began to be expectorated by soldiers around Ravi, with gaining frequency, as a racist slur. His promotions remained stalled until, during an interview where he was asked to prove his fluency in Sinhalese, he snatched up a newspaper, read aloud an article with machine-gun speed, and then wrote it up again for his examiner. He wasn't picked for a couple of positions that he applied for. When a friend in joint operations command recommended Ravi to relieve him, in a role that required translating intercepted Tiger communications, Ravi didn't get the job. Instead, the army hired Tamil-speaking Muslims for such posts. 'Why don't you employ a Tamil person?' Ravi asked. 'I'd say they didn't ask me because my parents are living in Jaffna, and it's a big compromise. I understand that. But why don't they even offer? "Ravi, why don't you come help us out? We'll get your parents out of there. They've been here, they can live here. We'll make it work.'"

In Panagoda once, a Muslim officer known to Ravi fell into a spot of trouble and was placed under house arrest, in a newly whitewashed building with barred windows. Hearing of his friend's situation, Ravi went to visit him, standing outside a window and conducting a conversation through the iron grills. 'At some point, I turn around, and there is a guy, one of the junior staff, spying on me from under a tree, standing there and watching me,' he said. 'So anyway, I finish and I turn to go back, and I see him running ahead of me, all the way back to the officers' mess, where there is a billiards room, where I have left my briefcase. So maybe they are going through the stuff in my briefcase? The way he runs, it looks like he is going to tell them I am coming back.'

In fact, Ravi felt doubly alienated by the war—not only from the army but also from his own community. This struck him with force one day in 1984, on a train from Jaffna to Colombo.

Ravi's father had retired in the previous year, but after he witnessed the mayhem of the riots, he abandoned his plans of settling down in Colombo. Instead, he built a house in Jaffna, where he owned a patch of land; then, when he was offered some temporary work in the Middle East, he took it. So in 1984, when Ravi's grandfather died, it was left to him to represent the family at the funeral. 'They did tell me not to come to Jaffna, because the Tigers are kidnapping and killing police, ambushing the army here and there.' Ravi went, nevertheless. 'Then I am in the train, coming back to Colombo, and out of the window, I see these guys in sarongs, riding motorcycles, holding rifles. And I thought: "Holy cow, imagine if they know I am in the army." They would have taken me right there. I realize it's not safe for me to go to the north any more.'

It wasn't good for Ravi's career as an officer, either, to be seen travelling frequently to Jaffna, trips that might goad paranoid army intelligence units into doubting his loyalties. 'I don't want to be a suspect, and I never know who is dealing with whom,' he said. To his dismay, other Tamil officers were changing their names; a Natarajasingham he knew became a Rajasingha, and another officer replaced his Tamil father's surname with that of his Sinhalese mother. 'But it's a weakness. And I know people are laughing behind their asses if you change your name, because they're thinking: "Look at that guy. He can't handle it."'

In Colombo, Ravi stopped going to Wellawatte entirely, and he cut down his visits to Tamil temples. 'Not that I'm religious. But I go to the temple just to keep in touch with my culture and my people, or to see if anybody I know from my schooldays is dropping by. I don't see anyone.' Occasionally, he would buy a copy of *Veerakesari*, and he would read it over dinner at Greenlands, a Tamil restaurant. 'That is all the Tamil culture I get, when I am missing my family. Otherwise, you finish work, you go to the bar and find a waitress, and you drink. That's the only thing you have. I was completely depressed. Basically, after 1983, for a long time, I didn't talk Tamil at all.'

This was the first time Selvy spoke to me. 'It's true. When he met me, his Tamil was awful. He was that out of practice.' She giggled, and after the bleakness of the last few hours, it sounded as startling and refreshing as the world's first laugh.

Ravi and Selvy were introduced to each other by their families in the mid-1980s. She had been living and studying in Wellawatte, and they began talking to each other regularly over the phone and then meeting whenever his schedule allowed it. There was no complicated courtship, but in recounting that slice of the past, Ravi seemed forever unsure of his chronology, as if the years had been pureed into one another. Selvy served patiently as his aide-mémoire. 'Selvy, when did I go to India for training?' he would holler towards the kitchen. 'It was 1986, no? Or 1987? Was it 1988?' In fact, Selvy would correct him, it was 1989. Ravi had told me earlier, with unimpeachable certainty, that they had been married in 1986; it would be a full year before I learned that the wedding had happened in 1988.

It was not easy for a Tamil army officer to marry into a Tamil family—to convince your fiancée's parents that, although your colleagues may rain bombs on their Jaffna neighbourhood tomorrow, you will keep their daughter safe and happy. Selvy's parents liked Ravi well enough, but one of her five brothers refused to speak to him and tried mightily to stop the marriage. 'I mean, they were affected by the army, and the way they grew up, they naturally thought that the army was evil. They insulted me many times.' Twice, though, Ravi nearly came to blows in such circumstances. 'The first person I almost punched is her brother. Then there is another gentleman, a former Tamil politician, back home. And Selvy is related to his wife, so we visit them, and he is introducing us around. He tells his uncle: "Uncle, by the way, do you know this guy? He was in the army. He was a major." And the way he said it, laughing like it was a joke—I almost punched him too.'

In 1992, Ravi asked to be retired, but his request was denied; instead, he received a circular telling him that all retirements were being curtailed, and that the army, struggling and failing at the time to capture Jaffna, was so desperately short of staff that it was offering incentives to retired officers to lure them back into service. Ravi already had a conditional visa from Canada, a document that would allow him to emigrate if only he could convince the army to let him go. Fortunately for him, the visa came through in early 1994, not long after D.B. Wijetunga became the president of Sri

Lanka. 'I have a friend who knows him closely, so I talk to this person, and he says: "Don't worry, I'll take care of it."' His release from the army, Ravi thinks, might well have been the last official document that Wijetunga signed as president, because he relinquished the post soon after, in November 1994. If not for Wijetunga, he said, 'I think I would have been stuck there.'

Near midnight, or perhaps past it, I must have flagged visibly. It had been a long, cluttered day, and it wasn't finished yet; I lived a clear hour and a half away by bus and train and bus again, assuming they all still operated at this hour. 'This is awkward,' I said. 'But I think I have to go. I don't want to miss the last train.'

'Don't worry about it,' Ravi said. 'I'll drive you home.'

'It's an hour and a half away,' I protested feebly, not really wanting to dissuade him at all.

'So what? It'll be a night-time drive. Selvy, let's take a night-time drive.'

The Hummer had been blocked, in its driveway, by Ravi's son's car, so Selvy had to run in to get the keys and back it out. 'Civilian life!' Ravi snorted. 'People don't work as a team in civilian life. She knew we were leaving, but she didn't move the car. I find it difficult to adjust to that.' He said this as he watched Selvy through the windshield, and it warmed me that his exasperation was so flecked with love.

My head felt heavy, stuffed so full with information that it pounded against my inner temples. Ravi was chipper, though, joking around about setting me up with a date in Toronto. 'You're single, right? You aren't married? We know some nice Tamil girls here. Selvy, you should think of somebody.'

In the long evening of the war, Ravi had pored often over Google Earth, squinting to make out the damage that had been inflicted by the army upon the north. He knew, he said, how the war would end. He knew the army had been strengthening its resources through 2005 and 2006, and he knew that the world had changed after 9/11, that governments suddenly had tacit international sanction to launch unrestrained attacks against those they considered terrorists. But he was still horrified by the shelling of the civilians in the no-fire zones; that he hadn't expected. 'It's population control, in a way. Already one million Tamils have left the country, another hundred thousand or maybe more have died, and the youth is all gone. There are more women than men there. There are too many widows, and too many soldiers running around. Testosterone levels are high in that area. You do the math. You know what's happening. In about 20 years, in the north and east, there will be more Sinhalese people, and all this Tamil Eelam concept will vanish. Everybody will be speaking Sinhalese. So it'll be done.'

'Are you happy here?' I asked. 'You're glad you came away?'

'Hmm,' Ravi said. 'Initially, I'm not too happy. I was more comfortable in the army than when I am new in Canada. It is unbelievably stressful.' He struggled at first to find work he could do, given his background in the army, but he had now worked 14 years in the correctional department. 'Maybe it's not what I wanted to do with my life. But the job is easy, the money is good, and I'm raising my children and my family, making new friends. Now I'm comfortable. Now I feel like a free person. Now I feel like a human being.' It was a strange thing to hear from a man in self-imposed exile from his homeland. On the other hand, it sounded just right from a man who had been nothing but an outsider at home. His exile had begun long before he left Sri Lanka for good.

8

ON MY WAY to Canada, I had stopped in London to see Raghavan and Nirmala, who lived near West Harrow. It had rained all weekend—not heavily, but in a bitter, pestilential, soul-straining way. The Metropolitan line of the Tube was closed for maintenance precisely until the West Harrow stop, so I rode a succession of double-decker buses and then tramped through puddles for a couple of kilometres to reach their house. The sky was the colour of tin. I arrived with wet feet, feeling bleak and worn. Nirmala, who knew it was my birthday, took one look at me and declared: 'You're eating lunch here. I'm cooking Tamil food. At least you can eat as if you're back home.' Through the morning, dense, steamy clouds, seeded with the smells of cumin and pepper, forced themselves into the living room from the kitchen.

Raghavan was sprawled on his sofa in his sweatpants, watching *Dr No*, and fresh box sets of *Mad Men* DVDs were stacked on top of the television. It was a Sunday, and I prickled with guilt for yanking him out of his torpor. He didn't seem to mind, though. Like a big cat, he uncoiled himself and sat up straight. His stubble had come out fuller than ever over the weekend, and he scratched absently at it as he spoke.

Just as the 1980s had disillusioned Ravi, they had disillusioned Raghavan; in fact, Raghavan had come crashing down harder because he had been so much more idealistic, had entertained such glittering hopes for the Tigers. 'All of us had faith in the armed struggle, even though we had no idea about how to conduct it.' Prabhakaran, however, had swotted up on guerrilla tactics like a morbid schoolboy. Somehow, he had found a copy of *Teach Yourself Shooting*, a book published in London, and he studied it intently. He cleaned and oiled his Smith & Wesson every day, and he spent hours in target practice. He always allotted himself extra rations of bullets; he needed them, he said, because it was him the police desired to kill most of all.

The Tigers melted into the jungle and invented their own training programme: first some furious physical exercise, some running and squats and crawls, and then shooting practice with small arms and shotguns. They lived in huts amidst palmyra groves, spending longer and longer lengths of time in the Vanni, until Raghavan lost contact with his parents altogether. Late in 1977, when the police clattered into his family's house in Jaffna to ask where Raghavan was, his brother suggested they try an uncle's house in Batticaloa. He wasn't lying; he honestly didn't know that Raghavan was not in the country at all, that he had paid 200 rupees to a smuggler to sail him across the ocean to temporary refuge in India.

Raghavan returned to Sri Lanka in 1978, to a new camp that Prabhakaran had set up near Madhu, a town south and west of Jaffna. That April, T.I. Bastiampillai, a police inspector who had been investigating an assassination committed by one of Raghavan's colleagues, unwisely raided the Madhu camp with the help only of a sub-inspector, a sergeant, and his chauffeur. Bastiampillai was a Tamil, but he had been extraordinarily obsessed with crushing Prabhakaran and the Tigers. 'If I get hold of your son,' he had once cautioned Prabhakaran's mother, in the early days of the young militant's career, 'I will break him into a hundred pieces.'

In Madhu, Bastiampillai blundered in at 5 a.m. 'He had underestimated us,' Raghavan said. 'He didn't think we would fight.' The three officers—one with a sub-machine gun, one with a double-barrelled shotgun, and one with a pistol—found five Tigers in a hut and ordered them to come out. Most of the militants' arms had been stashed, for safety, in a small tree house high above their heads. They had a shotgun but not the time required to load it, so they emerged with their hands over their heads, protesting that they were only local farmhands. 'Then we grabbed their guns. We took them by surprise. We didn't even talk to each other. One of us attacked, and then by some internal communication, we all attacked.'

The Tigers shot the three policemen and the driver, and then they stole the car; it was discovered later, roasted to a crisp. They kept the policemen's weapons for themselves; for years thereafter, Prabhakaran would show off Bastiampillai's revolver to new Tigers. Bastiampillai's body was found after three days, severely mutilated.

'They thought we had done that, but we didn't. It was the animals in the jungle,' Raghavan said, his voice so even that he might have been discussing a ruined flower bed. He looked calm and unwavering into my eyes, and I wished desperately that I knew if he was lying. 'Bastiampillai was seen as a terror and a traitor. Now, if I think back, I don't think he tortured people. He beat his detainees, but later I heard he treated them well also.' Raghavan paused. 'He was a police officer, and this was his job, which was fair. But at that time, we didn't think about these things.'

After the killing of Bastiampillai, Raghavan said, the country began to fear the Tigers, and the Tamils began to respect them. Their membership increased; if Prabhakaran had not been so picky about new recruits, there would have been many more than the 60 or 70 guerrillas who trained and lived together in 1979. The first signs of tyranny had, by now, crept into Prabhakaran's leadership of the Tigers. In 1978 or 1979, Raghavan learned that Prabhakaran had killed two of their comrades, one because he wanted to leave the Tigers and return home to Batticaloa, and the other because Prabhakaran thought he might defect to a rival militant group.

Prabhakaran told Raghavan about what he had done. 'My impression was that he felt bad about it, but he said he had no choice. Several of us found it difficult to stomach this. If you've been living together as comrades, this makes you very uneasy.' Prabhakaran, he said, had developed the rudiments of a messiah complex. 'He never apologized for anything he did, never critically analysed his own actions. Never.'

Did he argue with Prabhakaran about these murders? I asked.

He didn't. Not so much as a quibble. 'You tended to accept them for the sake of the organization, even if you didn't agree. So I didn't raise it with him again. But that was the point when a lot of us started to think about the structure, started to have doubts.'

The years between 1979 and 1982 were fissile times. The Tigers cleaved and cleaved again, as members quit or were kicked out. After Prabhakaran expelled a senior Tiger for breaking his oath of celibacy, a minor mutiny ensued, and he abandoned the group for a spell, joining the rival Tamil Eelam Liberation Organization (TELO) instead. 'He tried to convince me to join them,' Raghavan said. 'But the cadre were weak. They were mostly sitting around watching movies. It was a part-time job for them.' Prabhakaran realized this as well. By the first few months of 1982, he had pushed his way back into leading the Tigers, biding his time in India and mustering plans for his men.

Late one night in May 1982, after Raghavan and

Prabhakaran had watched a film in Pondy Bazaar, the frenetic core of Madras, they were walking down the road for dinner when they spotted Uma Maheshwaran. This was the unchaste Tiger—the one Prabhakaran had cast out of his fold, and the one who had then formed the People's Liberation Organisation of Tamil Eelam (PLOTE), with the same tired words scrambled into a new name. Raghavan and Prabhakaran broke out their guns first. After the shootout, it turned out that Uma Maheshwaran had escaped, his friend was hit and bleeding, and Raghavan and Prabhakaran had been corralled by a crowd into a road that led straight to the police station. They would be detained for three months before they jumped bail and sneaked back into Sri Lanka.

Raghavan still has a photograph, a neat square clipping out of a Madras newspaper, showing himself and Prabhakaran after their arrest. 'Prize catch,' the caption trumpets. There are 10 policemen accompanying these two Tigers, the constables in unsightly shorts and pith helmets and an officer in trousers. Prabhakaran looks puny and nondescript. His shirt sleeves are folded up to his elbows, and his right hand is held, by a policeman, with the swinging looseness that accompanies a stroll on the beach. Raghavan, though, is tall and has a feline stride, his tight white T-shirt tucked into his bell bottoms, and his hair so thick that it resembles an afro. The photo is too grainy to be able to say this with certainty, but it seems as if he's smiling, as if he's enjoying the attention.

We pored over the photo. 'When they were arrested, the policemen were sure that Raghavan was the leader and Prabhakaran was the assistant,' Nirmala said. She told me how, one morning in 1978, when she had been teaching at the university, a student pounded in breathless to say that he had just seen a posse of Tigers hold up a People's Bank branch. 'And there was a foreign fighter with them. He must have been from Lebanon or Palestine or something,' the student huffed to Nirmala. It was only Raghavan, looking as languid and exotic as ever.

But Raghavan felt empty and unhappy after the Pondy Bazaar shootout. 'I told Prabhakaran: "This isn't going to work. We're all going to end up killing each other."' The Tigers by now numbered over four hundred, arranged so tightly around Prabhakaran that they crowded out dissenters and disagreement. Spies reported upon spies, and all of them ferried news back to Prabhakaran. 'If you wanted to be recruited into the Tigers, he would first ask you: "If your brother joined PLOTE tomorrow, would you be ready to kill him?"' Raghavan said. 'It was sickening. He wouldn't ask you if you would be ready to fight the Sri Lankan government. He'd ask you if you could kill a PLOTE member.'

This was what distressed him, I realized with discomfort— not that they had to kill other people, but that they wound up having to kill other Tamils. Murder was an acceptable weapon, as long as it was pointed in the right direction. An orchestrated death was murder if it felled one of your own but simply a component of the armed struggle otherwise. I recalled what a former Maoist in India had once told me, about being imprisoned for 'annihilating a class enemy'; it had taken me a full minute to work out that he had killed a man. War mangles words just as efficiently as it mangles bodies.

Raghavan was once more in Madras, in 1985, when he decided that he wanted to leave the Tigers. He had met and fallen in love with Nirmala, who was living in a safe house in the city, having been spirited there from Sri Lanka a year earlier. Madras was thick with Tigers in hiding, and Prabhakaran's meddling reach extended even here. 'It was like living in Stalin's Russia,' Nirmala said. 'All of us were tailed. We would go into an office to sit at a table, and automatically, with our fingers, we would check the underside of the table for bugs.' If they ever gave Prabhakaran advice, it was disregarded. 'It was like blowing a conch into a deaf man's ear.' In 1986, one of Nirmala's friends procured for her a fake Indian passport, and she flew under the name 'Christine Edwards' to the United Kingdom, where she was granted asylum. ('An Anglo-Indian name,' she said, 'because my English was so anglicized, and because I always wore blouses and pants, not saris.') Raghavan joined her not long afterwards.

What a succinct cautionary tale, I thought to myself, and how instructive in violence's habit of spraying out of control. I mentioned this out loud. It must seem so regrettable now, I said, that the Tigers ever picked up the gun.

Raghavan corrected me swiftly. 'Maybe we were too quick to take up arms. But I don't have any problem with an armed struggle in a certain sense. Obviously it would be ideal if there were no need for an armed struggle at all, and if people can get their rights peacefully. But was it likely to happen?' He thought not. 'I still don't know if there was any other way. And people portray Prabhakaran as a monster . . .'

'Of course he was a monster,' Nirmala called from the kitchen.

'That's your opinion!' Raghavan shot back.

'What do you mean, that's my opinion?' Nirmala said hotly. She had stormed into the living room, a spatula still in her hand. 'The atrocities committed by the Tigers, during the end of the war in particular—you can't deny it!'

Raghavan didn't reply. Either he didn't want this argument to play out in front of me or he realized the futility of his own position. He looked at the television, and in that profile, I could see that some of the muscles in his jaw were tight and pulsing.

I waited for a while, also watching *Dr No*, and then I asked Raghavan how he had felt in May 2009, when the Tigers had finally been defeated. 'I was angry and sad.' His voice had dropped back down to its drawl. I preferred it when he was heated, I thought; he seemed truer then, somehow. 'Angry with the state, but also with the Tigers, that they had conducted the war in this way, without caring about the Tamil people. And sad because, whatever was said and done, I knew these people. Even when Prabhakaran was killed, I was sad.' His flat, unsentimental tone was utterly misleading. Later Nirmala would tell me that, on 18 May 2009, when news of Prabhakaran's death had broken, Raghavan had gotten drunk at home and wept complicated tears—for his comrades, for his estranged and cruel friend, for the vast toll of a campaign begun with mere black flags and Solignum graffiti, for the devastation of a cause he still believed in, and for a fight that had somewhere gone very horribly wrong.

THE NORTH

1

THE BUSES TO Jaffna left from Wellawatte, from a rough, packed-earth parking lot where they all first idled, snorting and impatient like bulls in a bull pen. The fumes would have been intolerable had it not been for the breeze that swept in from the sea, which was a stone's throw away, on the other side of a railway line. These were the private bus services, where you were assured a 1000-rupee seat, air conditioning and a near-functional suspension; the rickety government-run buses left from a giant terminus close to the railway station, charging only a few hundred rupees for a cramped ride.

The first time I took a bus to Jaffna, I nearly missed it. I was halfway to Wellawatte before I realized that I had forgotten my passport at home, and I had to leap on to the bus just as it was pulling out of the bull pen. My seat hadn't been resold, fortunately. Next to me sat a priest in a white smock, a black sash around his waist and a chocolate-brown Bacardi cap on his head. Across the aisle, an older man in a safari suit was on the phone with somebody in Jaffna. He would reach in plenty of time for the wedding the next day, he was promising. Then he hung up, shook two pills out of a bottle, put them into his mouth, knocked his head back and swallowed them whole. His stubble glinted silver in the near-darkness. He'll have to shave before the wedding, I thought.

I fell asleep, but woke up frozen a few hours later, my nose icy and numb. The bus was ferociously air-conditioned, and

I saw now that the others had been prepared for it. My priest had slipped on two cardigans, and the man in the safari suit had wrapped a fleece around himself.

For the rest of the 11-hour journey, I sat half-awake and shivering, feeling the road change under the bus's wheels. Through the ancient capital of Anuradhapura and until Vavuniya, the highway was smooth, but as it entered the Vanni, the tarmac started to fall apart. The very sound of the wheels transformed, from a satisfied hum to a grinding protest. After Kilinochchi, the road crumbled even further, the highway here still pitted and disfigured from the war, and its shoulders so pulverized by the movement of heavy army vehicles that they had turned into dust. The bus transmitted each scar and lesion of the road as precisely as if somebody were pummelling me in Morse code. I curled my body into a tense coil and waited for daybreak.

Between Vavuniya and Kilinochchi, at 2 a.m., we stopped at the army checkpoint in Omanthai. Two soldiers boarded the bus and moved through the aisle, checking the ID cards of Sri Lankan citizens. I was a foreigner, so I was asked to get off, go into a tin-roofed shed, show my passport, and fill out a form explaining why I was going to Jaffna.

To see a friend, I scribbled, my fingers still frozen from the air conditioning.

The army officer looked at the form and then handed my passport to an assistant, who walked away with it into another room. I could hear the high whine of a photocopier. In 2011 and 2012, this elaborate screening was routine. Some areas of Sri Lanka were still closed off to foreigners and journalists, but although travel to Jaffna did not strictly require the Ministry of Defence's permission any more, the strained air in Omanthai suggested that the soldiers could send you back to Colombo at will.

The officer asked me a question in Sinhalese. I told him

that I didn't understand. None of the army personnel there knew Tamil—a strange staffing arrangement for a checkpoint inspecting buses to Jaffna—so the officer barked, in English: 'Address, Jaffna address?'

'A guest house,' I said. I wrote down the name, wishing he would hurry up, fearful that my bus would forget me and leave without me. I sat on and waited for the passport. Even this far into the night, the checkpoint was hardly silent; loudspeakers had been rigged up around the army sheds to murmur a continuous loop of Buddhist chants, puncturing the calm.

After I was cleared, I climbed back into my seat and tried unsuccessfully to sleep. Then I took to staring out of my window, making out dim details of the Vanni's landscape: its flattened terrain, the carpets of low vegetation that were anchored in place by palmyras standing tall as pushpins. After Kilinochchi, the smudgy light of predawn revealed wrecked houses, buildings with their roofs blown off, and sprawling army camps. Often, the road was bounded, on either side, by kilometre after kilometre of bright yellow security tape with the word 'MINES' printed on it in three languages. The bus trundled on stone-and-mortar bridges over a brace of lagoons, past stretches of paddy fields, and finally, under a low morning sky, into Jaffna, which was just shaking itself awake.

The Jaffna highway, the 320-kilometre A9, starts from Kandy in the hills, descends into the plains and runs nearly spine-straight up the country. It crosses a small stretch of water near the defunct salt pans of Elephant Pass before developing a crick in its neck, bending westwards into its home stretch and ending at the ramparts of the Portuguese-built 17th-century Jaffna Fort.

Almost all of the civil war raged around the A9's northern

segments, and the road became a useful dipstick to assess the army's fortunes. In 1984, the A9 was closed to civilian traffic, and as the Tigers snatched enough of the north and the east to begin administering their own de facto state, they came to control almost a third of the highway. Vavuniya, lying 115 kilometres south of Jaffna, turned into something of a border town, complete with bureaucratic formalities like entry and exit permits; a short distance from Vavuniya, the Tigers' hold over the land became complete.

During a brief lull in open warfare, between 2002 and 2005, the government managed to reopen the A9 until Kilinochchi, but the road was shut down again in 2006, when the fighting resumed. Only in early 2009, a few months before the end of the war, could the army capture Elephant Pass and deliver the entirety of the A9 back to the state. The railway line between Colombo and Jaffna had snapped during the war and had never been rebuilt, and flights were rare and expensive, so the A9 was always more than just a highway. It became the sole, fraying thread binding the north to the south, holding together the notion of an undivided Sri Lanka.

Jaffna is a small town made large by the war. It took perhaps seven minutes to drive through the entire town in an autorickshaw. Broken houses and small temples and big temples and palm trees and matchbox shops flickered by, and then suddenly there was the highway, reaching out to the next settlement on the peninsula. Was this all of it? I thought, and marvelled at what a massive dent this little town had wrought in its country's soul.

For strategic reasons, the capital of Tiger-held territory was Kilinochchi, but Jaffna was the Tigers' spiritual fount, the town that would have been the capital of an independent Eelam. Prabhakaran was born on the peninsula, as were the ideologies that drove the Eelam movement. 'The people of

Jaffna have a siege mentality,' somebody once told me. 'They have the ocean behind them, so they always feel defensive, like they're trapped in some way, and they act out against that.'

They've been trapped often. Jaffna was invaded first by the Portuguese, then by the Dutch and ultimately by the British; during the civil war, it was both lost and won through a siege. In 1990, the Tigers beat back more than two hundred soldiers into the Jaffna Fort, where they remained, kept alive by air-dropped rations, until they were evacuated 107 days later. The army regained Jaffna in 1995, after a 50-day siege that forced the Tigers and hundreds of Tamil families to flee southwards, past Elephant Pass and into the Vanni.

Nearly every time I came to Jaffna, I stayed opposite the St John Bosco School, in a little guest house with two dogs. The larger of the pair snoozed perpetually in the yard, but the smaller—a dachshund—nipped at my heels as I walked in through the gate, slung his bratwurst of a body up the steps to my room on the first floor, and deposited puddles of warm liquid in the corridor. The owner, a burly man clad always in a white singlet and a blue sarong knotted halfway up his chest, watched the dachshund's antics with granite impassivity.

Around the corner from the guest house was a sight common to Tamil towns: a pond full of jade-green water, and adjoining it, a tiny temple to Ganesha. I never saw the iron gates to that temple open. Whenever I walked past its candy-striped wall, on the empty, shaded lane leading to my guest house, I wedged my face into the grillwork of the gate and peered into the temple, at its cubbyhole of a shrine and its immaculate red-oxide floor. I imagined myself sitting there of an evening, as the sun extinguished itself and the sea breeze bustled into the temple. It looked like the most serene spot on earth.

Jaffna brought back vivid memories of Madras as it was in the late 1980s, so I initially concluded that the town had been frozen in amber, and that with the end of the war—with the construction of new houses and the return of a hubbub to its commercial quarter—the resin was only just beginning to melt. This was a mistake, although maybe it was an understandable one to make: Jaffna's houses were rambling, crumbling structures; its streets were quiet and narrow and, at night, frighteningly deserted; its manners were old and courtly; its vacant plots of land were permitted to cover themselves in luxuriant poison ivy rather than be converted into apartment complexes or sneaker showrooms. But war provides for no stasis. How can it, when life is unnaturally circumscribed, and when whole lives can be subtracted from existence? Even the urban physiognomy of Jaffna had not so much fallen into disrepair as it had been shoved hard into decay. Jaffna was not suspended in amber; it had been prevented from renewing itself in the ways that a town normally would.

Late in the afternoon of my first day in Jaffna, I flagged down a trishaw and asked to be driven north, on the road towards the port of Kankesanthurai. Afternoons in Jaffna are not always hot, but they are never anything but bright. The sun scours the horizon of all colour, bounces off metal and tarmac, and throws shadows that are sharp and stark.

All along the road, on either side, were stretches of empty houses, some of them so consummately wrecked that they looked like strange outgrowths of stone rather than disintegrated structures. Their roofs had surrendered and caved in, and their walls were being patiently split asunder by the roots and trunks of trees. Out of the windows of some houses, plants and creepers burst dramatically and unexpectedly, like torrents of vegetal vomit. The oldest houses were skeletal, some of their ribs pitted with bullet holes or craters from nearby explosions, and their front yards reclaimed by Jaffna's native shrubbery.

In gloomier weather, the houses might have inspired

melancholy, as if their very abandonment clouded the sky. But that afternoon, with a merry wind mussing the tops of the palmyra trees and the light strong and clear, they seemed merely like clues provided to crack larger puzzles. What could have transpired here, for people to flee their properties in such wholesale fashion? (And Jaffna people at that, because as somebody once told me, your average Jaffna man would readily admit: 'All I want out of life is to live in Jaffna and drink Jaffna's water.') Why, even though there had been no fighting in Jaffna for years together now, did the houses remain so resoundingly vacant? It was like some iron law of economics had been overturned, and in the sudden devaluation of these homes—from meaning everything to the families they sheltered to meaning nothing—lay the magnitude of Jaffna's distress.

I had come to this road because of an encounter earlier that day. In the morning, I had wandered into the university campus, thinking only of walking among its butter-coloured buildings, feeling not very sure of myself in this storied, unfamiliar town. I sat around on a low wall that bracketed a corridor, watching students rush about with purpose; as classes started up in parallel across the campus, the corridor emptied suddenly, as if a stopper had been yanked out of a bathtub. I peeked into a couple of large rooms that had been converted into exhibition spaces for art students, but it wasn't until I passed them a second time that I remembered a conversation from Colombo, about an artist named T. Sanathanan, who worked at the university.

I found him in his office on the second floor. Sana had a perfectly shaved head, coal-dust stubble on his chin, and heavy eyes set behind his rimless spectacles. His face was always utterly unflappable; even a smile, I came to feel, would be too severe a storm upon that placid sea. Two of his works, out of a four-painting series called 'Darkness, Not the Night,' hung on the walls of his office. One of them featured an eight-armed being in the throes of some extreme aggression, three of its hands firing off revolvers; a muscular blue angel hovered above. In the second painting, yet another eight-armed creature held its head in its hands, its legs mired in some vortical quicksand, with a sand clock draining in the foreground.

Sana was obsessed with the physical detritus of the war: objects that had transcended their mundane purposes to become repositories of painful memory. Once, in 2004, he curated an exhibition at the Jaffna Library, where he asked people to bring in anything that reminded them of the previous 25 years. Then, with such an article in his hand, using it as a pass key, he would ask about the story behind it. People told him about the slain daughters whose dolls they had brought with them, about the names on death certificates, or about the hut that had been reduced, by shelling, to the ash he was holding. Fishermen brought him bottles of seawater, representing the ocean upon which, for security reasons, they were no longer permitted to sail.

When they had received 500 such objects, Sana and his students slipped them into bell jars, and they placed these bell jars, on red velvet cushions, on the shelves of the library. One part of this project of Sana's was the edifice of the library itself, which had been burned down in 1981, along with its 100,000-odd books and manuscripts, by Sinhalese rioters and even policemen. Archival photographs of the library after its bout of arson show a hollow husk of a structure, its white walls splashed with soot, its roof damaged by miniature shells.

The library had been rebuilt and reopened in 2003, during the ceasefire, but it was still largely bare when Sana mounted his assembly of objects. In a building destroyed as a part of a war, memories of the war returned to take the places of books on the shelves. 'The symbolism was almost too much to handle,' Sana said. After the show, he went to India to finish his doctorate, and since he had not figured out how to return things to people, and since nobody returned to claim anything, he had a friend stuff the exhibits into plastic bags and bury them.

Sana spoke carefully and deliberately about his work, as if he needed to keep some distance from the accumulated pain of these artefacts, lest it overwhelm his life. If he had a medium at all, in fact, it was pain; he used it as deftly as paint or clay. He mounted another exhibition in Vancouver in 2009, asking the Sri Lankan Tamil diaspora to submit items that reminded them of home. 'One woman gave me an 11-year-old bouquet,' he said. 'She had to leave Sri Lanka in 1998, because of the war, so she had an arranged marriage with a man she hadn't even seen. She came to Canada, and she met him for the first time at the airport, and he had been carrying this bouquet.' Sana also got more than one bottle of MD Jam, manufactured by Lanka Canneries. 'In Canada! Where you get so many other brands of jam!' he said. Even his exclamations were gentle, reined-in creatures. 'I'd say to them: "You're boycotting Sri Lankan goods, but you're continuing to buy this damn jam?"'

He had been going now on little excursions around the peninsula, as research for his next project, tapping more reminiscences and distilling them into his work. This time, he was asking 80 people, from across the north of Sri Lanka, to recall their homes—homes they had left and never seen again, or homes they had left and miraculously returned to. He would request them to sketch a crude floor plan and, in the process, tease out of their mind an abiding memory associated with the house. He planned then to collate his own artistic rendition of this memory, the roughly sketched floor plan, and his more precisely drawn one, binding 80 such tripartite profiles of loss into a book called *Incomplete Thombus*.

A *thombu* was a colonial document that registered ownership of property, but in a society that was once as static as Jaffna's, the *thombu* stood in for a person's very antecedents. The wisecrack 'Don't give me your *thombu*!' was meant to interrupt somebody who was reeling off his personal history. The oldest existing *thombus* are documents made out of palm leaf, written in Sinhalese or Tamil, with the Dutch emblem printed on them. The identity of a plot of land, in those days, depended very much on the identities of adjacent plots of land. 'So the *thombu* would say that on the east side of this property is so-and-so's house, and on the west side is so-and-so's land, and this was done in the confidence that these things don't change in a major way over time,' Sana said. But in a war, of course, they do, and in a place where your home was—even for official purposes—defined by who your neighbours were, this was major change.

In this manner, Sana hit upon a wellspring of stories.

A doctor first outlined his drawing room and then carefully sketched in his piano; in the 1990s, a shell had fallen on the house and reduced the piano to splinters. One man in Kilinochchi recalled that he had come back to his house to find it razed to the ground, but that a chicken cage, made out of three bicycle-wheel rims welded together, was still mysteriously intact. People tended to remember trees. 'It was almost as if making a house into a home involved having a tree that you or your father planted,' Sana said. Later, when I hunted down Dutch *thombus* from the 1860s at the National Archives—thick, long volumes, longer than my forearm, with tea-coloured leaves and neat cursive hugging faint ruled lines—I noticed something similar. Almost every registration of land made careful note of the trees standing on the property. It was as if they pinned the deed of ownership to the earth beneath.

Another man talked less about his house than about a pumpkin patch in the garden, which had grown out of a single seed that he had carelessly tossed away in his youth. A lawyer refused to abandon his home because it contained hundreds of deeds and legal documents pertaining to other people's homes. In Kilinochchi again, a young woman told Sana that when she, her father and her brother had to leave the three-room house they had constructed with their own hands, they unscrewed the doors and windows from their hinges and defiantly carted them along. A girl who had returned recently to Jaffna broke into sobs when Sana asked her what she thought of when she thought of home; indicating her handbag, she said: 'This is enough for me. What do we need with a house? If you have a house, you can always lose it again.'

A Muslim butcher had to flee Jaffna just as he had finished building his family a new house, ordered out of town, along with thousands of other Muslims, by the Tigers in 1990. He locked the door and kept the key prominently on the outside sill of a window. 'If the Tigers or anybody comes to search the house,' the butcher told his wife, in Sana's recounting of the tale, 'at least they don't need to destroy the door.'

Sana paused here, and I wondered if his eyes were prickling, as mine were, at this quiet and beautifully futile act of resistance. By voluntarily giving the key up, the butcher had retained a slim degree of ownership; he had ceded the house, rather than having it snatched from him. Twenty years later, Sana said, the butcher and his wife came back to Jaffna and discovered that only the basement remained of their hope-filled house.

Sana was too young to remember the Black July riots vividly, although he told me that he sensed tension at home and among his neighbours, in the village of Thavady. Tamils were flooding into the peninsula, by boat and train from Colombo or by buses from elsewhere in the country, and the streets were wiped scary-clean of people after curfew fell every evening.

'My house was in the middle of fields,' he said. 'You could see the road in the distance, so you could spot problems coming. On the other hand, in that kind of situation, leaving the house becomes a problem as well, because you're out in the open.'

When the first aerial bombing of Thavady happened, Sana and his family had no idea what was going on. 'We didn't know what it was for. At that time, there were still so many fantasies about airplanes, and we certainly didn't expect bombs.' So they stood in the courtyard of the house, craning their necks up to look in wonder at the aircraft, until it deposited a bomb in an opposite corner of their plot of land, demolishing his grandfather's rice mill. Sana still remembered how acrid it smelled. After that, the sight of an airplane was traumatic.

This would be Sana's incomplete *thombu*, I thought: a small house, fields in every direction, and an airplane poised in mid-raid.

The bombings continued. His family built bunkers for safety, shallow pits scooped out of the earth, ready to be jumped into at a moment's notice. Sana learned to tell, from the texture of the sound, when a plane was circling around on a bombing run. 'They would just be ploughing the sky. Up, down, up, down. And on each run, there'd be a bomb.' At night, he sat under a coconut tree outside his house, listening to the plane, wanting to sleep but unable to, and reading with the help of an oil lamp.

The *Incomplete Thombus* project, Sana said, must have been born out of a sense of personal crisis that he developed as he saw Jaffna's social fabric being ripped apart and restitched along strange new seams. His own village was now fully populated again, but with people who had moved there from other villages in high-security zones.

'We went recently to find a friend's house somewhere,'

Sana said. 'We couldn't find it, so we knocked on the door of another house on that street and asked: "Do you know where Sabanathan's house is?" The lady said she didn't know. I said: "They should be around here. They're from this area." And the lady replied: "They may be. But I'm not."' Sana waggled his head in sadness. 'This is what happens. Homes become mere houses. Without any displacement, I found that I have been displaced.'

2

SITTING IN MY room, I looked at my notes from my conversation with Sana and thought: yet another catalogue. Death certificates, damaged dolls, prosthetic limbs, ash. The war was a beast of the wild, and all this constituted its distinctive spoor. But even more remarkable than the things that the war broke with its very touch were the things that outlasted the war altogether.

In the guest house where I stayed on my first trip to Jaffna, an ancient Fiat car stood decomposing in the courtyard, coloured such an uncommon shade of orange-red that it was impossible to tell where the paint stopped and the rust began. The window next to the driver's seat was permanently rolled down, so I was able to stick my head inside and see the length of plastic tubing that had broken free out of the dashboard, the gear shift that was really just a long stick ending in a hollow golf ball, and the peeling cloth lining the panels of the doors. It smelled of stale, trapped, heated air. Surprisingly, the tyres were kept inflated, and the registration plate—CY 3488—was still screwed into place. The car must have been at least fifty years old, to judge by its design: a high, curved bonnet, a body that resembled a carapace of some metallic animal, a sturdy luggage rack affixed to the top, and a running board. Christopher, the caretaker, thought that the car belonged to the owner of the guest house, but he had never asked, and he had never seen it being driven anywhere. 'I'm not even sure it will run now. It's just there.'

Jaffna was full of vintage cars, and many of these others were in better fettle. They trundled through the town's inner streets or up and down the road to Kankesanthurai: Morris Minors, Morris Oxfords, Vauxhall Victors, Volkswagen Beetles, Fiat 110s, Austin Cambridges, unrecognizable Toyota models that had been dropped from production lines decades ago. Some of these, in use as taxis, were always to be found parked in a row outside the Jaffna Teaching Hospital, their paint jobs—of eggshell white or periwinkle blue or lilac, even the colours sounding old-fashioned—fading in the sun. Whenever I walked through an unfamiliar neighbourhood, I took to peeking over the gates of houses to see if I could spot another specimen. It seemed a miracle that these cars even existed, no matter how wheezily they ran. One afternoon, walking along a narrow lane, I thought I would be bowled over by an apple-green Morris Oxford coming up behind me. But I needn't have worried; it was crawling slower than I was walking.

I mentioned this to M. once. M. was a friend, a middle-aged man upon whose knowledge of Jaffna I had come to rely. The past here was such a foreign land that I felt I needed a Virgil to sort through its souls, and M. turned out to be that patient, long-winded guide. I asked him questions, and he delivered answers in bold pronouncements. In rare instances, I'd discover some of his answers to be inaccurate or misconceived. But it helped, in my initial weeks, to lean upon his confident assessments, until I learned to make my own.

We were wheeling about town on his moped, and I had braced my notebook against his back to note down the details of an antique car we had just passed. This had become a habit, although I don't know why. I have no particular fascination for automobiles. Perhaps they were visible reminders of the past I was trying to uncover, or perhaps I had caught the habit of cataloguing everything.

M. asked what I was writing, and I told him.

'It's just striking, M., that apart from the big modern cars belonging to the United Nations or the other NGOs, the only other cars in Jaffna are from the 1950s or the 1960s.'

'That's Jaffna for you,' he said, his words half-eaten by the wind. 'Jaffna people will always stick to the brands that they consider prestigious. If it's a cycle, it has to be a Raleigh cycle. If it's a sewing machine, it has to be Singer. If it's a radio, it has to be National. Whatever brands came here first, they stuck to those. This is a stodgy city.'

The more prosaic explanation, which M. must have felt he didn't even need to mention, was that the war had frozen modernity at Jaffna's doorstep. Nearly every car on Sri Lanka's roads is a heavily taxed import, and when the Tigers controlled Jaffna, no such new cars were allowed past the government's blockade. After the army regained the peninsula, in any case, the town's economy had been wrecked so thoroughly, and so many of its inhabitants had fled, that nobody remained with the money to buy expensive imported vehicles. So the cars that had once been spanking new in the decades before the war continued now to creep about Jaffna, antebellum relics on the move. They were driven more often than not, I noticed, by grizzled men. Both cars and men had been tossed aside by the war for not being sufficiently able-bodied, but these discards had survived where their fitter counterparts had not.

The cars were emblems of the war in another way. One of the country's first language agitations began in 1956, when the government ordered that the licence plates on all vehicles— even on private cars—bear the Sinhalese alphabet *Sri*. The Tamils rebelled against this imposition. In January 1957, protesters in Jaffna threw themselves in front of a local official's car, demanding that he switch over to the Tamil

Sri; other Tamils, including some members of Parliament, painted Tamil *Sri*s on to their cars' licence plates, and they boycotted public buses that sported the Sinhalese *Sri*. When a squad of 40 Sinhalese-lettered buses was dispatched for use in the north, the campaign grew more heated. Tamil political parties tried to efface the Sinhalese *Sri* by force, tarring it over with the Tamil letter; in the south, pro-*Sri* mobs—including groups of Buddhist monks—responded by blacking out Tamil signboards with tar, even managing to paint over the Tamil 'Left Hand Drive' legend on the prime minister's Cadillac. A Tamil parliamentarian claimed that some Tamils, who fell into the hands of Sinhalese mobs, 'had the Sinhala *Sri* painted on their foreheads, on their faces, and a lady was forced to take her jacket off and the Sinhala *Sri* was painted on her back.' The *Sri* agitations segued smoothly, tragically into the ethnic riots of 1958.

The Sri Lankan government insisted that the *Sri* was merely symbolic, and not to be read with indignation or concern. But Appapillai Amirthalingam, a Tamil politician, called the *Sri* a 'stamp of inferiority.' In Parliament, he raged:

> *If this is such a minor matter, why do the Sinhalese people worry so much about it? No, it is not such a minor matter. The Hon. Minister of Labour said that the letter Sri is only a symbol. I agree, but as far as the Tamil people are concerned, the Sinhala Sri is certainly a symbol of their eternal slavery in this country, a slavery which every self-respecting Tamil is not prepared to tolerate in his territory.*

The one vital lesson that the Tamils learned during the *Sri* campaigns, M. told me, was that non-violent protest and civil disobedience achieved nothing of substance: 'I remember my father telling me this, because he had seen peaceful protesters get beaten up.' Even the otherwise temperate Amirthalingam grew incensed in his speech, and in doing so, he inadvertently twitched aside a curtain to the future:

> *I say in all humility, as a member of the great Tamil race, which has held its own against all intruders at all times of history, that even if only one Tamil man is left in this island, he will fight to the bitter end and to death to assert our rights.*

Over my weeks in Jaffna, I grew more and more curious about these long-lived cars, and about the men who had tended to them through the war. I talked about them endlessly, and finally somebody gave me the phone number of Ayathurai Santhan, 65 years old, Jaffna-born and Jaffna-bred, and owner of a 1960 banana-yellow Ford Prefect 105E. He had only bought it in 2011, for 110,000 rupees, from a dealer in Colombo; earlier, he had owned another Ford Prefect, and prior to that a Peugeot 203.

'All old cars,' I marvelled.

'Yes,' Ayathurai said, 'although, you know, people started calling them "old cars" only a couple of years ago. Before that, they were just "cars."' He screeched with laughter at his joke.

The longest drive Ayathurai and I ever took was out to Casuarina Beach, which lies across a causeway, on the northern tip of an island called Karainagar. He picked me up one morning, bringing with him his mechanic of two decades, a puckish man named Sundaralingam. Ayathurai, a talkative writer of short fiction, called him 'Sundaram' and referred to him as something of a family doctor. He had worked to restore the car when Ayathurai bought it: 'It took five weeks. When Master first saw it, it was coloured a dull grey. He didn't sleep for so many nights on end. He sat up looking through books to choose the colour he wanted.'

Now the Ford Prefect never embarked on a journey without Sundaram lolling in the back seat, spitting invective at passing bicyclists; Ayathurai needed him in case the car ever broke down in the middle of nowhere. On our trip to Casuarina Beach, I saw Sundaram at work only once, when he had to tweak something in the car's engine. He bounded out of the car, scattering the lapful of boiled sweets he had been consuming, and burrowed into the hood. His hands were a wonder. They seemed to be half metal themselves, the fingernails black with years of conglomerated grease, and the skin hard, swollen and callused. Where each of my fingers had three definite segments, his were so cut up and striated that they looked like they had dozens of jointed parts.

'Touch them,' he said once, proffering his hands to me with inordinate glee. It felt like I was touching a patch of badly laid tarmac.

Casuarina Beach was more than an hour and a half away, and Ayathurai's driving consisted of a series of small, nervous tacks across the road that further elongated the journey. He hugged the steering wheel, the pomade in his hair gleaming in the sun, his spectacles half-dark, and his neat moustache quivering with tension. At the slightest apprehension of trouble, he would shoot off two quick bursts on the horn. Sometimes he would see a speed breaker too late and emit a disappointed 'Ohh!' as we went over it at cruising speed. From behind me, Sundaram issued warnings to Ayathurai: 'The road isn't all right at all, Master. Master, watch out.' At its fastest, on fifth gear on open lengths of highway, the car hit 48 kilometres per hour, and at this speed it suffered from bouts of ague. Each wheel felt like it was trying to escape in a different direction. In this juddering manner, Ayathurai drove us to Karainagar, on a road that wound through fields of paddy, past Jaffna College, where he had once been a civil engineering lecturer, and near the Varadaraja Perumal

Temple, where Prabhakaran had shot and killed Alfred Duraiappah.

When Ayathurai was a boy, his father had owned an Austin 8, a boxy British four-door saloon manufactured for a few years on either side of World War Two. Ayathurai was in love with this car; one of his earliest photographs shows him, at the age of perhaps one and a half or two, standing in the car, rear door open, as if he were just about to get out. The car continues to feature in photographs over the next two decades; in the last one, Ayathurai looks 18 or 19, and he is standing in swimming trunks next to the car, leaning rakishly on its bonnet.

'The Austin 8 was my original love,' he told me once. 'My father didn't let anyone else touch the car, but I drove it for the first time when I was 14 or 15.' His father and his uncle had once driven out to inspect their paddy fields, taking Ayathurai and his friend along for the ride. The car was parked under a tree, and the two older men set off across the fields. Seizing the chance, Ayathurai asked his friend for the key to his bicycle, which luckily fit the ignition. 'So I drove it a kilometre and came back and parked it back under the tree. Except that when my father came back, the car was now facing in the opposite direction.' He subsided into giggles. 'Fortunately my father adored us, so he didn't say anything.'

Ayathurai purchased his first car, the black Peugeot 203, for 10,000 rupees in 1985, well after he had quit the civil service and returned from Colombo to Jaffna. The 1977 riots precipitated the move. 'Those weren't riots, they were pogroms, and there was a certain trauma in not knowing what would happen to you at any time,' he said. 'The good Sinhalese people were helpless, and every second you'd be hearing news of burning and looting. So I thought it was better for me not to have dealings with the south any more.'

Soon after he bought the Peugeot, the Sri Lankan

government began to squeeze the supply lines of petrol to Jaffna. 'I used to drive the Peugeot to Jaffna College, and then I had to switch to driving a motorcycle, and finally just a bicycle,' Ayathurai said. 'We'd have to stick a white flag on the vehicle to show we were civilians, because often there would be as many as four checkpoints in four kilometres.' After the Tigers seized full control of the peninsula, and after the government further restricted the movement of goods up to Jaffna, Ayathurai sold his Peugeot; it made little sense, in those times of privation, to feed expensive petrol into a car. 'It wasn't just petrol. We had no soap, for instance. And we drank our tea with jaggery, instead of sugar.' He drove for a few minutes in silence, his eyes roving anxiously over the road. 'But you know, I look back, and I miss those times.'

'Why?' I asked.

'Because we felt safe under the Tigers,' he said. 'You know what Gandhi once said? He said that in a really ideal society, a woman could wear all her jewellery and walk the streets after dark. That was what it was like. You could leave the doors and windows of your house open and sleep peacefully. That was how much people feared'—and then he corrected himself—'how much the Tigers controlled things.'

I asked Ayathurai how keen a supporter of the Tigers he had been. 'I did agree with their politics. Most people here did, because the Tamils were treated like aliens by the Sinhalese. Mostly, though, I feel sorry for them,' he said. This was a peculiar sentiment, I said; I had never heard anybody express pity for the Tigers. 'But yes, that's how I felt. Because they had some genuine ambition, and then it all went so wrong. They made their people suffer, and it was all in vain.'

At Casuarina Beach, the sand had been roasting all morning, and it filtered into my sandals and singed the skin between my toes. Ayathurai bought us biscuits and Elephant House cream sodas from an army-run snack kiosk, and we sat in the shade, on broken palmyra trunks. Periodically, Sundaram left us to wander along the shore, bent double, looking for strange seashells that had embedded themselves into the sand. A hundred metres away, a photo shoot was in progress. A male model posed in ankle-deep water, wind whipping through his hair; every quarter of an hour, he emerged on to the beach, changed his clothes, and waded back into the ocean for another round.

For most of the 1990s, after he sold his Peugeot, Ayathurai didn't own a car, but in 1999, he bought a well-worn Ford Prefect for 20,000 rupees. It had been retooled, at some point during the blockades of Jaffna, to subsist on kerosene, supplies of which were irregularly allowed up into the north for use as cooking fuel. Like many drivers in Jaffna at the time, Ayathurai took to carrying around small, invaluable bottles of petrol with which to prime his engine. 'You only needed two or three fluid ounces of petrol when you first started the car, and you needed to let the engine run for five minutes to allow it to warm up,' he said. 'But there were some problems with this kerosene business. It produced an unpleasant smell, and the floor of the car tended to get very hot. I had it for two years and then got fed up and sold it.'

The most sustained blockade of Jaffna occurred between 1990 and 1995, when the Tigers controlled the north and were thus given an unexpected taste of what it might feel like to run an independent Eelam with a baleful Sri Lanka next door. Farmers left their farms, unable to buy chemical fertilizers. Fishermen stayed home, unwilling to sail out into what were now high-security waters. Factories and workshops ceased work, and in Jaffna alone, more than eleven thousand skilled workers lost their jobs. Many of these newly unemployed drifted, inevitably, into the Tigers, enlisting to fight or to work in some of the Tigers' own factories, which manufactured weapons and boats but also sweets, soft drinks and leather. Rickety new professions were born, in which people collected meagre payments to wait in queue for somebody, or to cash a cheque for them, or to type letters for them. The publishers of the newspaper *Uthayan* went out every morning to buy any paper they could find—cardboard, brown paper, ruled school notebook paper—and thus printed their daily four- or two-page edition, filled with announcements of casualties.

Money started to behave in curious ways: the Sri Lankan government continued to pay the salaries and pensions of teachers and doctors, but the taxes on this income were paid to the Tigers. Properly speaking, though, the north was kept fiscally afloat by the Tamil diaspora; a Sri Lankan minister once estimated that the Tigers were raising, every month, between 3 and 4 million dollars in Canada and a quarter of a million pounds in Britain. Only food and other essential items were permitted past the blockade, but once they were transferred into Tiger hands, the channels of supply were distorted yet again. The families of Tiger cadres often ate free or were allowed to buy food for next to nothing; others had to pay 30 rupees for a kilogram of rice that cost 17 rupees in Colombo.

The blockades were designed to be impermeable. Ben Bavinck, a Dutch missionary working in Sri Lanka, spent months running convoys of relief materials up to the north, negotiating at checkpoints to push items through. In his diligently maintained diary, written in Dutch to occlude his opinions from Sinhalese and Tamil readers, Bavinck described the checkpoints at work:

> *Everything had to be unloaded and then re-loaded.*
> *Even the diesel tanks were emptied and then filled to*
> *a level commensurate with the distance to be covered.*
> *The air from the spare tyres was let out and the tyres*

*were removed from the wheel in order to check the
inner tube. After that the tyre was again mounted
and inflated. The military police was very strict but
correct. The checking lasted from 9 a.m. till 4 p.m.*

On another occasion, Bavinck complained to an army captain
about Jaffna's various shortages: 'When I spoke about the
scarcity of soap, he explained that this was a banned item
because the Tigers apparently use it to make their little
landmines watertight.' The food situation in Jaffna, Bavinck
wrote, was 'difficult but not alarming . . . There is however a
shortage of medicines. Even Panadol cannot be purchased . . .
There is no electricity and at night the darkness is total.'

Sundaram, who had set up his own garage when he was 22
or 23 years old, was forced by the circumstances to practise
a monkish version of the mechanic's craft, learning to do
much with little and finding new value in the jetsam of his
profession. He never met a car he couldn't repair; in fact, the
Tigers did not force him to fight because they required his
services as a mechanic. Without warning, they would come
to get Sundaram, and he would go with them and work on
their trucks and Mitsubishi Pajeros. Then they would give him
lunch, pay him, and drop him back home.

Most of Sundaram's work, during those years, involved
the conversion of petrol engines to run on kerosene. 'Petrol
was selling at 1000 or 1250 rupees a litre, whereas kerosene
was 250 rupees a litre or even less,' he said. 'I'd change the
manifold, and I'd make more space around the spark plugs,
and I'd charge 5000 rupees for the job.' Jaffna's mechanics had
no gas for welding, so they jury-rigged portable generators for
power. 'We never changed the engine's oil filters. We'd just
clean them out with petrol and put them back in. We never
threw anything away, because we had nothing to begin with.'

Spare parts were impossible to obtain, unless they were

cannibalized from dead cars. Sundaram bought old cars for 5000 or 10,000 rupees and stripped them clean. 'Some people became machinists, and they opened foundries and machine shops to manufacture duplicates. If you took a part to one of these shops and showed it to them, they'd take one look at it and reproduce it exactly.' Occasionally, he asked friends to smuggle things in past the blockade. 'I've had women put piston rings on their babies' wrists and say that they were bangles,' he said, snorting with laughter so that some cream soda leaked out of his nose. 'And they would put petrol into feeding bottles. At the checkpoint, they would tell the soldiers, "I need to feed my baby," and they would walk away for privacy. So the army wouldn't check to see what was in the bottles.' When, late in the 1990s, Sundaram moved to Qatar for a few years to escape the war, he felt maladjusted to a culture of plenty. 'Sometimes, even if a small part looked like it was mildly flawed, I'd be ordered to replace the whole thing, even though I could have repaired it easily.' He threw up his hands in mock horror. 'Such wastage! I couldn't believe it!'

Two days after our excursion to Casuarina Beach, when I was walking along Palaly Road to the university, I passed Kangu Garage. The gates were open, and when I peeked in, its premises were full of half-undone cars that had been manufactured half a century ago. The garage was really a small, unpaved patch of land, which tended to fill with slush when it rained. The only shelter came from two sheets of corrugated iron, hoisted up on wooden beams, with no walls and no proper floor. On sunny days, the roofs baked the air under them, making you feel breathless even as you stood in one place, next to a workbench or an engine block that had been scooped out of its parent car. Sick cars were parked and tended to in the front of the lot, the garage's infirmary; cars that did not make it were junked in the morgue, at the rear, where assorted tyres and corroding metal skeletons waited not for salvation but for salvage.

The chief mechanic at the garage was Nirmaladevan, the gruffest, most laconic man I had ever encountered. I loitered around his workbench, waiting for an opening into a conversation, but Nirmaladevan didn't ask me who I was, or if I had a car I wished to have mended, or even if I would kindly leave, since I had no apparent business to transact. Instead, he worked silently, his head down so that I could only see the top of his bald crown, framed by a circle of curly hair. A colleague could shout something in his direction, from another part of the garage, but Nirmaladevan wouldn't look up; at his most eloquent, he would convey assent or disagreement via a taxonomy of grunts. He appeared harried, and this puzzled me, because the urgency was so mismatched with the long, patient lives of the cars he worked on, and even with the unhurried pace of Jaffna itself. He flitted constantly between tasks— from taking a file to a piece of metal, to mixing a can of paint, to inserting himself under the body of the car—and to each of these he brought a ferocious concentration. In bothering him, I came to feel, I would be disrupting some phenomenon of nature, like the wretched boy who deliberately blocks the path of a line of purposeful ants.

The first two times I went to the garage, I came away without having said a single word; this was how dramatically Nirmaladevan shrank away from the world. On my third visit, after an hour and a half of standing around in the sun, I gathered my courage and asked if we might perhaps speak about his cars, if he had some time.

Nirmaladevan smiled, and this made me even more uncomfortable, because his smile resembled a grimace of pain. His face was smudged with grease, and he was hot and tired. 'It'll be difficult. You see how short-staffed I am,' he said, gesturing towards his crew of four.

'I could come back another day,' I said. At this, he relaxed. 'Yes, yes, that's good, another day. We'll talk then.'

Versions of this conversation occurred again and again. I came to the garage at different points during the next few weeks, trying to catch Nirmaladevan during a slow hour. I tried to be there first thing in the morning, before he had even bicycled in through the gates of the garage, thinking that he could spare some time and then settle into his labour in earnest. I went after lunch, hoping for an afternoon lull; I went on rainy days, when the mud made it impossible to work on cars in the yard; I went late in the evening, to catch him after he had tidied up but before he got on his cycle to pedal the 16 kilometres home. Each time, Nirmaladevan and I would talk a little, and then he would apologetically fob me off: 'You can see there's a lot of work to do today. Why don't you come tomorrow?' In his polite obstinacy, he reminded me of Dr Thurairaja, back in the hospital in Colombo.

But the garage was a fascinating place, and I was always reluctant to leave, so I was allowed to plant myself in a corner, or against a pillar, and watch the day unfold. Every morning, Nirmaladevan's crew arrived first, around half past seven, to open up the garage. They were men in their 60s and 70s, all nearly as wordless as their boss, shuffling about their workplace with a total economy of effort. The first man in switched on the radio, which buzzed and grumbled through the day; another took the communal kettle, went to a shop nearby, and brought back an inaugural instalment of tea.

Nirmaladevan came at 8 a.m., carrying a plastic bag full of flowers. He took his shirt off, picked up a broom, and swept clean the floor around his bench. Then he placed a flower next to a clamp on the bench, and two flowers apiece on top of portraits of Hindu deities that hung above a tiny storeroom. These propitiations done, he changed into his work clothes: a pair of shorts, cinched at the waist with a length of blue plastic wire, and a shirt that, as gradually as twilight changes to night, ran from its original grey at its shoulders into a greasy black at its tails.

Aside from brief breaks for lunch, cigarettes and tea, the mechanics toiled continuously until sundown. They rotated through the cars in the yard, but they held no conferences about what each car needed, and each man seemed to know instinctively what he was required to do when he switched projects. In fact, the smooth, complex interplay between the mechanics formed the best-functioning machine in that garage. Nirmaladevan sat at the centre of this machine, directing it by force of will.

I watched him keenly one afternoon, and while I could pick out no particular pattern to his work, there was a rhythm and a method that was choreographed almost into art. First, he slid into the wheelless maw of a Morris Minor, with its blinding new coat of black paint, trying to fix its front left axle. It must have been beastly hot under the car, but Nirmaladevan's legs—the only parts of him that were visible—didn't twitch once in 20 minutes. If I hadn't known better, I'd have thought he was napping.

But he slid out and transferred his attentions to the engine block of an Austin Cambridge—white, with blue tail fins— that had been pushed into the garage a week ago. He undid its nuts and bolts and removed other detachable parts, the ropy muscles in his forearms twitching like mice trapped under a blanket. He rinsed all these odds and ends in a hubcap filled with soap solution, and laid them out on a newspaper to dry, like biscuits on a baking tray. Then, for half an hour, Nirmaladevan tried to shape a piece of cardboard to fit precisely on to the surface of an odd trapezoidal projection of one part of the engine. Laying the card over the metal, he pounded it with a hammer, so that the oil and dirt on the surface imprinted themselves on to the card and gave him an outline to work with. He cut around this outline, pausing often to scratch his face with his scissors and to muse upon the cardboard, trimming and re-trimming until it fit perfectly. I never found out what he did with the card; he set it aside on his bench, drank deeply out of a plastic bucket of water, and lay back down under the Morris Minor.

Nirmaladevan had been working at the garage since 1975, six years after it opened. Its proprietor was a man named Rathnam, whom I never met; he was ill in a hospital in Colombo, I was told. In the 1970s, the garage used to import all its spare parts directly from London. 'And then, once the troubles started, we couldn't get anything into Jaffna at all,' Nirmaladevan said. 'If we were lucky, we got some spares from India, but more often we just took a part out of one model, modified it, and put it into another.'

Through much of the 1980s and the 1990s, the garage did little except refurbish cars to run on kerosene. A single such transformation took three days. 'We had to close down only once, during the war—in 1995.' In that year, when the Sri Lankan army was on the brink of retaking Jaffna, the Tigers tried to compel the residents of Jaffna and its outskirts— nearly half a million men, women and children—to leave the north and head south into the Vanni. It was an act of singular outlandishness, born out of some benevolent concern for Jaffna's Tamils, possibly, but also out of a desire to maintain control of the body of people that filled out the Tigers' ranks and funded them. Jaffna grew bare and solitary, its streets speckled only by soldiers; its citizens would wend their way back home after many weeks, unwilling to survive as refugees in the Vanni, their lives tipped into hiatus. Nirmaladevan and his men did not obey the Tigers' strictures and flee into the Vanni at all. 'We boarded up the garage and ran back to our villages around Jaffna,' he said. 'But in six months, we were here again, back at work.'

Every time I thought I had wormed myself into Nirmaladevan's confidence, he proved me wrong. One evening, he would be especially loquacious—which, for him, meant a ten-minute conversation without a spanner in his hands—but the very next afternoon he would not even accord me a grunt of welcome. I learned to read the hints, and if he appeared moody on any given day, I fell back upon my other haunt for old automobiles: the Jaffna Teaching Hospital.

From Kangu Garage, it took me 20 minutes to walk to the hospital, and as I rounded the final corner, the row of taxis came into view, parked between two trees in the middle of the road. The drivers—old men all; Jaffna's youth had been neatly digested by the war—stood like sentinels next to their cars. I hired them, essentially, for joyrides, but for some reason I thought this would insult their sense of purpose, so I always picked an arbitrary destination, usually clear on the other side of Jaffna.

All the cabbies drove in identical fashion, their hands always at 10 and 2, bodies inclined so sharply at 45 degrees that their chin often jutted past the steering wheel; it made them appear as if they were peering hard through the windshield to pick the road out of a snowstorm. The cars ran beautifully, with deep-throated purrs. A drive lasted half an hour, perhaps, and at the end of it, I stumbled out, dazed and high from inhaling the mixed smells of Rexine and hot metal.

I remember Natarasa best. Natarasa was a mournful man in his late 60s, who wore over his bald head a floppy blue hat with a broad brim, like a cricket umpire's. He drove a white Morris Minor 1000 that had been in Jaffna, in the hands of various owners, for more than half a century. It reminded me of the Ship of Theseus: so many parts of it had been replaced, over the years, that the question arose of whether it was even the same car any more. The seats were transplants from another car, so low that I could almost rest my chin on my knees. The brake and accelerator pedals were just pads of metal, and although they sizzled in the afternoon, Natarasa operated them with naked feet. The ignition mechanism had broken down, and a rough replica had been installed; to start the car, Natarasa had to turn the key and simultaneously stick his hand under the dashboard, as if he was tickling the engine and coaxing it awake. The car had its original ammeter, but the speedometer had been changed, and the new one was frozen permanently at 16 kilometres per hour. In the well of the front passenger seat stood a jerrycan of petrol; a plastic tube rose out of it and disappeared behind the dashboard, into the engine. It was, in essence, the car's petrol tank, right there next to my feet.

During the war, Jaffna's taxis had doubled up as hearses and ambulances, which was why they continued, almost out of inertia, to remain lined up outside the hospital. 'There were ambulances around, but they were costly,' Natarasa told me, as we drove beside the ocean. It was a day of shimmering brightness, and the water looked like blanched blue silk. 'And there was a real shortage of private cars, you see.' For a while during the 1990s, when the Tigers held Jaffna and Sri Lanka's air force sent bombers screaming over the town, Natarasa would be called in to pick up a body every day or every two days. Petrol was expensive, so he had to charge them 500 rupees per kilometre.

'I didn't want to charge them anything at all, but what could I do?' Natarasa said, looking sidelong at me. 'Most of them only had to go a distance of five kilometres or so, to the cemetery.'

'How many trips like that did you make?' I asked.

'How many?' Natarasa permitted himself a chuckle. 'How do I tell you this? Those days, I was driving my car more as a hearse than as a taxi.'

He fell silent for a while. I looked around the Morris Minor and pictured blood on the floor or the corpse of a woman in the back seat. In the summers, during the day, the smell of heat and gore must have been nauseating. I turned towards the window for some air. It would have been impossible to scour its insides enough, I imagined, and yet here it was, bowling along in the sunshine, its seats looking like they had never once been bloodied. The cars hid their history well, I first thought. Then I remembered that in their very presence on the streets, they were already giving the game away, pointing back towards Jaffna's bruised, miserable past.

3

IF I WANTED to write about him, my friend M. insisted, I should refer to him only as M. He was sure that he would fall afoul of the government in some way if he appeared in these pages in all his full-named glory. Yet, puzzlingly, he allowed me a free hand to portray him and his life, requesting only that I skip the odd detail.

'If you describe my father, for example, they'll know it's me,' he said, for instance, 'and then they'll come after me.' I could never tell if he was serious or cavalier when he spoke about these inchoate dangers; sometimes he could be both within the space of mere sentences. When I was leaving his house a second consecutive evening, after spending nearly the whole day there, he told me: 'You know, the army is watching my house. So now that you've been here two days in a row, they'll start watching you too.'

'This is a fine time to tell me,' I said, not without some alarm. 'Why didn't you mention this yesterday?'

In response, M. only snuffled in laughter, in the way that he did, breathing in and out rapidly, setting up a gentle breeze that ruffled the hairs of his thick moustache.

On the very first day that I met M., in September 2011, Sri Lanka scrapped its state of emergency, which had been in place for most of the time since 1971. But the Prevention of Terrorism Act—which had existed alongside the emergency, like an iron hand in an iron glove—remained in place, granting lavish freedom to security forces to arrest, seize, interrogate and detain people as they liked.

The army was thick on the ground in Jaffna—one soldier for every five civilians, I read somewhere. They clustered in large military bases on the A9 leading into Jaffna, occupied houses in the peninsula's main roads, grabbed land in strategic areas, and stood singly or in pairs at junctions and street corners, all bristling with arms, as if the war had never ended. Chiefly, the army watched for any signs of Tamils regrouping and perhaps rearming. They stationed observers outside the houses of politically suspect people like M. They required former Tigers to check in regularly at a police station. Relatives of dead or missing Tigers received surprise visits from the Terrorist Investigation Department, so that they could be grilled and their houses could be searched.

To organize even a social gathering of more than half a dozen people required police permission, and soldiers were then deputed to sit in on these assemblies: church services, town hall consultations, village committees. M. told me about a meeting in the university, called by faculty members who wanted to discuss the digitization of the library. 'A lieutenant colonel of the army burst in and, since this was the month of May, accused them of planning to commemorate the defeat of the Tigers two years ago,' he said. 'It almost came to blows. Then one of the calmer people there just invited the lieutenant colonel to sit in on the meeting. Obviously, he didn't follow a thing.' The more fantastic story, however, involved the temple priest who had invited his six-year-old granddaughter's friends home for her birthday. The party was broken up by the police because there were more than a dozen children in attendance and no police sanction had been sought for this gathering.

Under the unremitting gaze of the army, life became an act, to be performed for the satisfaction of the audience of soldiers. A walk must not appear like a skulk; a package tucked under one's arm must not look suspicious; conversation must be sanitized; thoughts of anger or rebellion must not show transparently on one's face. This is no way to live, and it was hardly surprising that Jaffna felt stifled and sullen, as if it had cotton wool stuffed into its mouth.

Once, a friend—a Sri Lankan journalist—asked me if it was easy to work undetected by the government.

'I think so,' I said. 'I mean, nobody has pulled me in for questioning or anything of that sort.'

'It's probably because you haven't written anything yet,' he said. 'But your cell phone is tapped, you know that?'

'What?' I didn't know that.

He thought he had seen my name once, in a defence ministry list of people whose phone conversations were being surveilled, or perhaps somebody who had seen the list had told him. 'And I'm sure they're keeping track of your movements—when you leave and come back, that kind of thing.'

The news provided me, first, with a cheap, subversive thrill, and then with a jolt of worry for some of my sources who had spoken to me over the phone. The government did not look kindly upon Sri Lankans—Tamils in particular—who spoke critically of the regime to unauthorized reporters. I began to review my phone conversations in my head, to determine if anything had been said that could be used against anybody I knew. My friend mistook my silence for fear. 'Don't worry, *machang*, they tap everybody's phone. Even my phone is tapped. The only thing it means is that they know you're a journalist.'

The security forces tracked journalists closely, so my activities in Jaffna—reporting, but under the guise of being a tourist—would have been deemed highly illegitimate. There were stories that the government wanted to keep out of sight: about the army's brutality in the final bend of the war, for instance, or about the casual shredding of the Tamils' civil liberties in daily life. I was never followed or watched, I think, but even the thought of the state's hot breath down my neck created a sense of close peril. People spoke with me nervously, unsure if I was who I claimed to be and of how much they should say. They transmitted their anxiety to me too, not all at once but gradually, so that it accumulated in my bones and infiltrated my dreams. There were always tales at hand of abductions, thorough thrashings administered by the police, arbitrary detentions, mysterious disappearances. The air held the rank odour of menace.

The days that M. and I spent together fell quickly into a pattern. In the morning, at perhaps a quarter past eight, he would pick me up after dropping his young daughter at school. He drove a metallic-blue moped and was somewhat portly, so I would sit behind him and gingerly hold his shirt, teetering on the edge of the pillion and praying that we hit no potholes. We would ride into the commercial heart of Jaffna, which really measured just three streets by three, and eat breakfast at Malayan Cafe, on the signboard of which the 'n' was so squeezed for space that it almost didn't exist. The cafe was old but spruce; it had marble tabletops, lofty ceilings with solid wooden rafters, and glass cabinets that displayed packages of biscuits and bottles of Horlicks. Frankly, I thought the food was pretty awful, and although M. agreed with me, he never took me anywhere else. So we would eat and talk, and M. would show off his talent for distinguishing the visitors from the locals around us. This was not always as easy as it sounds. 'You see him? You see him?' he once said, rolling his eyes to his left to indicate a silver-haired man waiting for his food. 'He isn't from here. He's wearing jeans. A Jaffna man of his age would never wear jeans.' This was how the city seemed to divide itself up for M.: between insider and outsider. It was not that he mistrusted outsiders or liked them any less; it was just that he was sensitive, first and foremost, to their being outsiders.

After breakfast, M. drove us to a vegetable market to do his shopping, and then we proceeded to his house, a small bungalow tucked into the quiet elbow of a street, with a shingled roof, cool red-oxide floors and a dusty, unpaved yard. His wife was already at work; he did not permit me to mention what she did for a living, or to mention her name or his daughter's. He would hand off his cloth bag of vegetables to an old man he called *Thatha* but who was not really anybody's grandfather; Thatha had simply attached himself to M. and his family during the tumultuous displacements of 2008–09, and now he lived with them and cooked for them and otherwise remained silently in his room. M. and I would sit in cane chairs just inside the door of his house, or outside in the yard, and we would talk, gently sweating in the day's mounting heat. From some nearby temple, paragraphs of music from a *nadaswaram* were delivered by the breeze, and they eddied around us as we spoke.

At some point after noon, M. would excuse himself to go pick up his daughter, and I would lean back and stare at the ceiling. The little girl, perhaps six or seven years old, would run at full tilt into the house, the red ribbons in her hair unravelled or askew, and M. would have to chase after her, asking her to change her clothes and to stow her school bag neatly away. We would eat lunch, big steel plates heaped with rice-and-curry, and then we would talk some more, until by the early evening M.'s students filtered in for their English tuitions. I would go home, sit on the steps of the shuttered Ganesha temple, stare emptily into the pond, and let my cluttered, turbulent mind come slowly to rest.

On other days, if I needed to be elsewhere in the morning, I would drop by M.'s house around 6 p.m. By this time, his 20-odd students—young men and women, rather than schoolchildren—would be seated in two parallel lines in the yard, practising their spoken English on each other. They could be left like this for a while, to discuss the weather or talk about their family, so M. and I would repair to our own chairs. He would give me a cup of tea, ask about the people I had met that day, and provide rapid rundowns if he knew anything about any of them. Every five minutes, he would turn towards his students and roar: 'Outer line! Move!' or 'Inner line! Move!' so that they could shift partners and begin a fresh conversation. This was my favourite time of the day, with the dusk haemorrhaging out of the sky, the tea strong and hot, and the students mumbling so softly and steadily that they sounded as if they were engaged in communal prayer.

Nominally, M. was a writer and a newspaper columnist, and he did write: he showed me books and articles that had been published, and he still emails me links to some of his pieces online. But in describing his past connections with the Tigers, he was ever nebulous, managing artfully, over weeks and weeks, to not answer my questions with any specificity. He only let on that he had worked with the Tigers from 1983 to 1985, when he had been put in charge of recruiting people from the spray of islands that emerges from Jaffna's coastline. After 1985, he told me, he grew unhappy with the direction Prabhakaran was taking and quit the Tigers. 'By this time, they had started killing people who spoke out against them, so I absconded,' he said. 'I lived with friends for eight or nine months, before I thought it was safe to go back to my life.'

He continued, however, to be a Tamil nationalist, writing columns in support of the Tigers' political goals and appearing as an analyst on the National Television of Tamil Eelam until, one day in 2006, Prabhakaran barred him because he had predicted the Tigers' imminent doom. To me, M. insisted that his columns were independent minded, and that he had often criticized the Tigers. But when I told Nirmala and Raghavan

about M., they suspected that he might have been a member
of the Tigers' propaganda unit through the 1990s and perhaps
even until the 2002 ceasefire. He certainly seemed to possess
an intimate knowledge of the Tigers—not only of their internal
mechanics but even of ephemera that could have accrued only
with long, sticky association.

'There are former combatants in this very group of students,
you know,' M. told me one evening.

I twisted around to squint at the gaggle of amiable
youngsters and to speculate about which of them might have
been militants. The girl without an arm, maybe? Could it be
that obvious?

'I recognize a couple of them,' he said, 'but even otherwise,
I would be able to tell. Some of them move in the way Tigers
were taught to move. And they call me "Master," which is
very much a Tiger thing. One boy has a scar in an unusual
place. I don't ask him how he got it.'

Another afternoon, he let drop a detail so delicious that
a full week went by before it struck me to wonder how
he had learned of it. In the endgame of the war, he said,
when a shrunken band of Tigers had been trapped on a
sandbar between the Nandikadal Lagoon and the sea, with
the immovable might of the Sri Lankan army cutting off
their only escape, Prabhakaran handed out CDs of a recent
Hollywood movie to his top leaders. The movie was *300*,
the tale of Leonidas and his pocketful of Spartans fighting
to their death against an overwhelming Persian army, as told
through cartoonish violence. 'He had seen the movie six
times himself,' M. said. 'He used it to prepare himself for
the end.'

'How did you know that thing about the *300* CDs?' I asked
M. much later.

He laughed and snuffled. 'I learn these things,' he said, his
eyes glinting behind his spectacles. I sighed. It wasn't the first

or the last time I resigned myself to the fact that I would only ever know M. so well and no better.

The extent of M.'s Tigerishness was further obscured by the way he spoke. His Tamil was highly literary, so jammed with rhetorical flourish that sometimes I struggled to follow along; it didn't help that the antique Tamil of Jaffna is a few beats away from the slang-filled Tamil I grew up speaking in India. In this baroque language, he would hold forth on abstract ideology. He had not published any columns since the war ended, to avoid drawing attention to himself, so I was providing him a chance to vent two years' worth of bottled-up ideas. 'I am a theoretician, Samanth,' M. liked to say, without any irony, and his harshest criticism of Prabhakaran was, in fact, that he was unsound on political theory. M. was the sort of man who classified others by their philosophical moorings. '*Avan oru* Trotskyite, Samanth'—'He is a Trotskyite, Samanth'—he said on one occasion; another time, about somebody else: '*Avan oru* existentialist.'

With time, I learned that the way to drag M. down from his aeries of political thought, to get him to describe how a man looked or what kind of training he got during his Tiger days, was to ask him questions in English. M.'s English was fluent, often elegant, but it was, for him, the more mundane of the two languages, and thus well suited to the crass materialistic answers I sought. It became a tacit but enjoyable tug of war between us, I looking to keep him anchored in English and M. forever keen to soar back up into Tamil. In this playful way, we conducted our conversations, and if it initially worried me that he was so difficult to pin down, I came to look upon him as a metaphor. No truth is ever easily accessed or clarified, but the process of inquiry can be revelatory in its own right.

I like people who tell long, meandering stories, and so I liked M. He liked me, in turn, because I brought him news from the outside world. He had only a sketchy Internet connection, and it had been years since he had left the Vanni. 'What's happening in Syria?' he would ask me, and I'd cull details out of the newspapers I had read and relate them to him. There was violence in the offing there too, I said. Then he'd ask: 'What's happening in Afghanistan now?' And out of all my piecemeal representations of the world, he would spin grand theories of political strife.

Once, during such a discussion, I asked him if there was ever a neat inflexion point beyond which Tiger supporters could square with their consciences the practice of warfare and the murder of civilians. What did it take to turn a Tamil to violence? It had been impossible for me to even guess at the answer; my imagination failed me. I had, I thought at first, been too spoiled by peace to understand when it became necessary to fight. But perhaps that was an answer in itself. There are as many answers as there are people—which means there is really no answer at all.

For some in Jaffna, it had needed little—far too little—to snap the human conscience, and there was rarely a direct path from cause to effect. Raghavan joined the Tigers because he had seen a scruffy romance to the life of a guerrilla; violence was an ineluctable part of this life, or perhaps even a part of its appeal. Other young men rationalized the violence away, convinced themselves that it was necessary. Prabhakaran himself chose his methods out of some abstract ideological anger, even though the state's discriminations against Tamils had never constrained his own life. On the other hand, there were thousands of Tamils with legitimate grievances who refused still to bless the Tigers' killing sprees. In between these extremes lay a full continuum of provocation.

M. began to feel some sympathy for the armed struggle, he said, after he felt the imposition of a raw hostility that could only be answered with hostility. He had turned 18 in 1983, the year of the Black July riots; in fact, the Tiger ambush that killed 13 soldiers and sparked the riots occurred just down the road from the house where we sat talking.

'After the riots, it became difficult not to be acutely aware of Sinhalese–Tamil relations,' he said. Like Sana, M. remembered vividly the ships from the south, full of Tamil riot refugees, docking at Kankesanthurai. Around him, Jaffna was being hastily militarized. Helicopters landed on his school's playground because it was near an army camp. Tanks groaned through the slender roads. Floods of armed soldiers took over the town.

'You would see one of these soldiers, and you would naturally start to think: "He is Sinhalese, I am Tamil. He has a tank, I have nothing. He doesn't have to show his ID card at checkpoints, I do. If he blocks the road, I must turn back."' To M., who was forever attuned to the presence of even casual outsiders in Jaffna, the arrival of the Sinhalese army must have been a mighty affront. 'That was when a germ of political consciousness was implanted in us.'

M.'s father, who had never believed in peaceful protest, now looked with fond favour upon the upstart Tigers and other sundry militant groups, but M. remained more circumspect. Like somebody who has had a long and bruising relationship with the power of semantics, he was careful always to say that he only 'helped' the Tigers and never joined them. 'They approached me, so first I created street plays for them,' he said. His first play—in which Kali, the wild-tongued goddess of destruction, demands of people that they sacrifice themselves for the mass struggle—was performed dozens of times across the peninsula.

'That was a good, fluid time,' M. said. An ant had crept up his foot on to his ankle, and he slapped at it and flicked away its corpse. 'Some of us could be political and still voice our objections to some of Prabhakaran's military adventurism.' In the Tigers' camp, he trained in firing small arms, but he was keen to play this down, so he dismissed it almost as child's play, as a rite of passage for every red-blooded Tamil youth of the era. 'I couldn't think of killing anybody. That was just my mindset. I'm a theoretician, Samanth. But a lot of my friends joined these groups.'

'And you didn't try to stop them?'

He shook his head slowly. 'No, I didn't.' M. never said that he found the slaughter of civilians abhorrent in itself. He gave me the impression, instead, that he baulked only at poorly strategized killing, his disappointment more clinical than visceral.

I asked other people about their turns towards—or away from—violence. I kept thinking that these must have been deeply considered choices, much agonized over. Now I don't know why I thought that. Maybe it was important to believe that the violence was committed as a last resort, out of due deliberation or immense desperation, because then I could comprehend it better.

It was Nirmala who admitted to the most dramatic change of heart, and who explained best how even someone like her—a sheltered Jaffna girl who became an ardent leftist and anti-war protester during her undergraduate days at Wheaton College, in Massachusetts—got pulled in, upon her return, by the gravitational field of the Tigers.

'I was initially dead against a separate Tamil state,' she said. 'We felt that the Tamil leaders of the early 1970s were a bunch of unreconstructed upper-class guys who wanted to maintain their sense of privilege.' Her husband at the time, a college lecturer she called Nithie, was from Sri Lanka's hill country, up near Kandy, and when she announced her decision to marry him, Nirmala saw how riven with divisions of caste and class the country's Tamils were. Jaffna's Tamils consider themselves to be of a finer pedigree than the Tamils of the hills, she said. 'So my extended family went berserk. Some of them didn't even allow me into their homes again.' In the face of such disunity, she thought then, there was little moral merit in calling for a united Tamil state.

At Wheaton, Nirmala had read Fanon and Sartre and Guevara, and she had accompanied her American boyfriend on a march to Capitol Hill when the United States began bombing Saigon. 'Jim. That was his name. I didn't marry the guy,' she told me, with a toothy grin, 'because I didn't want to be some small-town lawyer's wife. I wanted to come back and do big things.'

She returned to Jaffna in 1976, married Nithie, and began working as a teacher, but she said she didn't give the issue of Eelam sufficient thought until 1977, when a tense general election was followed by riots that targeted both Tamils and leftists. The new prime minister, Junius Jayewardene, had promised during his campaign to negotiate sincerely with the Tamil United Liberation Front (TULF), which was demanding an independent Tamil state. 'After he won the election, he reneged on this,' Nirmala said.

During the riots, a TULF leader accused Jayewardene in Parliament of not doing enough to protect the country's Tamils. Jayewardene responded with an infamous provocation:

> *People become restive when they hear that a separate state is to be formed. Whatever it is, when statements of that type are made, the newspapers carry them throughout the island, and when you say that you are not violent, but that violence may be used in time to come, what do you think the other people in Sri Lanka will do? How will they react? If you want to fight, let there be a fight; if it is peace, let there be peace; that is what they will say. It is not what I am saying. The people of Sri Lanka say that.*

'This is what JR said!' Nirmala exclaimed, misremembering the quote slightly, or remembering only too well her interpretation of its spirit. "If you want war, we'll give you war." Really, that was the turning point for me.'

When the riots shattered the order in Sinhalese-majority areas, the government's response was to police the north more ferociously. 'As soon as the army set foot here, the extrajudicial killings began. So Nithie and I talked, and we figured that it was our moral duty to throw our weight behind the Tamil movement. That became our theoretical position.'

Theory yielded soon to practice. Nirmala and Nithie began to round up school students and pitch them into protest marches. They hosted Prabhakaran and other guerrillas at home, offering up their veranda as a meeting space. The Tigers, numbering barely 20 at the time, did not hesitate to ask for help. 'A lot of them were from poor families, and they didn't know anything about politics. They barely knew where Palestine was,' Nirmala said. 'We presumptuously thought that we intellectuals could school them in political theory.'

What the Tigers really needed, though, was practical assistance: 'a sympathetic network,' Nirmala called it. 'Once they wanted us to get medical help for one of their cadre, who had a bullet lodged in him, during an accident with a firearm,' she said. 'My sister was a doctor, so I couldn't refuse. And when you start giving practical help, you get sucked in unwittingly.'

Then she cut herself off in anger. 'No, I shouldn't say "unwittingly." That would be excusing myself. I have to offer a big mea culpa for getting more and more involved in the early years.' At that moment, I admired her immensely.

In September 1982, when Nirmala was teaching at school, a Tiger barged into her class, saying that three of his colleagues had been wounded in an attack on a police station, and that they needed temporary refuge. 'I couldn't put them in my parents' house,' Nirmala said, 'because I was really more scared of my mother than the army.' She and Nithie lived in the same compound but in a smaller annexe, and she took the militants in there. They remained hidden there for two weeks before getting on a boat to India.

The police learned, in November, that Nirmala and Nithie had sheltered these three Tigers. Within an hour, soldiers had surrounded Nirmala's parents' house. 'There were more than a hundred of them,' she said. 'I think they expected a battle. They cordoned off the whole area and jumped over our walls.'

The house still stands, on Chetty Street, not far from the Nallur Temple. Nirmala's great-grandfather had built the house more than a century ago, but when I visited, her mother had already passed away and her father lived there alone: Rajasingham Uncle, 85 years old, tall and erect and so often shirtless that his skin had turned a deep mahogany. Behind the house was an unkempt garden—a two-acre patch of wild vegetation, really, where palm trees, mango trees and banana trees threatened to clamber over each other in their quest for space.

Nirmala's father had been at home that November afternoon when the army came. It was around 3 p.m. A little while earlier, a Tiger named Shankar had stopped by in the hope of a late lunch. 'He had come on a bicycle, I remember, because these young men had learned to push the gate open without even getting off their bicycles,' Rajasingham Uncle said.

Even though Shankar had left the gate ajar, the soldiers chose to leap over the front wall of the compound, right into clumps of Madras thorns. 'One of them came up to me and said: 'Go squat under that mango tree.' I told him: 'I'm not squatting anywhere." Instead, Rajasingham Uncle sat in an armchair and watched the raid unfold.

Nirmala and Nithie were arrested. Shankar tried to make a

run for it, zigzagging through the back garden, sprinting from tree to tree. A bullet found his stomach nevertheless, and when he scaled the rear wall of the compound, he was holding his entrails in with his hand. 'Somehow, he escaped, but nobody arranged for a doctor for him,' Nirmala said. 'Some small boat took him to India, but he died of septicaemia on the way. He was the first Tiger martyr.'

Nirmala never lived in that house again; from prison, she went directly to India and then to England. Seven years after the arrest, Rajasingham Uncle lost another daughter, and this time more permanently. Nirmala's younger sister Rajini—the doctor, a mother of two young girls, and married to a Sinhalese man—had joined a vocal group of Jaffna academics who deplored the Tigers' cold violence, criticized their tunnel-vision ideology, and wrote copiously about their grievous crimes. By way of punishment, the Tigers shot and killed Rajini one afternoon, when she was cycling home from the University of Jaffna's Faculty of Medicine. A report on Rajini's assassination read: 'The killer had waited at a relatively lonely spot that she would have to pass while rushing home from work to care for her little ones. He had even found the time, after Rajini had fallen, to park his bicycle and pump a few more bullets into her head, before making his escape . . . On hearing the assassin's shots, with the exception of a few medical students and some ordinary people, the rest ran away or shut themselves inside their homes. It was difficult to find a vehicle to transport her to hospital.' This was how Rajasingham Uncle and his wife saw two of their four daughters wrenched away from them by opposite sides of the war. This was the nature of the conflict, its brutality dispensed in messy and contradictory ways.

In the years between Nirmala's arrest and Rajini's murder, the Tigers threw their energies into becoming the sole Tamil militant group, the only game in town. This became a point of pride for Prabhakaran, and he established the Tigers' pre-eminence in the only way he knew how: by dealing death with a heavy hand. Death resolved everything. Prabhakaran was impatient with those who advised cooperation or negotiation—with theoreticians, as M. called them—and many of his Tigers, eager pupils, absorbed that attitude as well. 'They called us storytellers, or the "Lolo" group—people who talked all the time, "Lolololo," but did nothing,' M. said. 'Their essential questions were simple: "You want to come join us? Come join us. But will you fight? Will you die?"'

From being consummately beloved by their people, the Tigers started to inspire some fear and revulsion. 'We would have all agreed that the Tigers should have led the Tamil cause, because somebody had to fight the Sinhalese chauvinism,' M. said. 'But the heart weakens without democracy, and there was no democracy within the Tigers. They antagonized their own brothers by killing them.'

The murder that most distressed M. was that of the principal of the school he had once attended. 'His name was Anandarajah. He was a really genuine man, hot-tempered maybe, but very frank.' Anandarajah had sent the school cricket team to play a friendly match against a soldiers' eleven, but the students were first frisked thoroughly before entering the cricket ground. The Tigers considered this an insult to the Tamil community, and since they saw Anandarajah as the architect behind this loss of face, they shot and killed him.

In and around Jaffna, firefights started to erupt on the streets, even in the middle of the day, between Tigers and other Tamil militants. 'Somewhere along this road'—M. waved a vague hand towards the world outside his house—'they shot some rival militants and burned them alive. During this—and this is what shocks me more, Samanth—the Tigers were given cups of tea by the residents of the houses on the road! And cold bottles of soda!' The Tigers also took it upon themselves to kill thieves, rapists, traitors and moonshiners, permitting them no trial and awarding them summary sentences of death by lamp post. 'First they would be beaten. Then they would be tied to a lamp post, and the charges against them would be written on boards hung around their necks. Then they would be shot, in full view of everybody.' The corpses were left tethered to their posts for a day or two, their moral lesson sharpening even as they decomposed.

M. looked deep into me as he narrated these details, as if he was trying to judge how I would have reacted to these developments if I had been a Tamil in Jaffna. I wanted to think that I would have been repelled by the Tigers' methods, but I feared that these convictions would really not have been worth a dime. The Tigers sang the siren song of the tyrant most effectively. What we're doing is for the greater good of us all. Bear with us through these small excesses, and we will deliver you the promised land. It provided a useful life lesson: anybody who asked you to trust them despite minor infractions was not to be trusted at all.

Notwithstanding their growing cruelty, the Tigers continued to fill their ranks with young Tamils: foot soldiers to ambush army patrols, or to bomb buses carrying women and children, or to conduct missions involving certain death. This happened in one of two ways.

First, there were the volunteers, a generation or so younger than Raghavan, Tamil men and women to whom the question 'Why did you join?' came as a puzzle, as if I had asked them why they breathed or ate. Almost invariably, they responded with brief, simple sentences, and then they moved on to other matters. I never thought they were being evasive; they just seemed to think that the answer to that question was both unimportant and readily apparent. The moral decision that transfixed me so much had been made without any fuss—as a matter of course, even—by tens of thousands of people during the war.

I met one of these guerrillas in London, a 29-year-old I will call Adityan. He had joined the Tigers in the 1990s, fought through the next decade, and had somehow escaped the army's clutches after the last stand in May 2009. A year and a half later, he paid a huge sum of money to an agent to procure a passport and a visa to the UK, where he now lived in asylum. He sat in a suburban office for most of the day, employed by a fellow Tamil, trying to push through terrific boredom to perform data-entry work. Mostly, he sat at his computer looking through Tamil news websites or talking on Skype to his family in Sri Lanka.

Adityan was still guerrilla-fit: He had a body constructed out of lean muscle, without a trace of fat on his torso. I could see this because, within five minutes of meeting me, he proudly yanked up his sweater to show me a curved, livid scar running from breastbone to navel. An army sniper had once shot him in the belly, back in the days when he was deployed on the Tigers' front lines. 'My stomach looked like a coconut that you smash when you make an offering at a temple,' he said, but a doctor at a Tiger hospital managed to repair the damage and save Adityan's life.

Adityan grew up in Kilinochchi, and he argued with me that after the army bombed his school, he faced no real choice. 'At some point, the army was on one side of us and the Tigers were on the other side,' he said, in his low, assured voice. 'So of course I joined the Tigers.' The Tigers were always proficient at this, at persuading people that the only alternative available to them was life under the heel of a Sinhalese-dominated Sri Lanka. They ordered schools in the north to replace the government's history textbooks with their own Tamil-centric ones. On Heroes' Day every year—a day after Prabhakaran's birthday—Tiger deputations in civvies gave three-hour presentations in classrooms about Sinhalese atrocities; they took with them a television, a VCR and videotapes of some of their successful attacks, and they urged students to join their training programme. The Tigers were persistent, proficient wooers.

Even before he became a teenager, Adityan's existence—his potential, his ambition—would have been circumscribed severely by the ongoing war, and to this purposeless young man, the Tigers offered the only sort of structure that was available in these parts at this time. 'I left home and joined the Tigers because of my passion for Eelam, and now that passion has nowhere to go. It's searching for a target,' he said.

Did he never think that there might be other ways to use his passion? Other ways to stake out an Eelam?

There weren't any such alternatives, he said, and in any case, the Tiger leadership did everything—even kill other Tamils—for a sound reason. 'I see it as a process. First, yes, you do negotiate. But if that does not work, then you have to use violence to get what you need. Even if you have to bomb a school.' There was a swagger to that statement, a perverted machismo: only a real man understands the necessity of bombing a school.

Adityan was nostalgic for the 1990s, when Kilinochchi and Jaffna were administered thoroughly by the Tigers. 'Everything was pure Tamil—the names of streets, the names of newborn children, the names of houses.' You never needed to lock your house when you went out, and women could walk the streets safely even after midnight. This idyll had been constructed out of paralysing fear, of course, but it suggested—falsely but ably—that an independent Eelam under Tiger rule would be something of a perfect society. To people as accustomed to deep, deep imperfections as the Tamils of Sri Lanka, even a glimpse of utopia was powerfully seductive.

Then there were the conscripts, drafted into the Tigers by
pure coercion: first the compulsory recruitment of one young
adult per family, and then, as the war's turning fortunes
induced a manic desperation, the abduction of any able-bodied
teenager at all. Even in the mid-1990s, one Indian journalist
saw children, barely into their teens, walking about in Jaffna
in military fatigues and described to him as Tiger 'cadets': 'In
fact, some of us . . . were told by long-time contacts that child
recruitment by the Tigers had become so rampant that mothers
and fathers stood guard outside school gates to prevent "cradle
snatching." Thus drafted, these unwilling guerrillas would
be threatened that their families would come to great harm
unless they stayed put. So they stayed put, often turning into
cannon fodder, to be replaced by still more quaking, forcibly
recruited boys and girls.

What did he think of this? I asked Adityan.

He shrugged. The question didn't faze him at all; he
continued to lean back in his office chair, relaxed and amiable.
'I never saw this happen. These are stories that the Tigers'
enemies would spread.' Then, without a shift of rhythm: 'Even
if it did happen, it was necessary for Eelam. The children may
have even wanted to fight.' Denial and explanation, served in
tandem, for me to believe whichever I wished.

But these conscriptions did happen, of course, right until the
very end.

From Jaffna, early one morning, I travelled down to
Vavuniya and switched buses to head west to Mannar, on the
coast. The journey took most of the day. I slept fitfully until
Vavuniya and not at all between Vavuniya and Mannar, when
a hot wind gusted through the window and coated me with
fine dust. Next to me, on a two-seater that was really built
for one-and-a-quarter people, a plump woman perched with
a wicker basket on her lap. The basket was covered with a

damp blue towel, so I never discovered what lay within it; every 15 minutes, though, the woman would peel back a corner of the towel, peek lovingly inside, and satisfy herself that the contents were still intact or alive. I itched to ask her what she was transporting, but I refrained; the relationship between the woman and her basket seemed too personal to warrant such intrusions.

I had come to Mannar to meet a friend, an employee of a local church; he had promised to introduce me to a girl I will call Vasanthi, who had been impressed into the Tigers in the final years of the war. On his motorcycle, my friend and I drove into further clouds of dust, off the main highway and to a small church in an area called Manthai. I could never have visited Vasanthi in her house without calling attention to both her and myself, but the church was neutral ground. First we sat indoors, within a priest's lodgings, but when the anaemic breeze from the sole fan proved incapable of dispelling the stuffy heat, we moved to the veranda.

Presently, Vasanthi rode in on her bicycle, propped it against a wall, and sat down with us, beaming at my friend and examining me warily. She wore a black skirt and a blouse of vegetal green, and her hair had been sculpted into tight pigtails; she was 25, but she looked like she might still have been in school. She had a chronic cough, but also a sudden smile that tended to blaze across her face and vanish without a trace.

Vasanthi hated the Tigers, she said. 'They caught me when I was 21.'

'You were 21?' my friend teased. 'Hah! You should have been signing up of your own accord, at that age!'

'I knew you'd say that,' Vasanthi shot back. That smile again. 'Of my own accord? Never!'

In 2007, one of the fronts of the war had entered the region around Manthai, so Vasanthi and her family abandoned their house and sought shelter in a church in the town of Madhu, along with 500 other people. 'Initially, the Tigers didn't come into the church, but then gradually they did. And at that point the bishop told us: "I can't protect you." After two weeks, the Tigers ordered everybody out of the church, and the younger members of the group were abducted. 'They literally caught us by our hands and dragged us away. Women dragged girls, men dragged boys.'

The new draftees were sent to Kilinochchi for two or three months, to be taught how to fire guns, and then sent to defend north-east Sri Lanka. 'We didn't know the area, we didn't know what to do with the guns, we didn't know anything,' Vasanthi said. 'We suffered, stumbling around in the dark.' She was posted on what she called a 'defence line,' essentially serving as an armed sentry, first on a crumbling highway and then in the jungle. 'We had to build bunkers, and we'd take rice cakes and water into the forest with us, in plastic shopping bags. I ran away four times. I'd change into civilian clothes and run all the way to Kilinochchi in the dark, through the forest, staying away from the houses on the main road. We'd escape in groups of four or five people, or maybe eight or ten.'

The Tigers had asked her for her family's details when they had first abducted her; shrewdly, she had given them false names and addresses, but they had discovered the true ones nevertheless. The first time she escaped, she went to stay with a pair of aunts, but then she heard that the Tigers had, in retribution, found her father and taken him away, putting him to work cooking or digging bunkers. So she went back. Another time, she came to Kilinochchi to find that it was being shelled without pause by the army. 'We had hidden my sister away at the time, to prevent her from being taken by the Tigers as well. When they came for her, I offered to go back instead, to protect her.'

In February 2009, a few months before the end of the war, Vasanthi surrendered to the army. The soldiers treated her well, she said. They kept her for a year and a half in a detention camp, along with 3000 other girls, but they organized computer lessons and sewing lessons, and they distributed textbooks to those who wanted them. Before she was released, a soldier photographed her and noted down her address, and she was asked to write an exam that included questions such as: 'If a war like this were to begin again today, what would you do?' Then she went home, in October 2010.

For months thereafter, the local constabulary visited Vasanthi regularly, or she was summoned to the police station to fill out reams of forms, all to confirm that she was still there, that she had not decamped into the ranks of any new militant group. This was intrusive, but Vasanthi remained angrier at the Tigers.

'You should have been there in Madhu. It was a scene where Tamils were beating up Tamils and sending them to their certain deaths. It shouldn't have been like that. If this was really our cause, we should have wanted to go voluntarily. But we didn't.' This was the war the Tigers lost first, the war for the unconditional affections of the island's Tamils and for the uncontested right to fight on their behalf. Once this war was lost, once this earth was scorched, it could have been only a question of time before the Tigers lost the other war too.

4

EVERY TWO OR three days in Jaffna, I walked down the road and around the corner to an Internet cafe, on the first floor of a pink building, above a grocer's shop. I took off my shoes at the door, as instructed, and sat at one of the free terminals to check my email. Each computer sat in a half-cubicle of blonde wood, so that nobody could easily see what was on your monitor. Within this sheathed privacy, people conducted their work, quiet as mice, and then left.

One day, from the cubicle next to mine, I heard the low burble of a young man on Skype. The wood muffled the words but not the melting, teasing tone; he was speaking to his wife or his girlfriend, either way somebody who lived far from Jaffna.

At the end of half an hour, the tone changed. He seemed to be protesting something—once, twice, and then he gave in. He cleared his throat and launched into a love song from an old Tamil film. At first he sang with some embarrassment, but then more gaily, his voice almost fully off tune but impossibly endearing. I stopped mid-email and eavesdropped without shame.

He sang for five minutes or seven minutes, completing the song once but circling back to the first verse and going through it all over again. Some way through this second rendition, he must have signed off from Skype. He pushed his chair back with a scrape, went to the counter to pay, still singing merrily.

I peeped out from my cubicle and caught a flash of his purple shirt as the door closed behind him.

Time slipped noiselessly away in Jaffna, so that I never knew which day of the week it was. I took walks around the town, trying to find different routes to my regular haunts: M.'s house, Kangu Garage, the seashore, the university, the library. The library was good for ice cream. Tour buses from the south stopped regularly here, so that their occupants could gaze upon the palatial white building and imagine what it must have looked like in 1981, after it had been shelled and burned. The half-dozen Elephant House ice cream carts would stand back for five or ten minutes, giving the tourists their moments of contemplation. Then they would move in, to sell them orange bars and Cornettos.

Directly across from the library was a stretch of blasted earth, strewn with rubble, where even grass refused to grow properly. In the middle of this desolation was a statue of Sir Ponnambalam Ramanathan, a Tamil politician of the late 1800s who had been his country's solicitor general. I recognized him only because I had seen a replica, painted gold and in healthier shape, on the campus of the university. On this one, the plaque dated 5 October 1974, was barely readable. He still wore his tunic and held a scroll in his right hand, but his head was missing altogether, so that the central iron pole of the statue protruded above his neck, like a grotesque spinal column. Barnacles had grown on the underside of Sir Ramanathan's stone tunic and within the groove of his clenched left hand. From here, if you faced north, you could see, across a jumble of fishermen's shacks and polluted water, the curve of the peninsula, sweeping away like the blade of scimitar.

In the evenings, I ambled down a tiny lane next to my guest house, cutting across from one main road to another, to an empty restaurant where I was always the only guest for dinner. I read there for hours, and by the time I had eaten and was ready to leave, night had rushed through Jaffna. The lane leading back to my guest house had no street lights, and in that profound darkness, packs of stray dogs congregated, howling and barking with such fury that they seemed almost feral. I would walk the first third of the lane with as much calm as I could muster, but by then the dogs would be at my heels, snapping hard, and I would invariably sprint the last few steps into the gate, my heart going like a piston. One night, the dogs gathered right at the entrance to the lane, growling in concert. My nerve failed me. I lingered at the gate of the restaurant, and when a motorcyclist appeared to turn into the lane, I asked him for a ride.

Recalling how M. had told me about recruiting for the Tigers in the islands off Jaffna, a friend and I took an autorickshaw east, towards the sea. There are new causeways there now, springing off the mainland and leaping from island to island, all of them built by the armed forces, the tarmac smooth and sparkling. 'The Navy Welcomes You All,' read a sign at the first checkpoint. The causeways—wide berms, really—rose up out of the shallow water on either side; in the water, men stood waist-deep, fishing with tattered nets. Crows pitched and yawed around the fishermen.

More army bases on the islands: smaller ones, certainly, but still watchfully present. The causeways must have been built so that supplies could be ferried to the bases, I thought, and so that the army could do its job of routing out every last Tiger, wherever she or he was hiding.

'Where are you going?'

'The temple. On Nainativu.' That island had been renamed now, into the Sinhalese Nagadeepa, but I used the Tamil name still, just to see what happened. The soldiers waved us through, uncaring.

The islands were unlike any other place I had seen in Sri Lanka: flatter even than the Jaffna peninsula, if that was possible, and the land covered in sand so white that it looked like an alkaline salt flat. The road seemed to run through pulverized bone. We could see few villages, but they must have been there. Somebody needed to tend to the neat copra plantations and the groves of palmyra, and to pray at the small, perfect temples, their low red-and-white walls visible from miles away. We stopped once, on a curve of road, to slip and slide down a gentle hillock of sand towards the pale, hesitant blue of the sea. Surreptitiously, I stuck a finger into the sand and tasted it. The salt burned the cracks in my lips.

The gauntlet of causeways wound through the island of Kayts, then through Pungudutivu, and finally to Kurikadduwan. We had been virtually alone on the road for most of the trip, but at the Kurikadduwan jetty, where the road ended, we ran into a melee. Row after row of tour buses stood parked on a patch of pebbly ground, emptying themselves of Sinhalese tourists from the south. At the jetty, the navy operated one upscale launch across the water to Nainativu, with plush, blue-leather seats, but this was exclusively for VIPs. The other tourists all pulled on orange life jackets and poured into one of two ferries that sat low in the water. There were a hundred of us or more in our boat, all trying not to inhale the diesel fumes that roared from the engine. The low ceiling pressed down upon us, so that we were forced to bow our heads, supplicant even before we reached Nainativu.

The Tamil temple on Nainativu is an old, well-known one, and I was puzzled by the number of Sinhalese tourists who had flocked into the ferries to visit the island. But then the boat docked, and the first thing we saw as soon as we clambered on to the jetty was not the temple but a spanking new Buddhist *viharaya*, a modernist bell-shaped structure of burnished steel. The path to the Tamil temple ran through the complex of the *viharaya*, past a towering poster of President Mahinda Rajapaksa with arms raised in triumph, and under an archway that was still being finished by masons perched on scaffolds.

We inspected the *viharaya*, its matte grey dome marking the Buddha's visit to the island, one of three that he is claimed to have made to Sri Lanka. There had been a *viharaya* here earlier as well—only 70 years old, and so younger than the temple, and not nearly as large as it is now. After the war ended, the government started to renovate and expand the *viharaya*; for a while, massive framed portraits of Sarath Fonseka, the general who led the army during the war's final days, hung on the walls within, until Fonseka himself became a thorn in Rajapaksa's side. Now there was only Rajapaksa, larger than life, offering his tight smile of welcome.

Past the *viharaya* was a row of shops selling straw hats, Hindu and Buddhist baubles, and cheap sunglasses. Then we came upon the temple, built in worship of one of the many forms of Hinduism's mother goddess. This too was being refurbished, its blue-grey facade gradually being consumed by a riot of new colour. No presidential cut-outs welcomed visitors here, however. Mahinda Rajapaksa lent his august presence to only one of these two houses of prayer.

In the decades gone past, Nainativu's Tamils and its sprinkling of Buddhists had lived together in fine amity. Both the temple and the *viharaya* had been constructed by the residents, and the Hindu temple even timed its annual festival to coincide with Poson Poya, the full moon of early summer that commemorates the arrival of Buddhism in Sri Lanka. On the approach to Nainativu, this deep corner of the country, the *viharaya* and the temple appeared to stand shoulder to shoulder on the coast, in fraternal solidarity. Only if you went into one of them and looked upon the other did you understand that they also stood in opposition, the temple facing east into the island, towards India, and the *viharaya* facing the sea, towards Sri Lanka.

We returned to Kurikadduwan in the ferry and got into our autorickshaw, a little undone now by the heat. The ride back to Jaffna was silent and weary. The Jaffna day always developed in this manner: first a fresh morning, filling the sails of the spirit, and then a rough heat that becalmed you entirely.

On the mainland, we stopped as soon as we spotted a restaurant. We wanted not food, really, but something cold to drink.

'We have beer,' the waiter said. 'Tiger beer and Lion beer.'

'All right, we'll have the Tiger.'

Two or three minutes passed. Then the waiter returned and said: 'I'm sorry, sir. The Tiger is all finished. We only have the Lion.'

My friend looked at me, both our mouths agape. 'It's a good thing you have me here as a witness,' she said. 'Nobody would have ever believed that this conversation actually happened.'

5

IN SRI LANKA, ethnic divisions are lines drawn not in sand but in slush. The Sinhalese say of themselves that they are descended from Aryans from north India; the Tamils are Dravidians from south India. The drama of this racial opposition is more imagined than real. Nobody knows with certainty whether the Sinhalese were here before the Tamils. Both communities have lived on the island for over twenty centuries, and they have spent that time not only feuding but also intermarrying. Legend informs us that, 2500 years ago, even the progenitor of the Sinhalese race imported a Tamil princess to be his wife. Much as Sinhalese or Tamil nationalists wish to believe otherwise, Sri Lanka is a country of commingled blood.

The island's Muslims, slightly less than 10 per cent of the population, also trace their ancestry back to diverse sources: Arab traders who began to arrive in the 8th century, their Sinhalese wives who converted to Islam, Malays shipped over by the Dutch and British colonial authorities in the 18th and 19th centuries, and later immigrants from the Malabar coast of south India and from Pakistan. The census crudely divides this morass into two categories: the so-called Moors, who mostly speak Tamil and who make up nearly all of Sri Lanka's Muslims, and the Malays. When linguistic tensions began to grow, the Tamil-speaking Muslims kept a determinedly low profile; in broad terms, the Muslim community formed Sri Lanka's third-largest ethnic group, and it behaved as such, insecure and fearful, attempting to soothe the Sinhalese majority but also to maintain its ties with the Tamils.

Through the 1980s, the Tigers tried to recruit Muslims in the northern and eastern provinces, rallying them around the Tamil language. Somewhere I found three slim propaganda pamphlets that the Tigers had distributed to Muslims in Jaffna. Each is between 23 and 28 pages long, a little larger than a passport, and printed with tight Tamil text on cheap, now-yellowed paper. The first, from 1985, bears a Warholesque blue print of a tousle-haired man with a thick moustache: the first Muslim Tiger martyr, with the nom de guerre of Johnson. On their back cover, the other two pamphlets, from 1987 and 1988, carry a map of Sri Lanka, rendered in blue ink, showing the number of Muslims living in each district. Issued by the Tigers' political wing, the pamphlets depicted the Sinhalese race as a vital enemy to both Tamils and Muslims, and urged the Muslims to collaborate with the Tigers in fighting for a free Eelam. The Tigers premised these arguments not on passion but on the cool rationality of demographic statistics. The booklets packed tables of figures to demonstrate how, in the northern and eastern provinces, the Tamils and Muslims together dwarfed the Sinhalese; another table, for the district of Ampara, showed the Sinhalese population to be a steadily growing one, poised to draw level soon with the Muslim majority. Two of the pamphlets ended in identical sentences: 'For the Muslims living in Sri Lanka, their lives, their security and their sense of dignity can only be obtained in an independent Tamil state.'

Then, almost on a dime, everything changed. In the space of a few hours in October 1990, the Tigers emptied Jaffna of its 24,000 Muslims, suddenly and efficiently, the way a can of peas might be overturned and thumped on its end to dislodge its contents.

Abdus Salam heard about the expulsion on the radio in

Brunei, where he was working at the time, as a teacher in a girls' school. He had moved there in 1984, with his wife and children, but he had still regarded Jaffna as home, and his sister's family had continued to live there through the turbulence of the 1980s. None of them had seen it coming. A handful of Muslims had joined the Tigers, Salam said, 'but otherwise we kept out of their way. You know, the Tigers used to say about us: "The Muslims aren't participants, they're spectators." We just never took part in the Tigers' struggle. And maybe this was our punishment.'

Salam was a firm-limbed man, 73 years old, with a shock of white hair; in the very centre of his forehead was a black mark the size of a raincoat button, the skin charred after decades of resting on the hot floor during afternoon prayers. He lived not far from my apartment in Colombo, and he took me one day to his sister Razeena's house, a few hundred metres further down the road. Razeena's husband had died in 2000, and she stayed now with her daughter Rozmin, her son-in-law Mohammad Nawzan, and their children. Razeena, an elderly woman in a light-blue headscarf, had papery skin, mischievous eyes, a knowing smile and a viscous memory for details. Her heart was weak, and so she could only manage short squalls of conversation. After a few minutes, she would tap her ribs with her thumb and say: 'I'm going to stop talking now, for a while.' Then, while her daughter pushed the tale along, Razeena sat in placidity, gesturing and nodding. Around us, the children, three of them, bounced off various pieces of furniture, only half-listening to the story of how they had come to be born in Colombo.

For two or three months in the late summer of 1990, Razeena had smelled trouble. 'I would go out, and I would hear people saying that, in some time, Jaffna would be only a Tamil area. "Only temple bells will ring here." So I'd come back home and tell my husband, but he never believed me.

He'd say they were all rumours.' Towards the end of October, Muslims were turned out of Chavakachcheri, a town in the peninsula just south of Jaffna. 'Even then, in my house, I kept being told that we wouldn't have to leave. "We haven't done anything to the Tigers," my husband said.'

Razeena had taught arithmetic, home science and art at Khadija College between 1961 and 1982, before retiring to raise her children. In 1990, she was 55 years old. 'We were already living with one kind of fear because the Sri Lankan Air Force was bombing Jaffna.' Several bombs fell near their house on Moor Street, in Jaffna's Muslim quarter. In the week before the expulsion, a bomb destroyed a relative's house, killing nine people, because they had accidentally switched on a flashlight and the planes had spotted that from the air. 'We couldn't even pray properly, because we were afraid of the bombs.' They lit small candles of goat fat and placed them under a chair or a table, to hide the light. When they heard a bomber, they got under the bed, under loose stone slabs in the bathroom, because they had heard that was safe. Some nights, they even shifted their mattresses into the bathroom and slept there. In the last days of their stay in Jaffna, bombs fell two or three houses away, rattling their own home's foundations.

One of those days, a big brown mongrel dog with a bloody mouth ran past their house. Razeena was sure that this was a bad omen, and the family made up its mind to leave. 'The Muslims from Mannar and Kilinochchi and Mullaitivu were told to leave,' Rozmin said, 'and we heard these rumours that we would also be asked to go.'

For this sudden blaze of mistrust, no single explanation appeared to suffice. Perhaps the Tigers thought the Muslims to be divided in their allegiance to the movement, but although some Muslims were accused of being informers in the pay of the Sri Lankan army or the Indian Peace Keeping Forces, there were no incidents of monumental betrayal to catalyse these opinions. Minor clashes erupted between the Tigers and Muslim youth; after one such altercation, the Tigers cautioned the Muslim minority to avoid 'offending' the Tamil majority. In hindsight, the expulsion seems now to have been inevitable. The Tigers depended on paranoia and an exclusionary racism, using them as sharp-edged tools to whittle and shape the movement as they saw fit. It must have been easy for Prabhakaran to believe that the Muslim community would turn into a fifth column, just as it must have been tempting to purify his vision of Eelam a little further, stripping it of Muslims entirely, concocting a Tamil heartland that matched his own claustrophobic view of the world.

'Just two days before we were kicked out, a group of Muslims went to the Tigers and asked them: "We're hearing these stories. Are you going to ask us to leave?" Razeena said. 'And the Tigers said: "No, no, nothing of the sort." We trusted them so much.'

'To be on the safe side, my father went to the Tigers to apply for a pass for us to travel to Colombo, although we thought we'd only need to be here for a few months,' Rozmin said. 'We were planning to leave on 1 November.'

October 30 was a Tuesday, a sunny day that later dissolved in rain. The family was at home: 'None of us was working then, and in any case, there was no work to be done, so what else was there to do but stay at home?' Rozmin had woken late, and she was indoors, oiling and combing her hair. 'Around 10 o'clock, a vehicle drove through the streets, announcing over a loudspeaker that the men of every Muslim household had to report to the grounds of Osmania College for a public meeting.'

Razeena shook her head vigorously and held up nine fingers.

'All right, it was 9 o'clock,' Rozmin said. In fact, the broadcasts may have started as early as 7.30 a.m. 'I didn't hear the announcement clearly or see the vehicle, but my father was standing next to the gate at the time, so he heard it.' He came back into the house, asked his daughter to close all the doors and windows, and then left for Osmania College. As soon as the men had left Moor Street, a unit of armed Tigers began to storm the houses, raiding them for cash and jewellery.

'Did they come into your house?' I asked.

'No, for some reason, they didn't. But one of my neighbours burst into our house, crying, because they had taken all her gold jewellery,' Razeena said. 'I was making porridge at the time, I remember. It was only partly done. It remained undone.'

Her husband returned in a hurry, after 10 or 15 minutes. The Tigers had informed the assembly of men that Jaffna's Muslims had been given until noon to vacate their houses. 'If you fail to leave your area, we are not responsible for your young girls, your belongings and your lives,' a Tiger commander told the Muslims. Carrying only clothing and 500 rupees a head, they were to gather at Manohara Theatre, to be driven en masse out of town. 'My father was not one to show emotion,' Rozmin said. 'So he just told us to pack. 'Take your good clothes. You have two hands. How much can you carry, after all?"

Rozmin had spent the previous few days stitching pockets into the inner lining of her skirts and her mother's, and now they secreted their jewellery—40 or 50 sovereigns' worth—in these pockets. 'My father took his office bag and a small suitcase. He took that office bag of his everywhere. He took his school and college and work certificates, and he took mine as well.'

'Yes,' Razeena said, with the smile of a seasoned troublemaker, 'they didn't worry about mine.'

'We thought she would take them! She was usually responsible for her own things!'

The bomb that had shaken Moor Street a few days earlier had sent Razeena's books and papers tumbling out of their cabinets. There had been no time to organize and replace them. Without her certificates, she explained, she stood to lose her teaching pension. 'I had gone through a teacher training course, so I was eligible for a higher grade of pension than other teachers,' she said. 'Without that certificate, I wouldn't have been able to prove that.' Fortunately, Razeena found a classmate in Colombo and used her certificates to track down the records of the teacher training course and to apply then for the release of the stoppered-up pension payments. 'I didn't get my full pension, exactly, but yes, I got an approximate amount,' Razeena said. 'But how would I have produced my certificates, if they had demanded them?'

'You'd have had to tell them to ask Prabhakaran,' Salam said, and he cackled. Razeena looked only dimly amused by her younger brother.

Some of the family's other possessions—old clothes, groceries, small pieces of furniture—were given away to two part-time servants, a young Tamil girl and her father. 'They had come home to help out anyway, since we were supposed to be leaving in a couple of days,' Razeena said. 'We did exactly the sort of things we would have done if we were going away on a short visit. We brought things indoors from the courtyard. We locked all the doors and windows. Then, before we left, we checked the locks once again.'

By 11.45 a.m., the house on Moor Street was empty.

That morning, Moor Street and its adjacent neighbourhoods were lined with Tigers on either side of the road, every one of them armed, ensuring that the Muslims proceeded to Manohara Theatre and nowhere else. At the junction of roads near the theatre, the Tigers had set up checkpoints, where boys and girls with guns, some of them 15 or 16 years old,

searched the departing Muslims with cold thoroughness. The
women were directed into a house, where they were frisked
by female Tigers. 'They first took every piece of jewellery that
was visible,' Razeena said. 'My earrings and the rings on my
fingers. Then, during the frisking, I gave them the jewellery
from my skirt also. The skirt had a zip, so I was able to take
it all out easily and hand it over. They even made us undo our
buns of hair, to make sure there was nothing hidden within.
They had guns. What else could we do?'

The Tigers collected so much jewellery at this checkpoint
that they needed to bring out large plastic buckets to store all
this gleaming wealth. Many of the Muslim families in Jaffna
were well off, because they had a relative or two working in
the Middle East, sending home money. 'There was one old
lady in front of us who had stitched her jewels into her pillow.
She was hugging it to her chest, and she said she was a heart
patient and needed the pillow, so they didn't check it at first.
Then she came out, after the checking, and when she was
waiting for her daughter, she kept the pillow aside.' A Tiger
spotted the lady and her pillow, unsheathed his knife, and
came towards her. 'He just split the pillow in two, like that,'
Rozmin said, her hand cleaving through the air. 'You should
have seen the jewels that came falling out.'

Razeena lost her handbag. She had given it to a Muslim boy
who had already been checked, trusting that she could retrieve
it after she had been searched, but the boy was nowhere to
be seen when she emerged. 'There was a pension ID card in
it, and a chain that looked like gold but wasn't,' she said.
'He must have taken it for the chain.' From Rozmin's bundle
of possessions, the Tigers kept for themselves a calculator, a
wristwatch, sets of particularly fine clothes, and even a couple
of pens. In her handbag, they discovered a clutch purse with a
surplus of 500 rupees in it; they would have taken it if Rozmin
had not pleaded loudly that she would need the money to

travel on to Colombo. Around her, families lost the deeds to their land and houses, their lives in Jaffna effectively lacerated in front of their eyes. 'They didn't say this to us,' Razeena said, 'but I heard the Tigers tell other people: "All this belongs to the Tamil soil. You can only take yourselves with you."'

Even if the Tigers' motivations behind ejecting the north's Muslims are cloudy, the operation turned into an excuse for grand larceny; in all, according to an estimate, the Muslims lost 110 million dollars of land, livestock, jewellery and cash. In Jaffna, 35 wealthy Muslim businessmen were kidnapped and held for ransom, to make a further profit; when the wife of one of these businessmen asked to see that her husband was safe, she was told that his return would cost her 10 million rupees. Earrings were ripped off the ears of young women, often along with the lobes they decorated. Welfare certificates, especially those that entitled the poor to state benefits, were confiscated.

The checking ended only in the late afternoon, at 4 p.m. 'Throughout, they gave us no food or water,' Razeena said. 'Only in the evening, when we were finally let into the grounds of the Manohara Theatre, did some people bring us biscuits and fruits. Not the Tigers—just regular Tamils who cared.' Thousands of people were packed into this small swatch of land, and it struck Rozmin that they might all simply be shot. She didn't tell anyone else about this thought of hers. It was better not to seed further anxiety into their situation.

Late in the evening, small Tata buses arrived to transport the Muslims away. They ran for their bus, Razeena said; people who, just a day earlier, wished only to stay in Jaffna were now desperate to leave. 'We could run easily. We had lost everything, hadn't we? So we had no weight to carry. The bus was swerving all over the place, but somehow we all squeezed in.' There was music playing on the bus, Razeena remembered, a song that went: '*Kaakeyare kaakeyare, enga pogire?*' In Jaffna Tamil slang, a Muslim was often called '*kaaka*,' or 'crow,' Salam said. 'That was the song: "O crow, O crow, where are you going?" Maybe it was a pointed jibe or maybe it was just a coincidence, I don't know. By that time, the Tigers were producing so many songs of their own. This might have been one of theirs.'

'The song sounded so terrible,' Rozmin said. 'Our hearts were absolutely broken.'

Their bus left Manohara Theatre at 6.30 p.m. and drove to Kerathivu, a town south of Jaffna, near Chavakachcheri. There the passengers were made to wait, in remorseless rain, for a ferry that would take them across the Jaffna Lagoon to Pooneryn, on what the Tamils often call 'the mainland.' The ferry arrived at 9.30 p.m., and the crossing took 15 minutes. The ride was brief, but so many people had clambered on to its slick, greasy deck that some of them fell in and were left behind. The rain continued, driving its metallic pellets into the crowd on the ferry. 'At Pooneryn, there was a bus,' Rozmin said. 'It was a Tiger bus, and the driver charged us 500 rupees per person. We tried to argue with him: "You just chased us out. Why should we now pay you?" The driver replied: "Whoever can pay can get on the bus." So we paid.'

There was a bathroom break at 5 a.m., but thereafter the road had been washed out, and the bus refused to proceed. A group of 25 or 30 of them pooled together scraps of money, found a man with a tractor, and convinced him to load them up and take them further. At the last Tiger checkpoint, the tractor stalled in the mud, or maybe its owner was only pretending. So the family picked up their weary, banished feet and walked the last two or three miles, through no-man's land, to the first Sri Lankan army checkpoint on the other side. Nobody frisked them there; there was, palpably, nothing to search for and nothing to search. 'My cousin, whose wife was with us, had come from Anuradhapura to meet us at the checkpoint,' Rozmin said. 'He had left as soon as he heard that all the Muslims of Jaffna had been expelled.' On their way to a relative's house in Anuradhapura, hitching a ride on a truck, the family ate its first meal in 36 hours. 'We hadn't even drunk a sip of water until then,' Rozmin said. 'It was like we had no hunger, no thirst.'

By the time they reached Anuradhapura, it was near midnight, but none of them slept; their minds, agitated and feverish, allowed them no rest. They left for the railway station at 4 a.m. and caught the first train to Colombo. 'We went to Colombo literally in just the clothes we were in,' Rozmin said. 'They were all muddy and torn, and in the train, everybody was looking at us as if we were mad. We came to Colombo and went to the house of my mother's elder sister. They had no idea about what happened to us or where we were.' It was 10 a.m. on 1 November, a full two days since an autorickshaw with a loudspeaker had clattered through Moor Street and propelled its residents into exile.

Razeena and her family were among the fortunate ones. A citizens' commission report from 2011 catalogued stories from the expulsion that were bursting with pain and death. A pregnant woman went into labour in the jungle beyond Pooneryn, but the child died and was buried there, in the very spot where it was born, its life swiftly circumscribed by both time and geography. A man recounted how his mother-in-law drowned during the ferry crossing. Those who travelled by daylight found themselves trapped between the army and the Tigers, wide open to crossfire. 'There was this elderly person, he was struck by a bomb right in his chest,' a man told the commission. 'We were resting when this happened. He died on the spot. Since they could not bring his body, they buried it behind the mosque. They performed all the rituals. The other person was a friend of mine. He had no problems; it was his wife. She was travelling in a lorry. She was pregnant as well.

Suddenly a bomb hit the top of the lorry, and pieces of the bomb fell on her stomach. Blood started pouring out. She fainted and died on the spot. I can never forget this incident.'

'When were you able to visit Jaffna again, after 1990?' I asked.

Razeena had taken one of her intermissions, breathing deeply to calm herself and motioning me to wait for an answer. She described a rectangle in the air to Rozmin: Photos. Rozmin went into a bedroom and returned with an album.

During the 2002 ceasefire, Razeena finally said. 'In 1990, my neighbour had actually fled before me, and she had given me some of her jewels in a tin box, for safekeeping,' she said. 'I didn't take them with me. I buried them under a tree in the back yard.' The neighbour had begun to ask Razeena repeatedly for the jewels, and so she travelled to Jaffna just to recover them. 'The house had no roof, no doors, and no windows,' she said. 'It was just floor and walls. The compound walls were gone, and even a big gate that we had was missing.' In the photos, I saw how poison ivy had stormed into the house and how the back yard had been colonised by scrub and weeds. But the house looked damaged in odd, unnatural ways as well. 'The Tigers had dug up the floor, to see if anything was buried under there,' Razeena said. 'The yard was so overgrown that it was a miracle I found those jewels. I had to go to the house and dig many times before I found it, though.'

Salam went to Jaffna too, in 2003, nearly two decades after he had departed for Brunei. He had left his house locked up, but his title deeds had somehow been spirited through the Tiger checking posts by Razeena's husband. When Salam reached Moor Street, he couldn't recognise the house that had been in his family for over a hundred years; nearly every structure on that street had melted into anonymous lattices of brick and mortar, and a friend had to guide Salam to his own doorstep. He lingered outside for many minutes, apprehensive about encountering snakes within. Even after he entered, he was not certain about where he was. Through a crack in the cement floor, a tree had grown inside the house, and it seemed to bend and distort the space, making it foreign and unfamiliar. Then, in a corner of the house, Salam found a jag of polished slate: a chip off the blackboard that he had bought, in 1981 or 1982, to teach his children. That was how he knew he was home.

6

IF JAFFNA HAD been caught unawares by the events of that October, it had not been paying attention. The rupture of goodwill between the Tigers and the Muslims had begun already that summer in the east, in and near Batticaloa. The news must have drifted up north, but perhaps the Muslims of Jaffna had just ignored these terrible signals, or perhaps they had thought that the contagion would never be blown their way, which was pure delusion.

I went to Batticaloa, which sits right on the sea, on a filament of land that is so slender, and that is separated from the mainland by such an extensive web of lagoons, that it seems on the map to be of Sri Lanka and yet not of it. An amphibious town. The train from Colombo took a full night, and it brought me to Batticaloa on a moist, grimy morning. Batticaloa was always moist; perspiration was always one minor exertion away, and the air tasted sweat-sour. After the first few days, I saw that it was perilous to venture out in the afternoon; the sun and the humidity drained the life out of me, as if by some osmotic procedure. So I sat on the terrace of my rundown hotel, leaking sweat even when I positioned my chair next to a pedestal fan. Over the balustrade, in the courtyard below, a television crew was shooting audition reels for a reality show involving singing children. The crew sweated, the parents sweated, the heavily made-up kids sweated even more, especially when they were backed up against the trunk of a coconut tree and prompted to belt out old Tamil film songs. We were all bound together by sweat.

Batticaloa felt as limp as I did. As a town, it has been cuffed repeatedly by the hands of nature and geography. Its marshy terrain gave it the Tamil name of *Matta Kalappu*, or 'muddy swamp,' and the Dutch, who snatched the town from the Portuguese in 1638, called it 'a vile and stinking place.' Its lagoons teemed with crocodiles, their teeth sometimes so large, a visitor wrote in 1861, 'that the natives mount them with silver lids and use them for boxes.' Smallpox plundered life out of the local population. The low-slung skies hurled storms and cyclones at Batticaloa. An 1878 flood rolled away a herd of elephants, and a cyclone a century later levelled everything in sight. The 2004 tsunami, twitched out of tectonic plates under faraway Indonesia, killed 13,000 people in Batticaloa and the adjacent district of Ampara, close to half of Sri Lanka's total death toll. Many old photographs show bridges and roads drowned under floodwater, as if an ancient lease had expired and the ocean was preparing to take Batticaloa away from Sri Lanka and back into itself.

One road leaving the Batticaloa railway station runs due south, spans a stretch of water, and proceeds into Kattankudy, a town that was, in the summer of 1990, almost 90 per cent Muslim. That June, a 13-month ceasefire had ended, and the Tigers, rearmed and reanimated, had been raring to assert themselves. On 3 August, during Friday evening prayers, they surrounded four mosques and attacked the Muslims inside with automatic weapons and hand grenades. One hundred and forty-seven people were killed; in two mosques alone, the Meer Jumma mosque and the Husseiniya mosque, standing not far from each other on perpendicular roads, 103 people died. As always, the Tigers announced themselves with the infliction of death.

If you know the history of the Meer Jumma mosque, you

find that it arrives too suddenly upon you: just one right turn off the main road and there you are. The mosque provides no preamble that allows you to steel yourself. It is a large, squat, powder-blue building, with a sprig of loudspeakers on a pole emerging from one corner. On that Tuesday, between prayers, it was as silent and patient as a cemetery. Outside its main iron-grill door, a black-on-yellow signboard hung on a mildewed wall, listing in Tamil every one of the 103 people who had died there and at Husseiniya. I wrote names down. The oldest was a man named S.M.M. Mustafa, 72 years old; the youngest were two brothers, M.S.M. Akram, aged six, and M.S.M. Tahan, aged eight. The congregation was a young one, and many 10- and 13- and 14- and 17-year-olds were slaughtered as they prayed for the capacity to lead good, worthwhile lives.

Indoors, the red granite floor was smooth and cool under my bare feet, but the pillars and the front wall of the mosque, near the *mihrab*, had been left untouched after August 1990. They were still pockmarked with bullet holes, dozens of them. Chunks of plaster had been bitten out of the pillars by grenade explosions. As I stood there, three men came in to pray, spreading themselves out through the large hall, facing the afternoon sun blazing through a hexagonal window.

I walked down the road and turned right to reach the Husseiniya mosque, which also bore, on an outside wall, a list of the 103 victims, fading blue letters printed up on a sheet of white flex. The Husseiniya was a much smaller mosque than the Meer Jumma, painted a florid purple-orange on the outside and Pepto-Bismol pink indoors. But I saw no evidence of the attack here at all: the walls were whole and unblemished, and despite the cobwebs in the corners, the mosque looked new, or at least newly renovated. Strange, I thought; this congregation seemed as if it wanted to forget, just as much as the Meer Jumma's congregation wanted to remember.

As I was leaving the mosque, an old man walked in, and he smiled and nodded. I went on for a few steps, but then on an impulse, I wheeled around and returned to him. His name was Sarabdin, and he was a long-time congregant at Husseiniya, having lived just down the street his entire life. He wore a blue sarong, a white skullcap, a white shirt unbuttoned down his chest, and a disciplined beard that hugged the line of his jaw.

I was confused, I told him. Why hadn't the Husseiniya preserved the scars of its attack, as the Meer Jumma had done?

But this Husseiniya wasn't the site of the attack at all, he said. 'This was built later, in 1991.' He pointed next door to an older building, which was locked and unused, consigned entirely to the past. 'That's the mosque that was attacked.'

'Were there any survivors here?'

'There were three,' Sarabdin said. 'I know one of them, my brother-in-law Ismail. He works near here, in a hospital. Do you want to meet him?'

I did, I said.

'Four young boys from my extended family died here,' Sarabdin said, unprompted. 'Two of them were my sons. Did you see the signboard? They were the two boys aged six and eight.'

I pulled out my notebook and showed him the names I had scribbled down: M.S.M. Akram and M.S.M. Tahan.

'Yes, yes, that's them.' He gave the notebook only a glance, as if he couldn't bear to look at the names for longer than a second. 'I wasn't here at the time. I was in town, in Batticaloa. When I heard the news, I came running all the way. Nobody knew at the time whether it was the army or the Tigers who did it. There was utter panic.'

The next morning, as we had arranged, I met Sarabdin at the Husseiniya mosque, and he took me to Ismail's house, a few steps further down the same lane. Ismail, a thickset man of 40, with fields of grey dawning at his temples, a watery right eye and quite perfect teeth, was somewhat taken aback; Sarabdin hadn't told him that we were coming, and he was just leaving for work. 'Will you come back in the evening?' he asked me, not hostile exactly, but wrong-footed by our arrival and therefore unable to be warm and welcoming.

I returned at 5 p.m., and we sat in Ismail's living room, where strips of patterned, chocolate-brown linoleum had been pasted out of alignment on the floor, so that it looked as if it was tilting and teetering, like the floor of a crazy house at a funfair. Ismail's blackened feet stuck out of his striped sarong; printed leaves drifted down the expanse of his white linen shirt, as if they were drawn by the gravity of his pot belly.

'I've spoken to journalists a couple of times before,' Ismail said. 'I don't mind telling you what happened that day. But I have a question for you first.'

'Of course,' I said. He wanted to know what kind of book I was writing, I thought.

'What good will this conversation do for me?' he asked.

I had no answer to give him. I had asked this question of myself often in Sri Lanka, uncapping deep wells of self-doubt. Even in ordinary circumstances, the work of a journalist can feel like that of a parasite, fattening itself on the time and memories of others but giving back nothing tangible at all. In Sri Lanka, the process felt especially voyeuristic, as I asked people to rehearse the pain of their lives so that I could write a book they would never read. 'Will I ever even see you again?' Ismail asked, and the honest answer was: probably not. I wasn't from Sri Lanka, so after this book was written and forgotten, I would, in all likelihood, visit only sparingly.

'It's important that these stories be recorded and told,' I could say, as indeed I did say to Ismail. It was true, but at the same time it must have sounded pathetic and hollow to a man whose relatives had been killed and who still limped because he had two inches of shrapnel nestled within his left thigh.

Ismail shrugged a shrug of immense politeness. 'What you can do,' he said, 'is take down my number and, when the book comes out, send me a copy. Will you do that?'

'Of course, of course,' I said, feeling even dirtier now for having been requested to do so little in exchange for receiving so much.

In 1990, Ismail, having just finished his A Levels, was working at a shop in Batticaloa, and he had watched ties between the Tigers and the Muslims grow flimsier and flimsier. There was history here. The two groups clashed first in 1985, and when the government created a home guard in 1986 and slyly staffed it with Muslims, relations worsened. The killings began the next year: 30 Muslim passengers on a bus headed to Kattankudy, dozens of Muslim policemen in Ampara, men and women and children returning from the Hajj. When a Muslim member of the Tigers was mysteriously murdered, 75 people were rounded up in Kattankudy for questioning and were never seen again.

Ismail's best friend was one of those 75 people. 'I was part of another group of around 50, and we were boxed in on the street by just three Tigers with guns. They kept asking us: "Who killed him?" We said we didn't know anything. When we were dispersed, we didn't know how to leave, because we were sure that if we turned our backs on them, we would be shot. We were saved, I think, because one of the Muslims in this group knew some Tigers well.'

The summer of the mosque massacres had been long and enervating. The army prevented Tamil civilians and traders from leaving or entering the district, so Kattankudy's Muslims, who were permitted to drive to nearby towns, became the sole source of provisions. In June, the Tigers stormed Kattankudy, imposed an ad hoc curfew, and raided the shops to resupply themselves. During this spree of looting,

when one Muslim man unknowingly wandered out of his
house, he was immediately shot. In July, the Tigers halted and
robbed a convoy of goods trucks; their Muslim occupants—
including one of Ismail's cousins—were first herded into a
house by the road and then taken outdoors and killed, all five
dozen of them. 'August was hot, and you could sense so much
tension in the air,' Ismail said. 'We had no food, and we had
no electricity, and we had no work.' At night, in the streets
of Kattankudy, neighbourhoods burned piles of tyres. The
tyres threw off clouds of reeking smoke, but the light of the
flames helped warn families of approaching dangers. This was
atavism, I thought: man regressing to the survival methods of
the wilderness.

'That day, 3 August, was really hot, and we were all more
tense than usual,' Ismail said. 'Could we go out? Should we?'
He attended afternoon prayers at half past noon, sat down
for an early dinner at 5 p.m. and then decided to visit the
Kattankudy beach with four friends. Around 6.30 p.m., they
left the beach to go back home. It was already dark by then,
and the street lamps were dead; only bonfires of tyres threw
any light at all on the vacant streets.

Ismail parked his bicycle at home, washed his hands and
feet, and crossed the road to the Husseiniya mosque in time
for the 8 p.m. prayer. With him were his two younger brothers,
aged 12 and 13, and Sarabdin's two sons. 'The prayer was
about half over when we heard a shot. It was just one shot,
somewhat far away, near the Meer Jumma mosque. I think
that was a signal to start.'

One of the worshippers at Husseiniya yelled: 'Shooting,
shooting! Run, run!' There were 35 people inside the mosque,
and only one door functioned as both entrance and exit. By
the time the congregants had risen to their feet, the Tigers
were at the mosque's outer gate.

'They told all of us to come out,' Ismail said. 'There was an old teacher of mine with us. He was disabled, with only one arm and one leg. He shouted back: "There's nobody in here with guns."'

"We'll shoot if you don't come out. We'll fire, we'll fire, we'll fire." Ismail emphasized how the warning was repeated in triplicate: '*Suduvom, suduvom, suduvom.*' He jabbed his finger in the air, as if he was ringing a doorbell with impatience.

It was difficult to tell how many Tigers were outside the Husseiniya, although Ismail could hear them conversing outside and even glimpse them through a window. 'They were in civilian clothing,' he said. 'Later, there was a rumour that the Sri Lankan army was behind the attack. But you can tell the difference between Tamils speaking Tamil and Sinhalese people speaking Tamil, which is how I knew it wasn't the army. And in any case, at the time, the Tigers controlled this area completely.' The mosque was surrounded on three sides, and through the windows in these three walls, the Tigers tossed in grenades. Then the barrel of a sub-machine gun was inserted through a hole in the decorative latticework near the door, and the firing began.

Ismail's father had contributed funds for the construction of the old Husseiniya mosque, and so he still had a key for the locked door. He took me in there now, hobbling as he crossed the road. The mosque had a sloping roof, shingles of red clay laid over a frame of round wooden beams. The grenades and bullets had perforated the mosque's walls and pillars, punching untidy circular holes in the masonry. The low, shallow basin where Muslims once washed their feet before prayers was dry. The mosque was hot; the air seemed not to move at all, as if it were still stunned from the events of two decades ago.

'This is where I lay, see?' Ismail pointed to a spot by the door. 'Two other people had fallen on top of me. They were bleeding all over me.'

After the first squall of firing, there was a lull. The Tigers, who had believed the door to be locked, found now that it was merely shut, and they pushed it open. Inside, the mosque was profoundly dark; an oil lamp had been lit to guide the prayers, but it had been extinguished in the confusion. Two Tigers came in, to sift through the bodies with harrowing thoroughness. The first Tiger, carrying a small flashlight, would point to people who still seemed to be alive; the second would finish the job. Ismail, already wounded in his thigh, was certain that he would die, but the two corpses lying on top of him kept him hidden from view. 'I thought of the people at home. What would they do? How would they cope with all these deaths?'

The Tigers heard a sound outside and left the mosque. There was another suffocating silence. Then the Tigers came back in and shouted: 'Everybody who isn't injured, get up. Come out and help us take the injured to the hospital.'

At this, Ismail's nephew, the six-year-old Akram, jumped up and, in tears, shouted: 'I want to go home. I don't want to be here.'

The Tigers put the barrel of a gun into Akram's mouth and fired. 'He was right by my feet,' Ismail said, 'and I couldn't do a thing to save him.'

Ismail's eyes had glazed over, and he wasn't looking at me any longer, or looking at anything in the mosque. I found I couldn't look at him either, so I stared down hard at my notebook, not really reading the words but tracing the cursive with my eyes anyway, from loop to loop. It gave me something to do.

There was one final round of shooting. The Tigers stood just inside the doorway of the mosque, framed against the awful night, and raked the floor again with gunfire. Ismail caught one of these bullets in his stomach. When they left, he heard a grenade go off at the intersection of roads near the Husseiniya—another signal, he thought indistinctly before passing out. The attack lasted a total of ten minutes. Ismail found this out later because a clock on the wall of the mosque, its face shattered, had stopped cold at 8.10 p.m.

Ismail spent the next two weeks in the hospital, intermittently conscious; in that time, the Tigers carried out a second massacre in Eravur, four miles north, ranging through that village's Muslim areas all night to kill more than a hundred people. For the next two years, Ismail was in and out of hospital, undergoing surgeries, learning how to walk all over again. He was frustrated, he said, by the helplessness of his community. 'We stayed away from the Tigers, largely, and we weren't involved in their movement at all. Even so, we received no guarantee of safety from the state.' After the slaughter at the Husseiniya, he forbade his Tamil friends from ever speaking admiringly of the Tigers. "Do it elsewhere, but not in front of me,' I told them. 'If you do, you're indirectly responsible for what happened to me."

He had photographs, he suddenly remembered. We were back in his house now, and he lurched heavily into the next room to retrieve an album, one of those cheap, commercial holders of happy memories that are sold in every corner store in the world. On its cover, a small blond boy in a straw hat and denim overalls snuggled up to a small blonde girl wearing Mary Jane shoes and a pink bow in her hair. In the album's first few leaves, Ismail's brothers and nephews clown around and mug for the camera; one photo, taken three months before the massacre, shows the four small boys packed tightly on to a green couch, Akram on the extreme left, his moon face clad in a smile. Immediately on the next page, he lies supine on the mosque's floor, his face turned to the left so that the camera cannot see the exit wound. As per custom, a strip of white cloth runs around his face, holding his jaw closed, and his wrists are also tied together, the body thus trussed in preparation for his burial. The floor around him is covered in blood; it speckles his white shirt and the skin of his arms. What is visible of his face, however, seems at first to be entirely unhurt; the right eye is closed as if in calm slumber, and only on closer examination does it become clear that his left eye, his left cheek, that entire hemisphere of his face, has disintegrated. In the space of a single page of a photo album, Akram's momentary life has come to a tattered end.

THE FAITH

1

EVEN AFTER MONTHS in Sri Lanka, I was getting the scale of the island wrong. I had come here with all the puffed-up arrogance of a visitor from a big country to a small one, so I was forever underestimating how long it took to reach one place from another. Three hours, I would think, tracing a route between towns just an inch or two apart on the map. But I would be misjudging the dimensions of real land, and forgetting about hills, war-ravaged roads, detours, and the stately trundle of government buses. I would arrive six hours later, travel-sore and out of step with time.

After one such trip back to Colombo, I fell ill. Having gone to sleep next to an open bus window, I had ingested a great quantity of dust, and my allergy symptoms gave way first to a raw wheeze and then to a bout of flu. I dosed myself with tea and rest, but when my temperature climbed, I went to the hospital for a prescription; I hoped, as I trudged through the lobby, to run into Dr Thurairaja, to gain comfort from his brazen health and geniality, but I had no such fortune. The general physician on duty sent me home, miserable, with ten days' worth of antibiotics.

For nearly a week, I glowed with fever. It was November, and even though the nights were filled with rain, the afternoons still prickled with heat. In my darkened bedroom, I shivered and sweated in turn under the blankets. My sleep shook with nightmares, but curiously, they had nothing at all to do with the Tigers or the civil war. Instead, they were spun out of high fantasy: ogres and chasms and space races. By calling up these absurdities, my mind revelled in its chance to distance itself from the stories I had been hearing over the past few months.

In between these dreams, I tried to read my way through the Mahavamsa, the great chronicle of Sri Lankan Buddhism. The previous month, I had bought a fat paperback translation from a bookstore near the university. On the maroon cover was a painting of a prince, a quiver of arrows slung over his back and a bow in his delicate hand, leading his men into adventure. During the time that the book stayed with me in my sickbed, it matched my temper perfectly. It too was stuffed with feverish detail—about how many cubits high a temple was, or how an army was assembled, or how a king hunted and killed a stag—and with looping, hazy narratives. The Mahavamsa and I kept each other infected with delirium through that week.

Even this unwieldy text is a condensation. Mahanama Thero, the monk who, in the 6th century CE strung together various Buddhist commentaries that had emerged over the previous few centuries, complained in his very second sentence: 'The account compiled by the ancients was too long and drawn out, and contained many repetitions.' Written in Pali, the Mahavamsa tells the story of Buddhist Sri Lanka between the 6th century BCE and the 4th century CE. It deals often with historical figures, but it is by no means a watertight history; monks have reworked the Mahavamsa over hundreds of years, tailoring its lessons to the political agendas of their kings and filling in the gaps—of the early years in particular—with their distilled imaginations. Even so, to Sinhalese nationalists, the Mahavamsa serves as the foundational epic of their civilization. The epic has no hero. Or rather, the hero is Buddhism itself, this fledgling faith that faded away in its home country of India but that flourished and grew powerful on this speck of an island.

In 483 BCE the Mahavamsa records, on the very day the Buddha passed on, Prince Vijaya washed up on the shores of Sri Lanka. He was the eldest son of a brother and a sister, who in turn were the children of a human princess and a lion. In what is now Bengal, Vijaya had been a brash, irresponsible prince regent. He and his followers were 'of evil conduct . . . They committed many intolerable crimes of violence.' To pacify his enraged public, Vijaya's father rounded up the prince and 700 of his men, ordered them 'to be shaved over half of their heads, the sign of a slave or a person banished to be shunned by all,' loaded them on to a ship, and sent them far out to sea.

Once in Sri Lanka, Vijaya the roustabout abandoned his ways of delinquency and ruled in peace for 38 years. His descendants believed themselves to be of Aryan stock, from northern India, and not of the Dravidian race of south India, and they called themselves the Sinhalese, after *simha*, the Sanskrit word for 'lion.' According to the Mahavamsa, it was to this civilization that the Buddha referred when, on his deathbed, he told his disciple Sakka: 'Vijaya . . . has reached Lanka, together with seven hundred followers. My faith will be established in Lanka. Lord Sakka, protect diligently Vijaya and Lanka.' Two centuries later, when the Indian prince Mahinda came to Sri Lanka, bearing the teachings of the Buddha, he met and converted the Sinhalese king Tissa, a direct descendant of Vijaya's brother. The Mahavamsa thus gives Sri Lanka to the Sinhalese twice over: first by celebrating them as the island's original settlers, and then by bestowing upon them the emphatic protection of the Buddha.

From Vijaya, the book straggles and meanders, cycling through an endless list of kings and kingships. My favourite discursion was a compact slice of royal history from one of

the chronicle's byways. The king Yasalakatissa, who had
come to his title by killing his older brother during a water-
sports festival, had a gatekeeper named Subha. Subha was
the spitting image of the king, and so Yasalakatissa draped
Subha in royal regalia and seated him on the throne. While the
courtiers clustered around the impostor and sang his praises,
Yasalakatissa, having dressed as a gatekeeper and stationed
himself at the door, shook with laughter at the ingenuity of
his jape.

> Then one day Subha addressed the ministers while the
> king was laughing, 'Why does this gatekeeper laugh in
> my presence?'
>
> He had King Yasalakatissa killed. Subha then
> reigned six years. Even when the truth was later
> discovered, he retained his throne and became known
> as King Subha.

Rarely is the Mahavamsa this wry and succinct; mostly its tone
is ornate and self-serious. It is a book with many missions.
One of them is to provide proof—such as it is—of the antique
enmity between the Sinhalese and the Tamils. Another is
to supply the country's Buddhists with a moral imperative.
Sri Lanka is, as decreed by the Buddha himself, the ultimate
refuge of his faith, so any measure—even violence—is
permissible in the protection of Buddhism.

The backbone of the Mahavamsa is the legend of
Dutugemunu, the most celebrated of the Sinhalese kings who
defended Buddhism and kept the Tamils at bay. He is the very
embodiment of the epic's moral lessons, and a full sixth of
the Mahavamsa's length is devoted to him, beginning with the
grisly omens of his birth, in the 2nd century BCE. His mother,
the Queen of Great Merit, experiences an unusual craving

when she is carrying him: to drink the water that had washed the sword used to behead the chief general of the Tamil king Elara, and to do this while trampling upon the general's severed head. Worried about this urge, she consults her Buddhist soothsayers, who advise her to indulge this morbidity. 'The queen's son will vanquish the Damilas, unify the kingdom, and will make the Faith shine,' they say.

Dutugemunu yearns, even as a young prince, to do nothing but fight the Tamils; when at first his father recommends restraint, Dutugemunu sends him the clothes of a woman, a sneering gift. Elara and his Tamils seem to roil his soul. Why does Dutugemunu sleep curled into such a tense, cramped ball? his mother asks him once. He replies that on one side of him is the ocean, and on the other side, across the river, are the Tamils, massed together, ever eager to push him off the island. 'How can I lie down with my limbs outstretched?'

The most curious aspect of the Dutugemunu story is that his sworn enemy is a fair and benevolent king. Elara arrives in Sri Lanka as an invader, it is true—from the Chola kingdom in Tamil Nadu—but the Mahavamsa describes him as an upright man, 'ruling impartially to friends and enemies during lawsuits.' He appears to present no danger to Buddhism at all: he visits and prays at *viharayas*, and he feeds and showers wealth upon communities of Buddhist monks. His zealous responsibility towards the faith even touches a moment of shimmering drama when, having accidentally damaged part of a stupa with his chariot, he lies down on the road and insists that his head be severed by the chariot's wheel, as an act of penitence. 'O great King, our Teacher does not counsel injury to others for whatever reason,' a monk says to Elara. 'Rather, seek forgiveness by restoring the stupa.' Elara is just and pure, but he earns Dutugemunu's anger, and deserves in due course to be slain, solely because he is a Tamil king in Sri Lanka.

The war between the Sinhalese and the Tamils is protracted

and bloody, lasting 13 years, but the final showdown between the two kings is brief and anticlimactic, occupying barely a full page in my translation. Dutugemunu builds 32 concentric barricades and places himself at the heart of this fortification. After one of Elara's mightiest warriors crashes through these barriers, Dutugemunu mounts an elephant and rides out to fight. Elara hurls a spear; Dutugemunu ducks under it. Dutugemunu's elephant impales Elara's with its tusks, and at the same time, Dutugemunu drives his spear into Elara, mortally wounding him. In a trice, the central battle of the Mahavamsa has ended.

It is the postscript to the war that offers the most revelatory and startling commentary on Dutugemunu's life. Despite his newfound wealth and his peacetime luxuries, Dutugemunu wanders gloomily about his palace, too often remembering the carnage he wrought on the battlefield and worried over the deep karmic deficits he has incurred. The elders of the Sangha, the Buddhist clergy, notice this and send a delegation of eight monks to minister to his anguish.

'In truth, venerable sirs,' Dutugemunu tells the monks when they arrive, 'how can there be comfort to me in that I caused the destruction of a great army of myriads of men?'

'There is no hindrance on the way to heaven because of your acts,' one of the monks assures his king. Slaughtering Tamils is no moral mistake. Only the equivalent of one and a half men died at Dutugemunu's hands, according to the Sangha's official arithmetic, because the Tamils 'were heretical and evil and died as though they were animals. You will make the Buddha's faith shine in many ways. Therefore, Lord of Men, cast away your mental confusion.'

Being thus exhorted, the great king was comforted; his kill rate would never disturb him again. He does, however, recall that, once upon a breakfast, he ate a red-pepper pod without consciously setting aside a portion of it for the Sangha, as was the royal practice. 'For this,' he decides, 'penance must be done by me.' A hierarchy of sin springs into being, in which dishonouring the Sangha by denying it a due share of a red-pepper pod counts as a graver transgression, worthier of penance, than massacring thousands of Tamils on the battlefield.

Once I had read about Dutugemunu, I recognized his presence all around me. Modern Sri Lanka remembers Dutugemunu more than any other figure from the Mahavamsa save only the Buddha. In the tabloids, I read about one or the other of two ongoing movie projects that were filming the story of his life. I saw schools, hotels, roads and restaurants named after him. Units of the Gemunu Watch regiment of the army were scattered across the north of the country, tasked with the responsibility of watching for signs of new dissent among the Tamils. Who better than the Gemunu Watch, I suppose somebody in power had reckoned, to keep the Tamils in line?

But it was Mahinda Rajapaksa, the president who had won the war, who called up Dutugemunu's ghost most vividly. It was as if he believed that his entire life had been ordained to culminate in this momentous military victory. He was born in 1945, nine years before Prabhakaran, into a sprawling political family from the Sinhalese heartland in the south. His uncle had been elected to a state council and his father and cousin had been members of Parliament; Mahinda himself became the country's youngest parliamentarian at 24.

It seemed, for a while, that Mahinda had a career of no definite focus. He became a lawyer. He became an ardent trade unionist. He worked as an assistant at a university library. He acted in several movies; once he played an army brigadier, cast in the role by a director who said he was looking for a stentorian voice and a commanding tone. Through it all, he sidled slowly into politics, going to prison for three months in 1985 as part of a purge by the government at the time. In the 1990s, he headed a few ministries, assembling for himself a reputation as a champion of human rights. He secured the presidency first in 2005 and then again in 2010, a year after he won the war and a year before I moved to Sri Lanka.

When I arrived, Mahinda was inescapable. His face was everywhere, plastered across the country, from tip to toe: hair slicked back, moustache draped thickly above his upper lip, jowls smooth and shiny. He dressed always in a chalk-white ensemble, with a maroon sash looped around his neck; in one of his hands was looped a golden talisman on a chain, which he worried without pause. Even when he smiled, he glowered. He looked every inch a strongman—politically, but also physically, as if he could snap your neck himself, instead of having to order his bodyguards to attend to it. Abetted by Mahinda, his family had followed him into the government and into Parliament: brothers, a son, a niece, nephews, the vast Rajapaksa clan moving into the Sri Lankan state as if it were an ancestral house.

Mahinda had already begun to style himself, with great deliberateness and brazenness, after Dutugemunu. On the website of the Ministry of Defence—which was run by his brother Gotabhaya—an essay appeared in late 2010, comparing the feats of Mahinda with those of Dutugemunu. 'The question arises,' the essay fawned, 'as to who could be greater.' There was no room here for an ambiguous answer: Dutugemunu had it easier. He never had to contend with meddling foreign forces—other countries, NGOs, or the media—and, for him, 'the modalities of waging a war were not restrained by issues of human rights and other instruments of international interventions.' Mahinda, who muscled past these problems and still won the war, proved to be a leader 'picked by history,' outshining Dutugemunu convincingly. Somewhere

I heard it said that the Rajapaksas were commissioning historians to produce an updated Mahavamsa, to include their own accomplishments of protecting Buddhism and reuniting Sri Lanka. I was never able to find out if this was just cynical speculation or if it was the truth.

Sycophants scrambled to fall in line to burnish this link between Mahinda and Dutugemunu. One of the most surreal of such displays came from the pronouncements of Jackson Anthony, a television personality who described himself as a veteran historian, and who had once hosted a dull television series consisting only of his commentaries on the Mahavamsa. He had interrogated the past, Anthony said, and he had arrived at the conclusion that Rajapaksa was not only a direct descendant of Dutugemunu but also related by blood to the Buddha himself.

Anthony grandly explained his revelations during the season finale of *Ranaviru Real Star*, an *American Idol* knock-off that was conceived by the defence secretary Gotabhaya Rajapaksa and produced by his ministry. The contestants in *Ranaviru Real Star* were members of the armed forces, singing their hearts out for the chance to win a house worth 20 million rupees. During the finale, Gotabhaya sat next to the evening's chief guest, his brother the president, looking upon a circular black stage built to resemble a gramophone record.

Anthony sat off to one side, behind a desk, wearing a glistening black tunic, his head shaven to billiard-ball smoothness and his beard immaculately trimmed. He had notes in front of him, but he rarely referred to them; even extempore, he spoke in fluent classical Sinhalese, firing the occasional simpering smile towards the president, waving his hands and pinching his fingers together in Italianate gestures. 'We are indeed extremely happy about this new beginning. We are well aware that this is not just any beginning, but one that will be engraved in world history,' he said, referring to the finale's opening ceremony but, not very obliquely, to a post-war Sri Lanka.

Anthony went on. Earlier in the opening ceremony, 10 burly men, representing the 10 legendary warriors of Dutugemunu, had marched up to Mahinda and presented him with a missive. 'It occurred to me that this was an incident complete in meaning, in every aspect, for two primary reasons,' Anthony said. 'The first is because this is the ultimate moment in the history of Sri Lanka's governance. If King Dutugemunu were to send a royal message to any head of state of post-independence Sri Lanka, he would naturally choose our great military leader.' The camera panned to Mahinda, who allowed himself a long, slow, implacable blink. I couldn't tell if he was embarrassed even in the slightest, or if he knew well in advance—or perhaps had even directed—the contents of Anthony's lavish introduction.

The second reason, Anthony continued, was the 'generational pull' of Dutugemunu upon the Rajapaksas. In the modern Sri Lankan region of Giruwapaththu, a 12-year-old Dutugemunu was believed to have engaged in and won a debate, with a man far older than him, on the subject: 'The political heritage of this country belongs to us.' Anthony tortuously traced Dutugemunu's ancestry back to Amithodana, the Buddha's uncle. And today, he said, Sri Lanka had a leader who had unified the country, and who hailed from the Rajapaksa family, which was rooted in Giruwapaththu. 'Therefore it is fitting that a leader from Giruwapaththu, destined to lead a free and independent Sri Lanka into the future, would be chosen to receive a royal message from his great ancestor King Dutugemunu. It is fitting that this message should be delivered at an occasion where the war heroes of the country are being felicitated.'

At some point during this speech, Gotabhaya and the rest of the audience fell into gentle applause. Anthony beamed. The president sat on, hands clasped in front of him. I recall that he laughed toothily once, either because he was sharing a joke with his brother or because Anthony had said something especially obsequious. Otherwise, though, he wore no expression at all. He just absorbed these conferrals of greatness and divinity without flinching, accepting them as his due.

2

SRI LANKA FELT claustrophobic, boxed in. It felt like a country in which somebody was deciding, top-down and in a tearing hurry, what the country ought to be, what its history ought to convey, what its people ought to aspire to. The pincers of this ideology were tight around my windpipe sometimes, leaving me breathless. Everything was being re-engineered to fit: the image of the president; road signs and road shrines; the past itself. The very landscape of the country was being altered, as if Sri Lanka could be terraformed into its intended future.

The signs of this vast redesign were everywhere in the north and the east. New Buddhist stupas rose in shattered towns, their splendid milky finish in sore contrast to the ruin around them; sometimes they were situated mere kilometres from existing Hindu temples, as if posted there in deliberate face-offs. In Kilinochchi, the Tigers' former capital, a giant dun-coloured statue of a seated Buddha had been erected. Nearly 30 such statues had been constructed along the A9 between May 2009 and February 2012, provoking one Tamil politician into protest against this 'cultural intrusion'; one of these statues, he claimed, had even been built over the rubble of a newly demolished Hindu temple. If they weren't stupas or Buddhas, they were Bodhi trees, planted so artificially—in the middle of their own enclosure, set prominently apart from the other vegetation on the shoulder of the A9—that they were transformed from objects of nature into objects of political sculpture.

Many of these installations were cared for and guarded by the military, which left no doubt about the side on which the state landed. Under the directions of Gotabhaya himself, the government began to build nine Stupas of Triumph, one in each of Sri Lanka's provinces, to celebrate the victory of its armed forces over the Tigers. In the small northern port of Dambakola Patuna, where the king Ashoka's daughter Sanghamitta is said to have landed carrying a sapling of the original Bodhi tree, the Sri Lankan navy built a large Buddhist *viharaya* after the war. Some of the Buddha statues along the A9 sat just outside the walls of sprawling army camps, such that it was difficult to tell who was watching over whom.

A little way past the checkpoint at Omanthai, a young Bodhi sprouted out of a high, grassy mesa; a cage of fine netting stood around the tree, protecting it from insects. When we got out of our car and wandered closer, a young man came sprinting out of a tin shack nearby. He wore Puma trackpants and an olive-green T-shirt with the legend 'Vijayabahu Infantry Regiment.' The regiment was housed, he said, in the 561 Brigade camp, across the highway; four soldiers from the 561 were deputed permanently at the tree. 'We did all this five months ago,' he explained. 'It was all marsh here before that. We had to drain it and raise the ground to various levels, and we planted this grass, and we laid the path.' It sounded like hard work. The highway itself, meanwhile, remained cratered and difficult, promising rupture to even the most resilient of vehicle suspensions.

The town of Chunnakam sits in the very centre of the final rounded spur of the Jaffna peninsula, and from here the road to Kandarodai constricts of its own accord, like a malnourished capillary. It bends through dense groves of palmyra trees, which refract the light through their leaves and toss strange tessellated shadows on to the tarmac. Small Hindu shrines went past the open door of my autorickshaw—at first as blurs and then as sharper images, as we slowed and slowed, before turning off into a sandy, empty parking lot. On a mat, a woman sat next to her king coconuts, big red-gold bubbles that looked as if they had fallen to earth, in intact bunches, from the tree above. To her right, through lengths of barbed wire strung across staves, the low grey-white hemispheres of the complex shone dully in the sun.

Kandarodai is an old Buddhist site, but the domes are newer. In its state of full-blown ruin, there had been only circular bases of stone, approximately sixty of them, the small burial mounds that had once been built over them having long crumbled away. On a couple of dozen of these bases, these new limestone domes—the stupas—had been reconstructed in recent centuries, the tallest of them still shorter than a grown man; the other rings on the ground remain vacant, grass thrusting through the cracks. The domes had character, each pitted and weathered in distinct ways, but they were all equally inscrutable. The human eye skittered right over their roundness and came away with nothing.

Visitors were not allowed too close to the stupas; they were kept back by an ankle-high fence of electrical cable and by paper 'No Entry' signs pasted on to the trunks of trees. Plastic Buddhist pennants, resembling cheap polythene grocery bags, flapped from clothes lines looped from palmyra to palmyra. An orange Buddha had been installed inside a glass display case, his eyes cast downwards, gazing at the lotuses sewn out of satin and placed in front of him. Another Buddha sat inside a gloomy tin-walled prayer hall with a floor of pistachio-green tiles.

Kandarodai's Buddhist ruins are surmised to be 2000 years old or more, and since they are among the most ancient relics on the island, the question of who built them had come to matter very much. This was what the civil war had been fought over, after all—this gnawing doubt over who was here first, as if the country were a gold mine and latecomers could be treated as claim jumpers.

For a long time, Kandarodai functioned as a pure ruin, not publicly attributed to belong to any particular civilization. That was left to the scholars and their journals. Some of the literature on Kandarodai referred to potsherds that have been excavated, bearing Tamil Brahmi script and dating to 300 BCE but I never found out where these were kept or even if they truly existed at all. A Smithsonian expedition had, in 1967, found types of pottery similar to the megalithic culture of south India, as well as a plaque depicting a version of the Hindu deity Lakshmi, which was discovered below a layer of Buddhist remains. No Sinhalese texts mentioned Kandarodai until the 10th century. So, tentatively, historians thought Kandarodai to be a Tamil settlement—or rather, a settlement first populated by Dravidians who arrived from south India in pre-Christian times.

In the renewal of Sinhalese nationalism after the war, this line of reasoning was being neatly reversed. At the site, a signboard, written entirely in Sinhalese, was affixed to the outer wall of the prayer shed. It announced:

> *The history of the ancient Kadurugoda viharaya goes back to the time of the Buddha . . . It was first noticed in 1917 by the Jaffna District Judge Paul E Peiris who wrote about it, and from 1917 to 1919 they excavated here. They found Buddha statues, painted tiles and coins from the Anuradhapura and Polonnaruwa periods . . . This temple was destroyed because of the cruel actions of the Dravida king Sangili who ruled in the 16th century . . .*
>
> *Folk tales also tell of how the Buddha, after resolving the dispute between the kings Chulodara and Mohodara, rested here at Kadurugoda for a*

while . . . The historic Kadurugoda viharaya, which
tells of the glorious Sinhala Buddhist past, is a national
treasure that must be protected for future generations.

I couldn't read the signboard, of course; I took a photograph
of it, so that I could have it translated later. Every sign at the
site—even the 'No Entry' printouts—was only in Sinhalese,
even though we were in the heart of Tamil Sri Lanka. On
the road leading out of Jaffna, freshly erected signposts had
pointed to 'Kadurugoda' and not 'Kandarodai,' boosting
a Sinhalese mutation of the site's Tamil-origin name. Very
methodically, the story surrounding Kandarodai had been
taken apart and rebuilt.

I walked around the stupas for a while, kicking a stone
through the grass, looking sneakily for a gap in the electrical-
wire fence through which I could get closer. Then I went into
the prayer hall and stared at the Buddha. The floor smelled as if
it had just been washed and mopped. A young monk was sitting
next to the altar, a thin rug of stubble on his shaven head. I must
have coughed on the antiseptic fumes because he opened his
eyes, grinned at me, and lit a fresh tuft of incense sticks.

When I came out of the prayer hall, I thought I might stray
a little beyond the complex's immediate perimeter, closer to
the woods. That was when I saw the rough army hut and
some other structures hunkering down beneath the trees. A
small contingent of soldiers had been deployed at Kandarodai.
They wore fatigues, as if they needed to be prepared for some
sort of dramatic action, but in reality they looked bored and
purposeless. When I tried to wander into the woods, I was
dissuaded by a soldier who smiled but waggled his finger in
severe warning. It must have been the most strenuous thing he
had done all day.

Once a version of history had been propounded, it
needed also to be protected—by the military sometimes, as

at Kandarodai, or by the nationalists. Nobody can say with certainty whether the Sinhalese civilization in Sri Lanka predates the Tamil one; the earliest ancestors of the Sinhalese as well as of the Tamils came from India to Sri Lanka a couple of millennia ago, perhaps even within decades of each other. So to lay down an immutable narrative that favoured the Sinhalese required the co-option of the very science of history and archaeology.

There were anecdotes in the air about how nationalism warped these fields of study. The very first rumour I heard to this effect had it that Sri Lanka's archaeologists were only allowed to dig down to a certain depth and no deeper, for fear of discovering pre-Vijayan Tamil relics. Fortunately, this turned out to be as ridiculous as it sounded. But there were other, more substantiated accounts. One archaeologist's excavations were interrupted by a squad of belligerent monks; another archaeologist told me the story of how, some decades ago during a meeting of the Kandy National Museum's board, his colleague mentioned accidentally that there was no evidence to prove that the Buddha visited Sri Lanka three times. The monks who sat on the museum's board were enraged. 'My God, it was a hell of a thing!' this archaeologist said. 'If he wasn't so well known, we would all have been killed, I think.' Nirmal Dewasiri, a University of Colombo historian with a long record of challenging the government, told me that, thanks to his 'bad reputation,' he was sure of never again being given a licence to dig. A member of Dewasiri's faculty, who held some critical beliefs about Dravidian–Aryan theories, had refused to publish over the previous few years because he didn't want to arrive at any controversial conclusions. In Jaffna, the widespread presence of the army made it impossible to schedule excavations at all.

There was even a monk on the advisory board of the government's archaeology department. Ellawala Medhananda, upon whose patrician nose perched a pair of tinted spectacles, was one of the Buddhist monks who had founded the Jathika Hela Urumaya, a right-wing political party, in 2004. Medhananda was a member of Parliament and had written many books on history and archaeology. 'They call him Puravidya Chakravarthi. "The Emperor of Archaeology."' Dewasiri was beside himself with derision. 'He was the one who changed Kandarodai's name to Kadurugoda.'

For the rest of my time in Sri Lanka, I looked for ways to meet Medhananda, but with no success. I searched for a book he had written years ago, titled *Sinhalese Buddhist Heritage in the Northern and Eastern Provinces*, but I didn't find that either. Within the Department of Archaeology, though, Medhananda was an influential presence. 'He's an epigraphist, really, and he's useful in that sense, because he can read the Brahmi script,' Dewasiri had said. 'But he isn't an archaeologist, and he's a violent propagator of the Sinhalese Buddhist heritage.' Upon Medhananda's urging, in the years after the war, bands of archaeologists and monks had roved together through the north and the east of the island, trying to establish the antiquity of Sinhalese Buddhism in these regions, to reclaim them in some form of moral spirit soon after they had been physically reclaimed by the army.

And where there was nothing Buddhist to reclaim, there was always something Tamil to destroy. Subtraction worked just as well to weight the grand ledger in favour of the nationalists.

In Batticaloa one day, I read in a local Tamil newspaper that a unit of soldiers had, a few days earlier, rolled up to the Thanthamalai Murugan temple and razed a part of its complex. On a map, the temple appeared to be an easy two-hour drive out of town. Yet again I was mistaken; I had missed seeing a stretch of the backwaters that lay across the path, over which no bridge had been built. Not long into the journey, therefore, my autorickshaw stopped at a cove fringed by scrub forest, where a strip of poured concrete functioned as a crude dock; we had just missed one ferry, and the next would leave only after an hour. Flanking us were two other autorickshaws, packed tight with children going home from school. Men and women had abandoned their motorcycles and bicycles to sprawl under the trees, seemingly comatose from the sun. I finished my newspaper and sank into a stupor, staring at the oily, blue-grey water. I wished I could take a nap, but in the heat, even that felt like it would be too much effort.

At a quarter past one, the ferry belched its way in. As a vessel, it did not so much seem destined for the junkyard as born out of it: a collaboration of discarded metal, nearly all of it draped in rust. The ferry was essentially a long, arched platform on pontoons, with the letters NECORD stencilled on one side; on either end were gangplanks, thick, shuddering iron sheets suspended by chains. Autorickshaws drove up the gangplank first, followed by motorcycles and then bicycles; finally, pedestrians came aboard, filling out the ferry, slipping into the gaps like sand through rocks. When it seemed like no more passengers could be accommodated—and when even the gangplank had a couple of motorcycles perched gingerly on it—the operator grabbed a log and pushed the ferry off the bank. He did this in such a perfect way, though, that the ferry spun a lazy 180 degrees around on its axis, bringing the other gangplank on to the dock with a loud, agonizing scrape of metal on cement. Two more bicycles and a motorcycle could now be ushered on to this gangplank, their riders content with only a precarious grip on the chains next to them. The ferry operator appraised his craft with a critical eye, to be sure that there were no wasted square inches of space into which an additional pedestrian might possibly be inserted. When he was satisfied, he pushed away from the bank and pulled the cord on a Yamaha outboard motor that, after a few attempts, came to life with a bronchial wheeze. The passengers left behind peaceably drifted back into the shade to wait out the next hour.

Back on land, we drove on rutted roads through territory where the Tigers had once hidden and lived. The land possessed its own rhythm of visual relief: first a thick forest, then a stretch of flat, dusty land, then forest again, alternating in this manner kilometre after kilometre. Once, in the middle of absolutely nowhere, I spotted a badminton net strung up between two poles and wondered about the players who played on this makeshift court: who they were, where they came from, how far they walked or bicycled to come here and bat around a shuttlecock. After an hour, the terrain began to change, and a spine of rocky hills drew nearer; the skies shifted as well, filling with sheets of morose cloud.

The autorickshaw crept up the side of Thanthamalai, one of the lower hills, until we reached a broad ledge of rock and stopped. The temple lay at the end of one last ascent, up a flight of stairs hewn irregularly from the rock. The Tigers had left these parts in 2007. The temple had been renovated in 2011, the year before I visited. Its cornices and domes had been repainted in vivid blues, reds and greens, but the walls of the shrine had been rendered a deep, serious grey, and on that late afternoon they matched the swiftly darkening sky.

Near the foot of the stairs, three young priests were seated beneath a tree, their shirts off. One of them, Navruvan, a gangly man with an overbite, had been with the temple for 11 years, and he offered to put on a shirt and show me around. First we crouched through an opening in a barbed-wire fence and walked a few hundred metres up the hill to a small cave, where a holy man named Swami Muthiah had lived and meditated many decades ago. Further down from the cave was a rectangular structure with chest-high brick walls; within, a few pillars still stood, but the ceiling that they had once held up no longer existed. Sections of the walls had been freshly knocked through, and sprays of broken brick lay next to these gaping holes.

Until two weeks ago, Navruvan said, this had been a *mutt*—a hall of temporary residence for pilgrims who came great distances to pray at the temple and at the shrine of Swami Muthiah. 'Then around fifty men in army uniforms came with equipment, and they tore the *mutt* down. We hadn't been told this was going to happen, and we still don't know why it was done,' he said. 'Later, some of the people in the local police told us that a Buddhist *viharaya* is going to be built here.' The previous year, the army had asked the temple authorities for some of this land, but the request had been denied. 'This year,' Navruvan said, 'they just came and took it.'

The truth was simultaneously better and worse than the news in the Tamil press. The army had not destroyed any of the temple's old statues, as the newspaper article had claimed, and the temple itself was intact, gleaming now, upon its mound of rock, in a last gush of sunlight before the rain began. But the *mutt* had undoubtedly been demolished, and a *viharaya* was to come up in its place, sticking a thumb into the temple's eye. Standing on the top of Thanthamalai, looking at acres of vacant land in every direction, it would not be easy to regard the new *viharaya* as anything but a taunt, a stamp of Buddhist domination, a permanent reminder of the order of things in Sri Lanka.

3

IT WOULD BE a fine idea, I thought, to take an autorickshaw down the coast, from Colombo to the small town of Baddegama. In theory, autorickshaws went everywhere in Sri Lanka. You could, if your resources as well as the enthusiasm of your autorickshaw driver were deep enough, hire him to take you right across the island, from the west coast, over its central hump, to the east. A friend did this once. She reached Batticaloa from Colombo after a journey that lasted many hours longer than it would have by bus or train. Her bones needed a day to settle fully back into their joints, her back twitched in vicious revenge, and her finances were drained of several thousand rupees. The ride, however, offered a splendid view of the land along the way, she said. She didn't regret it, but for the trip home, she bought herself a ticket on an air-conditioned bus. The autorickshaw, already paid for, drove back empty to Colombo.

But perhaps Baddegama would prove an easier destination. I was being careful now, in reckoning transit times with a map, but even with delays built in, Baddegama lay only four or five hours south of Colombo. I also knew an adventurous autorickshaw driver, a Sinhalese man named Pial who had previously worked in the Persian Gulf, and who had learned Hindi there from his Indian friends. One of the dial-an-autorickshaw services I used had sent him to me once, and I was so delighted to meet a Sinhalese driver who spoke one of my languages that I kept his number. Pial owned a parrot-green autorickshaw that was roomier than the average three-wheeler, and for me he dug out his old cassettes of Hindi film songs and played them on his tape deck. As we rode around, the music spilled out from the speakers just behind my head. Every time a new song began, he torqued his slender body around from the front seat to see if I knew the words. He knew them, every time.

I mentioned this notion of driving to Baddegama to Pial when we had once stopped for tea somewhere in Colombo. He grew so tremendously excited that he swallowed a hot mouthful in a hurry and burned his tongue. 'I know the place! We should go!' He slammed his glass down on the table. 'Let's go next week!'

For almost all of the five hours it took to reach Baddegama, Pial kept to the A2, the highway that skimmed along the coast, running through the resort towns of Bentota, Induruwa and Hikkaduwa. Sometimes the beach was less than a hundred metres away, the sands slowly starting to spit heat as the sun rose higher and higher. The surfers had not arrived yet; they would descend later in the day, clutching their boards under their arms, so that in silhouette they were strange, finned bipeds. The wind blew busily in through the open sides of the autorickshaw, leaving its grimy fingerprints on our faces and whipping dust into our eyes. A couple of times we rumbled on bridges over the thin neck of an estuary; below us, pleasure craft from the resorts—jet skis, motor boats, kayaks—scudded through the water. Just before Hikkaduwa, Pial turned inland, and now we passed between fields of paddy, bursting with green life, with forests and small mountains hanging just over the horizon.

Baddegama means 'the village in the jungle,' and so that was what Leonard Woolf called the slim novel he wrote about these parts. Woolf lived in Sri Lanka between 1904 and 1911, working as a colonial administrator, walking or bicycling through the territory under his purview. This was how he came upon Baddegama. 'It was in, and of, the jungle; the air and smell of the jungle lay heavy upon it—the smell of hot air, of dust, and of dry and powdered leaves and sticks,' Woolf wrote. 'The jungle surrounded it, overhung it, continually pressed in upon it . . . It was a living wall about the village, a wall which, if the axe were spared, would creep in and smother and blot out the village itself.' In the novel, Baddegama is a fragile sliver of civilization, easily infected by the brutish nature of the forest around it, and full of the sort of primitive injustices that Woolf, as an official of the Raj, thought he was attempting to eliminate.

We arrived in Baddegama just before noon, but the town was coiled into a sort of night-time silence that made the presence of the sun feel like a mistake. Pial found nobody to ask for directions to the Buddhist monastery we were seeking, the Sripada Chaitya Viharaya, so we blundered around the streets for well on half an hour until he spotted a tiny signboard bearing the monastery's name and pointing up a hill. He switched the music off as we drove up. It was impolite, he felt, to signal your arrival at a monastery with a Bollywood fanfare.

The Mahavamsa had explained to me its rationalizations of violence, but it was only a book, its stories distant and difficult to interrogate. I was more curious about living, breathing monks—about what they saw as their place in society, and about how they squared their politics with the Buddha's philosophies. More than with any other religion, the non-Buddhist world has a rigid idea of Buddhism, fixed along dimensions of pacific thought and lofty deeds and high detachment. I was learning, in Sri Lanka, how Buddhism was just as fluid as any other faith, just as easily poured into new and unexpected moulds.

The presence of monks in the congested, compromised heart of politics, for instance, rubbed against Buddhism's disdain of worldly pursuits and temporal authority. The first monk in Sri Lanka to stand in and win a major election was Baddegama Samitha, the head of the Sripada Chaitya Viharaya. This happened in 1992; since then, many monks have followed him into the provincial councils and into Parliament. Even in Sri Lanka's 2000 years of Buddhist history, this was a strange development. In the Mahavamsa, the Sangha's elders did accumulate power, but while they exerted vast influence over their kings, they never sought to become kings themselves. The Buddha himself, after all, left his royal household and gave up his aspirations to the throne. Yet, confusingly, here were the guardians of his precepts talking themselves up in election campaigns, forming political parties, and desiring to rule the country.

At the Sripada Chaitya Viharaya, a young initiate told me that Samitha was at his prayers, and that he would then need to finish lunch before meeting me; in Sri Lanka, monks eat their midday meal and then nothing else for the rest of the day. I sat for a while in the veranda of a small house, gazing upon its front door, on which were glued red-and-white posters for the Lanka Sama Samaj Party—the Lanka Equal Society Party. This was Samitha's party, a venerable Trotskyist outfit with an elegant key as its symbol.

Samitha emerged after 45 minutes, contrite about the delay. He was a short, fleshy boulder of a man, not fat but densely built. Through the folds of his orange robes, I could see his arms, back and calves, all packed with muscle, and his ritually shaven head sat upon a neck as substantial as a bull's. When he took my hand, his fingers felt like thick young bamboo shoots. The cane chair on which he sat creaked but held. He looked vital and powerful.

'How was your trip here?' he asked. Even in the veranda,

practically outdoors, his booming voice created the impression of an echo.

'It was all right,' I said politely. I didn't tell him that I had taken an autorickshaw from Colombo. 'Not very taxing.'

'Good, good,' he said. He had a crescent-shaped hand fan, made out of straw, and with this he chased away a couple of flies that had settled on his head.

Samitha had not always been attached to this temple; at the age of 12, he was ordained as a novice at the Dutugemunu Viharaya, a kilometre away. He did not join the order willingly. He had been a miserable student, preferring to spend his time scrapping with other boys, acquiring such a reputation for delinquency that word reached the head priest of the Dutugemunu Viharaya. 'He caught hold of me in the temple one day and said: "Why don't you come to me, look after me and the temple?" Samitha said. 'He thought it would make me a better person, but he framed it cleverly, so that it sounded as if I was looking after him rather than the other way round.' What Samitha acquired at the monastery was not just an education but also an iron discipline, he said. 'I needed that. It gave me direction.'

On 14 March, 1978, Samitha was accused of killing a man.

According to the version that Samitha laid out for me, it happened like this. At the University of Kelaniya, just outside Colombo, Samitha was studying Christianity, Pali and Sinhalese, but most of his hours were swallowed by his duties as vice president of the student union. During a time of strife between the government and the country's student and labour unions, a posse of thugs—government-backed, Samitha insisted—entered the university campus, intent on roughing up some student leaders. At least twenty-five thugs, Samitha thought, armed with guns, swords and knives. 'So the students took chairs, broke them, and attacked with them, or they threw stones. I couldn't stop them.' Another student hit one of the thugs fatally on the head. 'I was trying to rescue him and pull him out. But he died, and they accused me, saying I killed him.'

Samitha went into hiding first, but then he surrendered to the courts. He was acquitted of murder, eventually, but the process took a full year, during which he was in custody for six months. 'After that, I asked the government to allow me to go to some other university instead of returning to Kelaniya, because that area was still a stronghold of those thugs, and I thought they would be out for revenge,' he said. 'They basically told me that they wanted the thugs to have their revenge.'

When he finished his undergraduate course, Samitha went to England in 1981, to study religion and politics. He came back in 1989, just when—quite separately from the Eelam war—a Marxist insurrection was being nipped violently in the bud. He saw more death then, he said, and he rubbed his hand over his head and sighed with weariness, and his body went suddenly limp, as if all the energy stored in those muscles had suddenly leached away. He had sheltered some Marxists in his monastery for a while, but when they went back into the world, they were swiftly arrested or killed. One young man, Samitha remembered, thought he would flit home to see his wife and children before returning quickly to the monastery. 'They cornered him in a field. He was unarmed, so he tried to pick up stones to throw at the troops. They shot and killed him.'

The scene assembled itself before my eyes: David armed with a stone, encircled in a paddy field like the ones around Baddegama, slain by Goliath in this particular telling. There wasn't any heroism in this. It felt peremptory and pathetic.

Samitha didn't always approve of the methods of the insurrection, but he did support some of its principles. He was, he said, a committed leftist.

'How does that happen?' I asked, genuinely puzzled. 'How

can you be a Buddhist monk and a leftist at the same time? Don't leftists want to shrink the role of religion in society?'

'But Buddhism does advocate socialist principles,' Samitha said. I was going to point out that the reverse wasn't true, that socialism didn't advocate Buddhist principles, but he had gone on. 'Everybody in the Sangha is equal. Only the elderly are respected more, not the powerful or the wealthy. The Sangha owns property jointly. There are no class distinctions. That was part of what attracted me to the order—the simplicity of the leaders around me. Many of them were high-class or middle-class people, educated people. They could have enjoyed all of life's luxuries, but they didn't.'

As the government slaughtered droves of young Marxists across the island, Samitha couldn't continue to stay above the fray. 'When this sort of thing is going on, I can't just say "I bless you" and so on,' he said. 'Even though I'm a monk, I can't accept the concept of karma.' But this was such an odd thing for a Buddhist to say that Samitha stopped immediately and reconsidered his words, absently scratching a mosquito bite on his arm. 'Or rather, I believe in karma, but I don't think it is the same as fatalism.'

I asked him what the difference was.

'Say your leg has been amputated,' he said. 'If you sit around waiting for food, you'll be a beggar your whole life. If you learn to do something with your hands, you'll eat, and you'll get respect. According to the Buddha, you shouldn't wait for your meals to come to you. Your own hands are the shelter for your head.'

The year he returned to Sri Lanka, he ran for a seat in the local divisional council and won. Three years later, he was elected into the council of the Southern Province, and in 2002 he became the first monk to serve in the national parliament. 'People were so surprised to see a monk campaigning,' he said of his 1992 run. 'But they needed somebody to stand up for them. The robe was a good protection for somebody to stand up and fight.'

Samitha made, I thought, altogether too little of the radical nature of his move. I said as much to him.

'Why?' he said. 'In Sri Lanka, especially during the imperialist era, monks have taken leadership positions. They led armed struggles even if they didn't take up arms themselves. People have always gone to the temple to get advice from the monks, and in turn they feed the monks. This sort of bond has compelled the monks to lead.'

But in the Mahavamsa, I said—

He cut me off. The world of the Mahavamsa was different, he said. 'Back then, the Sangha influenced the kings, but the monks never became more powerful than the kings. They were only advisers. But today, we have to realize that if the monks take a side, they can change the whole discourse. It's a very negative thing. Politicians know how to use us for their gains.'

Did he ever doubt himself, or fear the boldness of his move?

Samitha said nothing for some seconds. He was a skilled manufacturer of pauses that hung pendulously between us. 'I did have doubts,' he said finally. 'I would ask close friends: "Will this set a bad precedent?" The majority of them were for it. The hierarchy—the elders—didn't really say anything one way or another, but it was an encouraging silence.'

Given a voice in Parliament, Samitha discovered that what he had to say did not always go down well within the clergy. The Tamils of Sri Lanka, he thought, had honest grievances, and the war would resolve none of them. He also didn't believe that the Sangha's concerted rituals—the sermons, the processions, the mammoth ceremonies of worshipping the Buddha—would make any difference to the outcome of the war. He wanted his government to sit down and negotiate with Tamil leaders, and he even went north, on several occasions during the ceasefire between 2002 and 2004, to meet Prabhakaran and other Tigers, on fruitless errands of placation and negotiation. 'Immediately, the extremists portrayed me as pro-Tiger,' he said. In Sri Lankan politics, this was always the most damaging, ineradicable mud that could be slung at an opponent.

When snap elections came by in 2004, Samitha lost his seat. The Jathika Hela Urumaya (JHU), the party of the nationalist monks, freshly formed and bristling with shiny new ideas for a Sinhalese Buddhist revival, ate up half of Samitha's votes, including those from his stronghold: the population living around his monastery in Baddegama. 'I was thrown out by the very people who first elected me,' he said. His face twisted at the memory. 'In place of me, they started to elect racist monks.'

'Did you regret your decision to run in that 1992 election?' I asked. 'Because it means that you were the first one. You started off this trend of monks entering politics.'

This thought had occurred to him before. How could it not have? 'I don't know. I don't know. I don't know if I encouraged these extremist monks to stand. That worries me.' We can never be sure who will follow us through once we push a gate open, I thought.

The prospect of a surging Buddhist nationalism appalled Samitha. In the years after I met him, he made speeches in the provincial council, accusing the JHU and other Buddhist groups of trying to destroy the country, of touching off religious tensions, and of intolerance. 'Religion is a private matter. The state shouldn't be involved, but here the state is involved, and in a bad way.' Listen hard to the speeches of Mahinda Rajapaksa, he told me. 'At the end of every speech, he makes a wish, or a prayer, in a Buddhist tone. How do you expect minorities to rally around you?'

The bounce had gone out of Samitha during the course of our conversation, and for the first time I noticed that the porcelain whites of his eyes were glazed with red. He was drowsy, I thought, or exhausted.

Then three little boys in white shirts and blue shorts peeped around the corner of the house and sidled up to him, and Samitha brightened. They were orphans, he said, and then corrected himself. 'Abandoned boys, actually—not orphans. Around six of them stay with us, and they're just back from school.' He fondly mussed the hair of one of the boys and said, 'This one is a Catholic Tamil, in fact. He's studying Buddhism.' Then he looked up and added with alarmed haste: 'It's totally voluntary, you understand! Nobody's forcing him!'

Even more radical than a Buddhist monk in politics was a Buddhist monk advocating war and death. In the brief period between 2004, when Samitha was voted out of Parliament, and 2011, when we sat talking in his monastery, the fringe of the Buddhist clergy had moved further to the right. In 2004, the JHU was founded, and that was startling enough: a party that put up 200 monks as electoral candidates and sent nine of them into Parliament, and that needled its government to go after the Tigers more hungrily, to show no restraint in wiping the country clean of them. The JHU emphasized, in its manifesto, that Sri Lanka was a Sinhalese Buddhist state that could not be divided, and so no devolution of power to Tamil-majority provinces could take place.

After some years, even the JHU was deemed by some to be too timid in its protection of Buddhism. Two monks quit the party and established the considerably more right-wing Bodu Bala Sena—the Army of Buddhist Power—in the summer of 2012. Another set of monks helped start the Sinhala Ravaya— the Sinhalese Roar. On the Sri Lankan national flag, a lion grips a sword, but it stands with a placid majesty, as if it were armed only as a matter of course. On the flag of the Sinhala Ravaya, the lion is bounding forward, agitated and rapacious, its sword already thrust forward in attack. The Sinhalese roar is practically audible.

After I returned from Baddegama, I spent months trying to find and talk to any monk who could be considered Samitha's polar opposite, a monk out of the ranks of the Buddhist right. This wasn't easy. Several such monks could only speak Sinhalese, and I wanted to be certain, in my conversations with them, that I was losing nothing in translation. Others were wary about meeting an unknown journalist. My search foundered. Then, just before I finally left the country, a friend arranged for me to meet Omalpe Sobitha, who was, along with the Emperor of Archaeology, one of the founders of the JHU.

We drove up to Kandy to meet him. The Sri Lankan International Buddhist Academy in Kandy stands on Anagarika Dharmapala Road, named after the 19th-century reformer who cast the country's Buddhism into its modern shape. Dharmapala was not a monk but an *anagarika*; he wore the robes, and he adopted the faith's Eight Precepts, but he never shaved his head, and his sharp, saturnine features sat under a cowl of wavy hair. Through his searing speeches and writings, Dharmapala rallied Buddhists around a nationalist project, prodding them into resistance against both the colonial authority and the Christian church. Some of this involved reminding his audiences, forcefully, that Sri Lanka belonged to the Buddhists, and that the Sinhalese were a race distinct from the *hadi Demalu*, the filthy Tamils.

'Enter into the realms of our king Dutugemunu in spirit and try to identify yourself with the thoughts of that great king who rescued Buddhism and our nationalism from oblivion,' Dharmapala wrote, addressing the youth. Elsewhere: 'Ethnologically the Sinhalese are a unique race.' Before Christian imperialists and Hindu polytheists ruined Sri Lanka, '[this] bright, beautiful island was made into a Paradise by the

Aryan Sinhalese.'

A century later, Omalpe Sobitha also lamented Sri Lanka's fall from glory. The country, he had told a reporter, had become a den of vice, and he blamed the island's minorities—the Muslims, in particular—for introducing sins into paradise. In the same interview, Sobitha declared of himself and his fellow monks in the JHU: 'It is true we are racists. It is true we are religious fanatics.'

Articles on Sobitha appeared frequently in Sri Lanka's newspapers; the JHU was a member of Mahinda Rajapaksa's coalition government, and Sobitha was one of its most strident voices. In photographs, he looked frightening. He was eternally grim, and his toothbrush eyebrows on an otherwise hairless head lent him an air of ferocity. He reminded me of Mola Ram from *Indiana Jones and the Temple of Doom*. In person, Sobitha was polite, and he smiled readily, which should have been comforting, except that he had a sharp-toothed, steel-lipped smile, like that of a cartoon shark. His eyes had cloudy grey irises and pinpoint pupils, difficult to read and the more unnerving for it.

When we arrived at the academy, Sobitha was completing a lecture in a long hall full of students. We heard his amplified voice even outdoors, where we sat under a tree to wait for him. After he finished, we drove to another building on the campus in his black Nissan Caravan, which had been furnished with bookracks and document trays that allowed him to work on the road. Sobitha led us to a conference room and sat at the head of the table, steepling his fingers before him.

'Yes,' Sobitha said, but before I could ask any questions, he continued, 'So I can brief you . . . .' He trailed off, not because he was distracted but because he was assembling his thoughts. 'You see, Buddhism is the sole energy that has protected the nation, developed the nation, for more than two thousand three hundred years. We had that heritage . . . ' He went on like this for some minutes, lecturing us as he had his students. It was not easy to cut into his flow. He spoke slowly, with deep pauses, but he also seemed like he would brook no interruption. I decided to bide my time.

Sobitha and his colleagues formed the JHU because they thought Buddhism in Sri Lanka was in danger. The Catholic church was converting villagers away from Buddhism, and the country's prime ministers and presidents paid no heed to the Sangha's concerns about such missionary activities. Meanwhile, the Tigers were attempting to dismantle the country's social and political system. 'This concept of the traditional homeland of the Tamils is a baseless concept,' Sobitha said. 'There is no traditional homeland here for the Tamils. There are thousands of inscriptions from the 3rd century BCE in Sinhalese, but not a single inscription in Tamil.'

This wasn't quite true. But then he said, 'In the northern and eastern provinces, all those historical and archaeological sites belong to Buddhists,' and this was arguable as well, so I decided to jump in. Even according to the Mahavamsa, I pointed out, Tamils had been in Sri Lanka for at least two thousand years. 'Why would this not be their traditional homeland as much as it is for the Sinhalese?'

Sobitha deployed some circuitous logic: this was not the homeland of the Tamils because it was the homeland of the Sinhalese. 'The Sinhalese are the people who created this culture, developed this country, created this lifestyle and this nation. So this land is the Sinhalese homeland, and many other people also live here.'

I changed tack, worried about squabbling with him too much before our conversation had even warmed up. I asked him if there had been resistance within the Sangha when the JHU was established.

'Of course, of course,' he said. The Sangha had been split almost exactly down the middle, and some of the most influential priests advised their laity to vote against the JHU. 'They told people: "This is not the way of a monk,"' Sobitha recalled. 'We argued that we had tried to push our way outside Parliament but failed. So now we had to go into the house, where laws are made. That was our argument.'

Was there nothing in Buddhism that prohibited monks from getting into politics?

'Actually, at the time of the Buddha, this was not such a problem,' he said, and he permitted himself a metallic smile at his witticism. 'So of course, there is no such rule or regulation to prevent monks from entering politics.'

'So why did some monks think this was not the right thing to do?'

'Because they thought, having seen all the corruption and bad practices among politicians, that politics is a very filthy thing, and monks should not be associated with it,' Sobitha said. 'But politics is not bad in itself.' Good rulers, he said, made politically valuable decisions and were well remembered, as in the Mahavamsa.

'But the rulers in the Mahavamsa were always kings, never monks.'

'Yes,' he said, and it was an elongated 'Yes,' the stretched syllable giving him time to think. 'But most of the times the monks decided who would be kings, because the monks were closer to the people, they knew what public opinion was. The monks advised the king, and if the advice was neglected, they'd topple the kingship and select another king.' It was difficult to reprise that role in a parliamentary system, Sobitha said, sounding most regretful about the advent of democracy.

'Do you know *kari patta*?' he asked. 'Curry leaves. How do you eat *kari patta*? You get the food from the market, and you cook the food with the *kari patta*, and when you eat, you carefully pick out the *kari patta*'—he mimicked a careful diner sifting through his food with pinched fingers—'and you leave it to the side of the plate, and you eat the rest of the food. Monks had become the *kari patta* in this new system.'

'So the Sangha had less power?'

No, no, not exactly, he said. The Sangha possessed pure power already, by virtue of its intimacy with the laity, but the politicians were exploiting that intimacy for votes. 'The monks should do their own monastic duties, they tell us. The monks should meditate, or the monks should look after people in the temple. Don't come and get involved with us. This is what the politicians advised us.'

Being so intolerably ignored, there was nothing for monks to do but wade into the muck of politics. I thought this specious. No politician had sidelined the Sangha as thoroughly as Sobitha was suggesting; no politician could afford to. Monks had pushed through the passage of the Sinhala Only Act in 1956; they had forced the 1972 revision of the constitution that named Buddhism as the 'foremost' among Sri Lanka's religions. Monks sat on a Supreme Advisory Council, formed in 1990 to advise the president on Buddhist affairs, even though the Sangha itself remained autonomous; in 1997, a draft constitution nearly gave this council a hand in shaping and legislating laws, before it was sunk for other reasons. Monks scuttled constitutional reforms, in 2000, by taking to hunger strikes and sit-ins outside Parliament. Throughout these decades, politicians showered wealth and land upon Buddhism, enriching not only the Sangha but even individual monks. In the mid-1990s, when the government gifted Mercedes-Benzes to two prominent monks, the cars were sent right back. They would not be accepted, it was made clear, unless the government paid for the automobile insurance as well. The Sangha already had power; in a most un-Buddhist fashion, however, it craved more.

Sobitha was still talking. He had embarked upon a thesis that the Sinhalese Buddhists were Sri Lanka's most patriotic

citizens, because they constituted 99 per cent—his statistic—
of the armed forces that had fought the Tigers. This should
earn the Buddhists an especially high measure of respect, he
was saying.

'What about killing?' I interrupted. 'How does Buddhism
sanction killing?'

'We do not ask for any special favour—'

'No, no. I understand, about the respect. I was wondering
how some of the members of the Sangha condone killing
people, even on a battlefield, in the name of nationalism.'

In Sri Lanka, monks had participated in the civil war—not
by way of some inchoate sanction of the government's army,
but by actually pulling on uniforms, taking up weapons, and
trooping out to fight. For this too, the Mahavamsa—that vast
general store of precedent—supplied a historical parallel, in
the 500 monks that joined Dutugemunu's war party as it
marched out to slay the Tamils. The legend of the militant
monk had been created, Baddegama Samitha had told me, by
kings who wanted to draft monks into their armies to fight
first invaders from south India and then the colonial powers.
'I've seen some of my own monks leave the monastery and
join the army,' Samitha had said. 'I tried to convince some
of them to stay. I told them: "You're under an illusion that
you're fighting an enemy. You're not. You're fighting your
own brothers." But they left anyway.' It wasn't even altogether
necessary to quit the order to kill in the name of Buddhism. In
1959, a monk extracted a revolver out of the folds of his robes
and assassinated Solomon Bandaranaike, the prime minister,
'for the greater good of the country, race and religion.'
Nevertheless, young monks chose to discard their robes and,
with the fulsome blessing of elders less pacific than Samitha,
enlist to fight. The Sangha held up these men as heroes.

In Elephant Pass, near Jaffna, I saw a memorial to the most
famous of these lapsed monks, Gamini Kularatne. When he

was 20 years old, and not yet fully ordained, Gamini found himself on a bus that was ambushed by the Tigers near the village of Aranthalawa, in eastern Sri Lanka. Thirty-seven passengers—including 33 monks—died that day, sliced to pieces by swords or shot up by pistols or machine guns. Gamini, who miraculously escaped, left the order to join the army two months later, with the permission of his monastery's chief monk. He must have been filled with anger at the Tigers, which explained the bold, cold fury of his death. In 1991, during the battle to control Elephant Pass, Corporal Gamini saved his garrison from an armoured, armed Tiger bulldozer. Even as he was being cut to ribbons by machine-gun fire, he swarmed up the bulldozer's ladder, a live grenade in each hand, and flung the explosives down the hatch. What remains of the bulldozer now stands as the memorial to Gamini at Elephant Pass, its innards still mangled by the grenades, its skin blistering and peeling in the sun.

As noble as Gamini's martyrdom was, I asked Sobitha, wasn't Buddhism's directive against violence absolute? How could some monks of the Sangha encourage one of their own to bear arms? How could they urge their government to fight harder, kill more thoroughly?

'You know, the Buddha has not given such an extremist idea,' he said.

This was plainly false. The very first of the Five Precepts followed by Sri Lanka's Buddhists reads: 'I undertake the rule to abstain from taking life,' and in the *Dhammapada*, an anthology of the Buddha's sayings, is contained the instruction: 'One should not use violence or have it used.' There are no caveats, no escape clauses, no laxities of language that can allow for these edicts to be bent to convenience.

Still, Sobitha continued, 'The Buddha was not the *parama ahimsa vada*'—the proponent of ultimate non-violence. 'Again and again, he preached the middle way. The middle way, the middle way, the middle way.' Sobitha chanted the phrase sonorously, as if he wanted to drill it into me. 'Not only in our philosophical lives, but at every point of our practical lives, we can practise this middle way.'

'How can the waging of war be part of a middle way?' I asked. Sobitha's logic fascinated me. I wondered if he was even convinced of it himself.

'Because if one's enemy comes to you, you have to fight back,' he said. 'If that fellow is coming to kill you, you can't meditate and pray: "May you be well and happy. May you be well and happy." That is the impractical way.'

Sobitha leaned forward, and the conference-room chair squeaked under him. The faith needed to be defended from imminent dangers, even at the cost of human lives. He mentioned Nalanda, an ancient Indian centre of Hindu and Buddhist learning that was sacked and burned by Muslim invaders in the 1190s. 'What happened at that time?' he said. 'The Buddhist leader must have said: "Now the enemies are here. They are coming to kill. We can overcome them. Let us meditate. Let us extend love and kindness to all." What happened? Those people came freely, burned the books and the libraries, and killed more than three thousand monks. That library burned for three months.' He spoke as if this was pain that he had personally suffered only the previous day.

'Yes, but—'

'Wait, wait,' Sobitha said, and he leaned even further towards me, so that those leonine eyebrows were now inches from my face. He had snatched to himself the momentum of the conversation, and he did not intend to relinquish it. He was smiling, as a teacher might when he suspects his student to be on the brink of enlightenment. 'When I fight to save my life, I want to live not only for myself but also for my society. A Subramanian'—he jabbed a finger at me—'is made not only by your mother and father, you know. You are the property of society. A Subramanian is a good resource to the society. Therefore we need to continue living not only for our own selves but for the sake of society.'

It was an odd twist of the Buddhist principle of renunciation—not a renunciation of violence for the larger good of the soul, but a renunciation of non-violence for the larger good of the Buddhist nation. If there was a paradox here—in how Buddhism could be saved only by violating one of its most prominent tenets—Sobitha did not see it. Or perhaps he chose not to see it, which amounted to something worse, something more insidious and wilful and dangerous.

The most striking of Sobitha's explanations for his support of the war did not emerge during our conversation; it was narrated to me a few days later by Udaya Gammanpila, Sobitha's colleague in the JHU. Gammanpila was not a monk but a career politician—a sleek young lawyer who was, when I met him, the agriculture minister for Sri Lanka's Western Province. He occupied a long room in a government building in central Colombo, so long that it required nearly thirty paces to walk from the door at one end to his desk at the other.

When I told Gammanpila that I had talked to Sobitha the previous week, he asked: 'You met him in Embilipitiya?'

In Kandy, I said.

'Ah. Well, in his temple in Embilipitiya, he has a school and a preschool.' We had been talking, again, about the JHU's professed devotion to Buddhism and its simultaneous mongering for war. 'And Sobitha said this once: 'There are around one hundred kids in my preschool. Imagine one day that a mad dog came and started biting these little kids. The little kids start screaming. True, I started the day extending compassion to every living being, but now I have to make a choice. If I am to protect the kids, I have to kill or hit this mad dog. If I have to extend compassion to the mad dog,

I am not extending my compassion to the struggling little kids. So when I have to make a choice, to whom I should extend my compassion? My choice is the innocent little kids, not the mad dog." In the case of the civil war, the Tigers were the mad dogs, Gammanpila said, and the moral dilemma turned out to be no dilemma at all.

The analogy put me in mind of Dutugemunu, whose shadow so darkens Sri Lanka. The thousands of Tamils he had killed in the course of his own war were pagans with worthless lives. They 'died as though they were animals,' the monks had told him. Shrink the humanity of your enemy, and the fighting must seem easier, more just, less complicated. Warfare consists of several psychological tricks, not least the ones you play upon yourself.

4

ONE EVENING IN Colombo, Sanjaya dropped by, intending to collect me on our way to someplace else. I offered him a drink—beer, I seem to remember now, but given how the next two hours slipped clean out of our hands, more likely it was arrack. Arrack did that to you: it greased the passage of time. We sat around my apartment's dining table, with its thick tablecloth of bright, striped yellow, orange and red; the pattern hurt my eyes, but I never got around to changing it.

'You heard they pulled a Muslim shrine down?' Sanjaya asked.

It had happened in Anuradhapura the previous week. A group of Buddhist protesters—a busload, or two busloads—had arrived with crowbars and hammers, and they had taken apart a dargah, a small, old shrine to a Muslim saint. In this enterprise, they had not been stopped by the police or the local administrators. Anuradhapura was said now to be bristling with communal tension.

'We should go there,' I said.

'We should,' Sanjaya said thoughtfully. 'I know a guy who caught the whole thing on video. But we should wait for a while, let things cool a little.'

In those days, the Buddhist right was experimenting with straight thuggery. The Tamils, cautious and defeated, living under a crushing military presence in the north and the east, posed no present threat to Sinhalese Buddhism. So instead, the

Bodu Bala Sena and the Sinhala Ravaya—as well as the JHU, their milquetoast cousin—were re-training their energies upon Sri Lanka's Muslims. Unlike with the Tamils, no long skein of ancient hatreds between the Buddhists and the Muslims could be unspooled out of the Mahavamsa, no rankling grouses could be invoked as justifications for this new animus. But this did not matter. The Muslims were demonized, accused of eroding the country's Buddhist heritage. In the absence of ancient hatreds, chauvinism can easily rustle up modern ones.

The newspapers were filled with reports of violence and with pronouncements from some Buddhist leaders on how they expected Muslims to behave. The JHU demanded the closure of Muslim-owned butcheries that sold beef and forced the government to ban the certification of halal meat. The Bodu Bala Sena attacked a popular Muslim-owned clothing store in Colombo. Other anonymous groups painted pigs on the walls of mosques. Some protesters stormed into the Sri Lanka Law College in Colombo, claiming that its examination results were doctored to favour Muslims. Calls went around for particular mosques and Muslim shrines to be razed, ostensibly for being situated too close to Buddhist temples. Even proximity was unacceptable now. In the town of Dambulla, the chief priest of a local *viharaya* led a protest to 'relocate' a mosque, and he warned in the process: 'Today we came with the Buddhist flag in hand. But the next time, it would be different.' No one stood up to these threats; Sri Lanka absorbed them passively and sailed on. It was a frightening, sickening time, plump with hatred and hostility.

The Anuradhapura demolition happened early in September 2011. We went there in the very last days of the month, Sanjaya and I and another friend named Dinidu. From Colombo, we caught a night train to Anuradhapura, practically sticking our heads out of the open window for all five or six hours because our compartment was so stifling and airless.

The train reached at 3.30 a.m., and we were the only people to alight at Anuradhapura's small, low station.

'During the war, whenever they wanted to make a film in which the Jaffna station appeared, they would use the Anuradhapura station instead,' Sanjaya said. He stood for a few minutes and looked up at the building's facade, pearl white by moonlight.

'Machang, let's just find somewhere to sleep,' Dinidu said.

In the morning, we visited Sanjaya's contact, Rizvi, a local journalist himself. He was a middle-aged man with brawny forearms and white stubble. Either he had known that we would be videotaping him or he was a punctilious dresser even at home, because he wore a white shirt with knife-sharp creases and a neat blue-and-white checked sarong. His first language was Tamil, but he spoke to Sanjaya and Dinidu in fluent Sinhalese. Whenever Rizvi said something significant, one of them would aim a translation in my direction. I sat off to a side, on a divan next to a window, scribbling.

It appeared that Rizvi was fond of recounting the turns of bureaucratic wheels: petitions filed, orders issued and appeals counter-filed, deeds issued, public meetings held and reports written. From this mess of administrative detail, he was certain, a clear and potent truth would emerge. For Rizvi, everything had a procedural history, and for this reason he started the story of the dargah demolition by describing how he moved house in 1974.

Rizvi and his family used to live in a jumble of Muslim residences in the Sacred City, a zone wrapped around a giant Bodhi, grown according to legend from a cutting of the original tree under which the Buddha attained enlightenment. Some families had been living in the area for more than a century. 'We moved out because the drainage in that place was so awful. But technically, we still owned our house there.'

In May 2009, a minister ordered all the houses to be

knocked down without compensation. Two weeks later, the civil war ended, but Rizvi's family felt no joy because they were so distressed about the demolition of their home.

The dargah had been in the very heart of this neighbourhood, and once the houses were stripped away, it shone through prominently. It had been built to honour Sikkandar Waliullah, a Muslim saint and a healer who had been buried in Anuradhapura. No one had precisely established the antiquity of Waliullah's life, although Rizvi claimed that the dargah had found mention in literature for at least four hundred years. 'Every year, there was a festival here, an *urs*, when holy men used to come to the dargah, and hit themselves with hammers or stab themselves with knives, to prove the power of the shrine,' Rizvi said. 'This at least, I know, had been happening for more than fifty or sixty years, because my uncle remembered seeing it when he was a boy.'

The very existence of the dargah now rankled the Buddhist right, a plainly Islamic commemoration on Buddhist turf. The night before the Poya—or full-moon—holiday in June 2011, seven men on motorcycles drove up to the dargah. A Sinhalese man living in the vicinity realized they were armed with tools and crowbars, and he alerted the dargah's caretaker. On that occasion, some tiles on the dargah were damaged, but the job couldn't be completed. A band of Muslims confronted the seven men, the police arrived, and the wrecking crew was hustled out of the site. In response to the incident, a new, permanent police post was installed near the dargah, for additional security. 'You can see it in the video of the dargah's final destruction,' Rizvi said. 'You can also see that the policemen are doing nothing.'

Anuradhapura was hushed and wary after this episode, bracing itself for more trouble. Around this time, hysterical pamphlets started to circulate within the town. Rizvi had saved three of them for us; two were anonymous, but the third was signed by Amithadamma Thero, a Buddhist monk who was something of a firebrand in the local clergy. 'I was surprised to see that monks were involved,' Rizvi said. 'I would never have thought it possible.' The leaflets—all in Sinhalese—sealed the dargah's fate.

The first pamphlet called the Sinhalese 'the fastest vanishing race on the face of this earth,' and it worried that the country's biggest threats came from its Muslims, who were 'breeding like pigs.' There were further descriptions of Muslims, consisting of astonishing filth, and then:

> We need a pureblood king who can proudly say to the world that Sri Lanka is a Sinhala Buddhist nation. He should be brave enough to say: 'The other races that live here have to live by those rules, or they can leave.' We don't need multicultural, multi-religious ideas. There has to be one Sinhala Buddhist country in the world. This is that country . . .
>
> Do not sell your land and businesses to the Muslims. They are able to buy things for higher prices because of the money they get from their mosque and the Middle East for the breeding of their kind. You and I will die soon, but it is our duty to save this sacred land for the future generations . . .

The closing sentence was an instruction: to circulate the leaflet among Sinhalese Buddhists only.

In the second pamphlet, the authors attacked the administration for allowing the Sacred City to be defiled by the dargah and other non-Buddhist enterprises. To prevent a religious war, the dargah needed to be removed. 'Don't you cow-killing, beef-eating, Tamil-speaking people already have a mosque in Anuradhapura behind the post office? Don't make a joke out of our Buddhist heritage.'

The final leaflet was signed by Amithadamma Thero and dated 2 September 2011. Calling the dargah a mosque, he raged that its very presence in the Sacred City polluted Anuradhapura.

Who is responsible for this?

Corrupt politicians and certain robe-wearers who bow their heads and tangle a yellow robe about them but don't even follow the Five Precepts. Shame on the Sinhala Buddhist policemen who protect this mosque . . .

Shame on the IGP [Inspector General of Police] who is using the police to protect this mosque. May Mahinda and Gotabhaya who are good followers of Buddhism become aware of this soon!

Pious monks and followers:

To save the Anuradhapura Sacred City from this Muslim invasion, come to the Dakkhunu Dagoba on the 10th of September at 1 p.m.

There was no mistaking that final line. It was a loud, clear call to action.

Just after noon, Rizvi interrupted his slaloming narrative to go collect his daughter up from school. While Sanjaya and Dinidu sat on in the living room, paging through a trove of documents, I wandered outside. In the veranda, I ran into Mohammad, Rizvi's son, a teenager studying for his A Levels. Who were we? he inquired, out of curiosity. I told him, and then, just to make conversation, I asked who their neighbours were. He pointed out house after house; at the end he indicated a bungalow two doors away, where a Tiger suicide bomber had killed Janaka Perera.

Perera, a distinguished army general, had been campaigning for the post of chief minister of the North Central Province in 2008, and he had opened a party office on this street. A crowd had collected at the formal inauguration of the office, and Rizvi's brother and sister, as well as her husband, had all popped over. They were standing outdoors, in a covered veranda very similar to where Mohammad and I stood and talked. A man staggered into the throng, gibbering and gesticulating, pretending to be mad. Then he blew himself up. 'His head had split into two,' Mohammad said, 'and they found parts of his limbs on trees outside the house.'

Rizvi's sister and her husband died on the spot. His brother was taken to the hospital. A shard of home-made shrapnel—the bolts, nails and broken razor blades that had been sewn into the suicide bomber's vest—had embedded itself into his heart. But even this he might have survived, Mohammad said, had these fragment not been coated painstakingly with cyanide. 'He was also a journalist, like my father, and he dropped his video camera right there. A metal piece went into that too.'

I realized I had seen this camera, a Panasonic that Rizvi still used. It had been sitting on a cluttered dining table all morning, charging. When I went back inside the house, I looked more closely at the camera, and I could see the path ploughed by the shrapnel, a deep furrow running just above the tape deck.

When Rizvi returned, I asked him about the bombing that had killed three members of his family in one fell morning. He gave me a thin smile.

'Not just them,' he said. Then he counted away, on his fingers, the number of people his family had lost to the Tigers. His sister's father-in-law had died in a Tiger massacre of Sinhalese civilians in 1985, near the great Bodhi tree; 146 people died in three separate attacks in Anuradhapura that day. This man's son—the brother-in-law of Rizvi's sister—had been an assistant government agent in Muttur, in the

east, when he was shot dead by the Tigers. Then there were
Rizvi's brother and sister and her husband; Rizvi had run out
of fingers on that hand. 'Now I am the only one left,' he said.
I felt like a man who had picked at a loose floor tile and found
a stash of corpses buried beneath.

In response to Amithadamma's leaflet, a couple of hundred
people, under the bounding lion banner of the Sinhala
Ravaya, assembled near the dargah. A large bus turned up as
well, bearing men with tools and a few dozen monks. 'Some
friends had called me, saying that there was some trouble, so
I had gone there with my camera,' Rizvi said. A squad of 50
policemen had cordoned off the dargah, but Rizvi discovered
that this was to prevent the public from getting closer, rather
than to protect the shrine. He tried to get nearer, but one of the
policemen prevented him. 'He told me: "Don't go. These people
aren't here to speak or to listen to reason. They're behaving
badly."' Rizvi stood with a tight, fearful knot of Muslims on the
shoulder of the road, a hundred metres or so from the dargah.
    At 3.45 p.m., the assistant government agent, G.A. Kithsiri,
entered the scene. 'He came past us, and he said to me: "This
is foolish. This is foolish." I told him: "That's right. Please go
and end this."' Kithsiri strode away, towards the dargah. Rizvi
watched the remainder of the afternoon play out at a distance.
The wind snatched away so many of the voices that the events
seemed to be part of a tragic silent film.
    The monks had been squabbling with the policemen when
Kithsiri arrived. He engaged animatedly with them; Rizvi
could see hands being flung about, and shreds of shouting
blew occasionally towards him. Then Kithsiri pulled out a
cell phone and dialled a number. In the video, Kithsiri moves
away from the dargah and paces back and forth, plunged into
conversation. There is no way to tell who was on the other
end of the line. Later, Rizvi heard that Kithsiri had first tried

to calm the mob, telling them that he already had orders from the Ministry of Defence—Gotabhaya Rajapaksa's ministry— to demolish the dargah in the next three days, assuring them that he would attend to it. When the men insisted on finishing the job themselves, and right away at that, Kithsiri called his superiors and asked them what to do.

In any event, in the video, he appears to have received some set of definitive instructions. He hangs up and walks— reluctantly, to my eyes, as if his feet weighed many tons—back to the dargah, to speak to one of the policemen. Some new commands are snapped out. Then the police cordon ebbs, and the destruction commences.

We climbed into Rizvi's van, and he drove us through the Sacred City towards the location of the dargah. The Buddha loomed over us, the head and shoulders of a gigantic white statue visible above the line of scrub and low trees on the side of the road. Rizvi pointed out where his family's houses had stood before they were rubbed out in 2009. The access path to the dargah, from the main road, was blocked by an army barricade; we were allowed no closer. Rizvi didn't stop, for fear that soldiers would come over and question us; instead, he crept on slowly but steadily. From the van, we could make out only the low wall of the dargah's compound and some Buddhist bunting that had been looped around the trunks of trees. There was, of course, no dargah to see.

In Rizvi's video, the dismantling of the dargah is clinical and coordinated, and it holds a perverse allure that makes it difficult to look away. The monks are attired in their orange habits, but the other men wear white work gloves and carry just the right tools for the job. They have come fully prepared but also fully confident that they will not be stopped.

First the men hang Sinhala Ravaya flags from the branches of nearby trees; it is important to advertise the organization under the auspices of which these activities are being carried out. They peel away the sheets of tin that form part of the shrine's modest roof, chucking them over the waist-high compound wall with a clatter. Large Islam-green blankets of cloth covered Waliullah's tomb; these are yanked off and burned. Somebody found a couple of Qurans within the shrine, Rizvi told us; one of them was thrown down a well, and the other was shredded and added to the bonfire. We can't see this in the video, but the earth around the fire is littered with white rectangles that might be pages ripped out of books. A monk stands over the fire, superintending it with such care that he resembles an attentive chef stirring and peering into his pot. Another man with a long metal bar is trying to take down, or at least damage, the compound wall, and his pounding upon the brick sounds tinny and melancholic.

At some late point during the hour-long demolition, Rizvi managed to creep closer to the site and continue filming in brief bursts. By this time, the dargah has been pulverized into a mess of masonry. The fires have reduced and expired, and helices of smoke seep out of the embers. Much of the mob vanished after the shrine was pulled down, although on the soundtrack, we can still hear the occasional jab at the still-standing compound wall or the thunder of the tin sheets. The drama of the afternoon has leaked out, but a dazed air hangs over the small set of muttering onlookers; they are like the audience at a mystifying play, still trying to make sense of the plot, hanging around the theatre in the hope that an epilogue will provide some explanation. But by 5 p.m., it is all clearly over. In one of the last frames of the video, Rizvi pans away from the rubble and captures the police post that had been set up for supplemental security, a dark-blue booth with the words 'Solex Water Pumps' painted on it. A solitary policeman stands nearby. He dusts his hands off by slapping them against each other, looks towards Rizvi's camera and then looks away again. He is relaxed and calm. No strife seems to have stained his world at all.

ENDGAMES

1

M. AND I sat in the courtyard of his house, digesting our lunch. The afternoon was ringing with prime Jaffna heat, and we felt stupefied, incapable of conversation or even thought. This was when Arun dropped by on his motorcycle.

'This is a friend of mine,' M. said, waving a hand by way of feeble introduction. The hairs of his moustache were slick with perspiration. 'He teaches at the university.'

Arun said Hello and sat down with us.

'Tell Arun what you saw the other day,' M. urged.

I narrated the story of my trip to Anuradhapura, and of the razing of the Muslim shrine. Arun said he was unsurprised. In the new Sri Lanka, demolition was a vital tool of nation-building.

'I told Samanth about the graveyard in Kopay,' M. said. It was a two- or three-acre plot of land, east of Jaffna, that had functioned for years as the local cemetery for the village of Kopay. The Tigers had interred many of their fallen comrades here; they always buried their dead, regardless of their faith, figuring intelligently that the gravestones constituted a silent, effective form of propaganda. Operating by the same logic, the Sri Lankan army had erased the cemetery once the war was won. In its place, an army base had been constructed, right on top of the bones of bygone Tigers. The lesson, M. said, is that what is yours today may not be yours tomorrow.

'Samanth wanted to take an autorickshaw and go to

Kopay, to see the army base,' M. said to Arun. 'I told him that I don't think that would be safe at all.'

'I could take him,' Arun said. 'We could go on my motorcycle.'

This wasn't the response that M. was expecting to hear, and Arun seemed to be having immediate second thoughts himself. But we went nonetheless. M. loaned me a spare motorcycle helmet. 'It'll hide your face to some extent,' he said. Then he gave Arun instructions: 'Don't even stop the motorcycle by the side of the road. Just drive past a couple of times and come back here.'

Kopay does not lie very far out of Jaffna; Arun drove slowly, steadily, as if he was hoping for me to change my mind, but we reached the village in 15 or 20 minutes. We had to tail, for a while, a truck full of soldiers, and I thought I could smell the nervousness on Arun. He made me jittery too. We were on a major road, with plenty of other pedestrians and vehicles. On either side, fields of paddy and banana-tree groves stretched away from us. It was the least ominous setting I could imagine. And still, here was this ridiculous anxiety, seeping out of two men who were going out to look at a building.

Most of the military base was not immediately visible from the road. On the first pass, Arun had to point out to me, through a thicket of trees on our left, the white walls and pistachio-green roofs of the prefabricated sheds. Then the trees fell away, and the large, grey gates of the army compound came into sudden view. We proceeded further down the road, and then Arun looped back and drove by the base again. 'I don't know how many Tigers were buried here, or how many civilians,' he said over his shoulder. 'But whatever—whether you dig up the grave of a Tiger, or whether you dig up the grave of a regular Tamil man, or a Muslim or a Sinhalese man—that is still some mother's son who is buried there. That should have been respected.' A minute later, he said: 'If it had been a Sinhalese graveyard here, the Tigers would have left it alone.' I couldn't fully believe that, but I said nothing.

Emboldened by our drive-bys, Arun turned off the main road and on to a dirt track that would take us nearer the base. 'Pretend you're looking at the fields, not at the base,' he said, and so I stared hard at two farmers sitting on a tractor, ploughing a small parcel of earth. We came to the end of the dirt track. 'Let's just sit on the motorcycle for a few minutes,' Arun said, 'so that we don't arouse any suspicion.'

Out of the corner of my helmet's visor, I sneaked glimpses of the complex to my right. It appeared new but deserted; only the occasional soldier scurried out of one building and into another. A Sri Lankan flag flailed on its pole. For the sake of appearances, we gazed into the fields a while longer, feeling like fools. Then we wheeled around and rode back to M.'s house.

Another erasure had happened in Valvettithurai, a fishing village on the north-western coast of the Jaffna peninsula. In Aalady Lane, where if you stood on the tips of your toes you could see the ocean, the army demolished Prabhakaran's ancestral house in April 2010, decades after Prabhakaran had ceased to live there. This was the house where he had grown up, the youngest of four children in a middle-class family. 'My world was confined to my house and the neighbours' houses,' he said later. 'My childhood was spent in the small circle of a lonely, quiet house.'

From the town of Jaffna, Valvettithurai lies an hour away by autorickshaw, west and north through the peninsula. The road runs through small villages and their adjoining paddy fields. I visited the village on an afternoon of strange, shattered light, as though the sun had temporarily been pulled a few million miles further from Sri Lanka. The ankle-deep water in the paddy fields gleamed emerald, illuminated from within. There was a moment, when we had halted to allow a troupe of goats to cross the road, when I could look around me and find it difficult to believe that a war had ever been fought here. I had never felt that way before in these parts, and I would never feel that way again.

In Valvettithurai, we stopped at a rank of autorickshaws to ask where we might find Prabhakaran's house.

'There's nothing there,' one man said. 'It has all been broken down.'

'We know,' I said. 'I just want to see the place.'

Another man set about providing directions. 'Go straight down here and take a left. You'll see an army booth. Go down the road to the left, drive slowly past where the house used to be, and come out at the other end. Don't stop the autorickshaw at all.' Then he said, 'Look, let me just come with you. The soldiers know I'm from here,' and he hopped in beside me. His name was Lalit Kumar, he told me. He had a scruffy beard and dark skin that had been so dried out by the salt air that it looked brittle. 'Where are you from?' he asked.

'India,' I replied.

He nodded, as if he had been expecting that. By now, we had reached the army booth, a lean-to consisting of a corrugated metal sheet held up by sandbags and cinder blocks. A lone armed soldier stood at the junction, and I could see two others sitting inside the booth. As we turned left, into Aalady Lane, the soldier on patrol followed our autorickshaw with his eyes, but he made no move to stop us. We had been permitted to make the turn, Lalit Kumar was confident, because the soldier had seen him accompanying us.

The first house on Aalady Lane was a bright green, single-storey affair with a sloping metal roof and a grey, unpainted compound wall on one side. To the right of that wall was a vacant lot, strewn with a few fragments of broken stone and bordered by thin grass and weeds. A cat and a chicken were fighting at the back of the plot, under a tree. This was what we had come to see—this absence of a house, this void on Aalady Lane. 'Prabhakaran's house was a lot like the one next to it,' Lalit Kumar said. After the war ended, as travel to Jaffna became simpler, people had begun flocking to see the house— Tamils, of course, almost by way of pilgrimage, but also curious Sinhalese tourists from the south. The army worried that Prabhakaran would be deified, and that the house would become something of a shrine, so it was knocked down. Even then, however, the visitors continued to come, now pocketing a fistful of mud or rubble as a souvenir. One night, trucks came in to carry away the debris and dump it in an unknown location.

Our autorickshaw crawled slowly past the lot, and when Lalit Kumar was confident that we were out of the soldiers' line of sight, we stopped next to a small tea shop. A bare-chested, bespectacled man in a blue sarong, sitting outside the shop, saw us alight and grinned: he knew instantly why we had come. We stood in the shade, next to the shop, for a few minutes, hands clapped over our eyes, looking at the nothingness.

'I never understood it,' Lalit Kumar said. 'What exactly did they think they were accomplishing by tearing the house down?' But the motivation wasn't born out of any pragmatism, I thought. The flattening of the house was an assertion of power but also an unwitting admission of fear. The government considered Prabhakaran's legacy to be so potent that every reminder of his life needed to be expunged. Even an infinitesimal trace of his memory could in some homeopathic way multiply in potency, spread through the bloodstream of the country's Tamils, and trigger more dissent and disaffection.

Prabhakaran's family moved out of Aalady Lane—out of Jaffna and Sri Lanka, even—after the Black July riots in

1983, when they fled to the town of Tiruchy, in south India. His father, Velupillai, disapproved so thoroughly of his son's chosen vocation that Prabhakaran was forced to visit his mother in secret, when she was alone at home. Prabhakaran's siblings never returned to Sri Lanka; they dispersed to Europe and Canada, where they are rumoured to still live. Velupillai and his wife, however, went back home during the fleeting ceasefire, living not in Valvettithurai but in Mallavi, a small town much further south of the Jaffna peninsula.

Through these years, Prabhakaran became the fulcrum of Eelam; the movement was no longer about what was best for the Tamils but about what was dictated by his whims and delusions. He kept himself safe for decades through his utter paranoia, refusing to trust even his closest colleagues, executing any Tiger who displayed even a tinge of insubordination or disloyalty, appearing rarely in public. He acquired, along the way, the habits of a comic-book tyrant. He kept three leopard cubs as pets; he ate orgiastic amounts of food, even when his men were surviving on spare rations; he pitted his guerrillas against each other in fly-swatting contests because he couldn't bear the odour of pesticide. He had become the despot of a banana republic that did not yet exist.

Even if it was in retrospect, M. was right about Prabhakaran. He was a skilled guerrilla strategist but a poor political one. He managed to construct, from within the jungles of the Vanni, intricate international networks of finance, and of drug and arms trafficking. For decades, he used these profits to equip his warriors well, and he pitched them into canny rather than vainglorious battles. But he misjudged the Sri Lankan state's ability and desire to keep itself whole; again and again, he spurned peace negotiations that he thought would not provide him the precise Eelam he wanted. He missed, too, the change in the world after 9/11, the sudden willingness among countries to bless each other's use of ruthless force against terrorists. Over time, Prabhakaran's political incapacity eroded even his considerable military acumen. In the final phase of the war, which began in the summer of 2006 and ended with his death in 2009, he was increasingly fighting battles that everyone except him knew to be lost ones.

Like waves of other Tamil civilians, Prabhakaran's parents left their Mallavi house as the Sri Lankan army advanced through the north of the country, in late 2008 and early 2009. Their path described an arc almost due north-east, towards the Nandikadal Lagoon, where they huddled not with their son but with other refugees, cowering under the ferocious shelling and trying to stay alive. A few days before the war ended, they crossed a causeway and surrendered, along with several thousand others, to the Sri Lankan army. Only towards the end of May, 10 days after Prabhakaran was killed, did the authorities realize that his parents were among the displaced crowds in the Menik Farm camp. They were shifted to a military cantonment, where Velupillai died, in January 2010, at the age of 86. His wife, Parvathy, returned to Valvettithurai, where she passed away in February 2011. By then, her house on Aalady Lane had long vanished, destroyed because of the war that her son had waged, the very war that had destroyed him as well.

2

THE FIGHTING ARRIVED at M.'s doorstep, when he was living in Kilinochchi, just before 2008 rolled over into 2009. For most of that year, the 57th Division had been combing upwards through the Vanni, capturing towns to the south and west of Kilinochchi: Madhu, Palampiddi, Mallavi, Kokavil. The Tamils in these areas, ejected from their houses, were herded by the Tigers into the parts of the Vanni still under their control. At the time, it was possible to fool yourself into believing this to be another cycle of evacuations, in which the army would hold these villages for a period, the Tigers would win them back, and the refugees would return. Back and forth, out of and then back into their homes, like tidal flows.

These movements had become routine during the war in the Vanni; I rarely met someone who had been displaced on fewer than seven occasions, and many people had gone through the process 15 or 20 times. Sanjaya had told me about a man in the north-east, a Displacement Expert, who had organized his whole life around the contingency of suddenly having to leave home. When the war first entered his village, a couple of decades ago, he took with him, to a refugee camp, only his most precious possession: his bicycle. At the camp, the bicycle was stolen. The second time around, he took his bicycle along again, and yet again it was pinched.

On the third occasion, the Displacement Expert knew what he needed to do. Despite the rush to flee the village, he wheeled his bicycle to a mechanic's shop, slathered it with grease, and dropped it into the nearest well. When he returned, after the fighting had waned again, his bicycle was still in the well, safe from both rust and thieves. This was such an effective trick that he deployed it the next 11 times as well. He still owned that same bicycle.

In December 2008, though, M. sensed things to be different; the fighting felt more urgent, more frenzied, more one-sided, more final. So he packed his belongings, counted his cash, and moved his family on to the road. The decision wasn't all voluntary. The Tigers wanted civilians to move with their cadre in one mammoth cloud, mistakenly thinking that the Sri Lankan army would curb its fire for fear of killing the innocent.

M. was not drawn easily into talking about this experience; the mechanics of the displacement were among the many subjects that he seemed to think too trivial for conversation. Then, one afternoon, perhaps to shut me up, he narrated the story of those weeks, and despite himself, he slipped into a reverie of remembrance. He forgot all about his tea, which grew cold on the floor next to the leg of his chair. After a couple of hours, a band of ants began, like courageous explorers, to skulk up the china and down the sheer sides of the cup's interiors.

'Initially, we thought we would remove whatever we could from our house,' M. said. 'Although we weren't as bad as some people, because I saw men unscrewing the doors off their frames and carrying them along.' M. paid a man with a tractor 15,000 rupees to drive him, his wife and daughter, and their belongings out of Kilinochchi. Alongside the tractor, heading east towards Mullaitivu, thousands of others trudged on foot, carrying whatever they could on their heads or on bicycles; eventually, when tractors and trucks could go no further, M.'s family had to walk as well.

'Even the vehicles moved slowly, because there were so many people on the road.' The mass of humanity reminded M. of 'a giant, wounded serpent.' Shells hailed down upon them. Trucks exploded. 'You'd keep seeing dead bodies along the way. The army was using para lights to guide the shelling, so it was like we were walking in perpetual twilight.'

From village to village, M. moved his family, trying to stay just out of the range of the front lines of the artillery: Ramanathapuram for a couple of months, Viswamadu for nine days, Udayarkattu for six days, Suthanthirapuram for 10 days, Devipuram for 20 days, Valaignarmadam for just over a week. 'In Ramanathapuram, I think, we found a proper concrete house to stay in, but that was taken over by the Tigers to be used as a medical camp for their fighters. After that, we stayed in tarpaulin tents throughout.' To hide from the shelling, people dug bunkers in the ground, covered over by tarpaulins. For additional protection, they stacked the perimeters of the bunkers with improvised sandbags—packs of loose earth sewn into the saris of women. As the months passed and pre-monsoon showers broke over Sri Lanka in May, the bunkers filled with rainwater.

M., the consummate intellectual, quickly had to grow expert at building temporary toilets. He described the procedure for me: dig a deep pit; install a barrel in there; nearby, lay a low base of cement with a hole in the middle; connect this makeshift commode to the barrel with lengths of PVC pipe, making sure all the while that gravity can pull the contents down into the ground. Where no such toilet was available, women and young girls preferred often to go without food, rather than wander away from their families in the search for privacy to relieve themselves. 'They knew that, early in the morning or late at night, the Tigers would be waiting, near a lake or by the sea, to forcibly recruit them into the fighting,' M. said. His nostrils flared with recollected anger. 'Both the

Tigers and the army were acting like devils towards the end.'

Although the government insisted that only 70,000 civilians were trapped in the Vanni by the fighting, the United Nations believed the figure to be closer to 350,000. The government gradually constricted the abilities of the Red Cross and the World Food Program to ferry food, shelter and medicines into Tiger-held areas, so commodities swiftly became scarce. A parallel economy prospered, in which people like M., who had money, could buy supplies at shocking prices.

'I had saved money for years, because I knew this would happen,' M. said. 'And then, in the displacement, I had to spend every rupee of it.' He paid 5000 rupees for a few tins of baby food, 2000 rupees for a kilogram of chicken or mutton, or 1500 for a bag of sugar. He bought a tent for 22,000 rupees; once, he parted with a thousand rupees for a fresh coconut. 'Whatever you wanted, somebody had somehow sneaked past the lines to sell it. At the same time, heavy, non-essential items were dirt cheap to buy, because who would carry it? You could buy a laptop for 2000 rupees or a diesel generator for 500 rupees.' The instincts that M. developed during those days had not fully faded even by the time I met him. 'Even now, when I buy something, I automatically tell myself: "Don't buy too much. We'll need to move soon again."'

The worst of it was the uncertainty—not a cosmic uncertainty, in which nobody at all knew what was happening to them, but an uncertainty peculiar to a networked world, in which the only people who did not know about the progress of the war were those confined within the very heart of the fighting. 'Any time anybody could raise a broadcast of the BBC Tamil service on a radio, that spot would become a gathering point for people,' M. said. 'Imagine! We had to listen to the BBC to even know what the doctors in our own displaced community were saying about us and our situation.'

Even in the sketchy form in which it emerged, the news out of Sri Lanka in early 2009 was grim, and it grew steadily grimmer. Several convoys of food and medicine were not permitted by the government to enter the conflict zone; neither were journalists. When United Nations staff did make it into the Tiger-held Vanni, they reported a refugee population so vast and chaotic that the UN's cars progressed inch by inch.

It became clear also that the army was either shelling indiscriminately or specifically targeting civilians. A no-fire zone would be declared, and once people hurried eagerly into its borders, they would be promptly shelled. In late January, when a UN team set up a camp in the so-called buffer zone, refugees erected hundreds of tarpaulin tents in the immediate vicinity, clustering around the UN bunkers for safety. Following conflict protocol, the UN team relayed its GPS coordinates to the Sri Lankan government; not long after, the army began to fire heavily and precisely upon the compound. Shells landed through the night. 'The scene at first light was devastating,' a UN report said. '[W]ithin 20m of our location lay 7 dead & 15 seriously injured. 1 dead infant was in a tree under which the family had sheltered and the 2nd decapitated infant was hanging from the wire perimeter fence.'

Further to the east, in Puthukkudiyiruppu, there was at least a hospital, but a UN staffer recorded its dismal state: 'Patients are stacked in every conceivable space, under tables, in hallways, outside, in the driveways. Most have serious to very serious injuries and a number have extensive burns. New patients with horrific injuries continue to arrive.' As refugees flocked into Puthukkudiyiruppu, the shelling followed them here too, and the hospital was assailed relentlessly. Patients—civilians as well as Tigers—died in large numbers. Simultaneously, the Tigers restrained people from crossing over into the relative safety of government-held territory; instead, Tiger gunners invited further army shelling into the no-fire zone by embedding themselves and firing from within the civilians clustered there. An eyewitness recalled how a man, 50 years old or thereabouts, remarked without rancour to a young Tiger amidst the frenzy of the shelling: 'Brother, at least at this stage, you must let the people go.' In response, the Tiger whipped out his revolver and shot the man where he stood.

The chaos and carnage, I had thought, could only be imagined, but then a Channel 4 documentary aired in the summer of 2011, stitching together many minutes of footage shot on cell phones by people who had been in the midst of the bombardment. The videos are filled with the thunder of shells landing from the sky. The injured lie on makeshift stretchers or on a tarpaulin on the muddy ground; some frames seem to be just littered with bodies, their blood mixing slowly into the puddles of rainwater. Two young girls, standing behind a waist-high barrier of sandbags, weep in high frenzy because they have just seen a parent die in front of their eyes. Men keen over the corpses of their wives. A medic furiously compresses the chest of a young man in a green T-shirt and then gives up, spent. The sound of raw, bewildered grief is everywhere.

Almost until the very end, the Tigers reached into their people and plucked out the able-bodied to press into service. Many of them were in their early teens. They would first be instructed to dig trenches and bunkers, or to erect tents; after a few days of such labour, they would be armed and sent to the front lines, where it was a near-certainty that they would be killed. It was difficult to tell if the Tigers were just playing for time, feeding the fight until some international agency forced the Sri Lankan government to cease fire, or if they believed, with hysterical optimism, that they could still beat the army back and hold on to a shard of the Vanni.

One afternoon, I rode with a couple of NGO workers to

Iranapalai, a village not far from Puthukkudiyiruppu, where palmyra trees stood beheaded by the shelling of 2009, their long, firm trunks pushing nutrients up to nowhere. I cannot recall now why we stopped at the bombed-out schoolhouse building; one of my companions, I think, had wanted to meet somebody who turned out to be unavailable. We had been driving for a while, however, folded up into the seats of an uncomfortable van, and so we decided to stand under a tree on the grounds of the school, easing the kinks in our spines. Behind us, a local official had called a small meeting of a few villagers, upon which we eavesdropped half-heartedly. On one of the walls of the school, a piece of Sinhalese graffito remained from when the Sri Lankan troops marched into Iranapalai in mid-March 2009: 'We came. The Tigers fled.'

A woman in a night-blue housecoat was standing next to me, looking into the villagers' meeting, and we fell into conversation. Her name was Mary Rosalind, and her husband had died in a shell attack on Iranapalai a week before the army captured the village. She told me she had two children and that when the Tigers came to their house in January 2007 to abduct her daughter, her son Jude—17 years old at the time—volunteered to go in her stead. 'I saw him last in November 2008, when he had come home for a few days,' she said. 'I know he was in a fight in January 2009, and I know from others that he was injured. So I assume he was captured by the army, but I don't know where he is.' Were there lists in Colombo, she asked, of Tiger combatants who were captured alive and were still in the government's internment camps?

There might be, I said, and I pulled out my notebook to record her phone number and Jude's date of birth. I wasn't sure I could help at all, but if nothing else, I thought I could pass on the information to the right NGO.

A young girl heard our conversation and came to me to ask if she could give me the details of her older brother: Rapael

Jayaratnam, 32 years old on the day that he was led away by the Tigers in March 2009, never seen again. I wrote this down as well.

By some atmospheric process, the whole schoolyard now suddenly seemed to know that somebody was recording the names of people who had been conscripted by the Tigers and still remained missing. More villagers walked over to us, in groups of four or five, hurrying to ensure that they caught us before we left. My two friends pulled out pads and pens as well.

'My sister Susainathan Susalini hasn't come home yet. She was taken by the Tigers on the road in Puthukkudiyiruppu, on 4 February 2009. She was 19 years old.'

'My sister Mary Justina was 17 years old. She didn't even see the results of her exams. They took her away immediately after she wrote them. This was on 6 March 2008. They came to our house and abducted her there. In September, some men came home—they were Tigers—and they told my mother that Mary Justina had died. They gave her a coffin, but it was sealed with bars and ropes. But later, after the war, in one of the displacement camps, a boy who knew one of Mary Justina's classmates, named Sena, said that Sena had seen her in Poonthottam, drawing water from a well. How could that be? Sena was in Jaffna, so a year later, my mother went to Jaffna to confirm this with him. She went there in May 2010, I think. Sena said that he had seen her, but that he did not remember when exactly this had happened. Now we don't know what to do next.'

'My younger brother Anthony Nishantan. He was taken on 5 January 2009, on the road in Matalan, when we were trying to escape the fighting. He was only 19 years old.'

Now people were rushing into the schoolyard from other parts of Iranapalai, flicking sweat off their brows, making straight for us. The word had spread like manic electricity.

Nobody asked us who we were, or which organization we represented, or if we were from the government, or if we even had any power to trace these missing boys and girls. They simply clustered around us, agitated but patient, waiting their turn to unburden themselves. The list grew: a 13-year-old who had once wandered too close to a Tiger encampment and was thought to have been snatched into the fold; a 20-year-old who agreed to join in lieu of his younger brother, only for the Tigers to come back the next day to take the brother anyway; a 17-year-old who had escaped the Tigers twice and had been found and yanked back to the front lines on each occasion. Unfailingly, everybody remembered the exact date of the abduction. These were the chronologies imprinted upon people's memories during a war: not birthdays or wedding anniversaries, but dates of disappearances, or of death by mortar, or of evacuation.

'My daughter Anuja was seized out of our house on 25 January 2007. She wasn't even 20. Two months after that, when we had fled from Iranapalai and were in Mullaitivu, somebody told our family that he had seen Anuja in a car there, outside a cooperative store. My husband went to see, but she wasn't there. Her brother Ananthan had to hide throughout that time, because he was afraid of being caught by the Tigers also.'

'My son, Janardhanan—the Tigers came to our house on 1 October 2008, and forced him to accompany them. He was 19 years old. Then on 25 March 2009, the Tigers took me to a place where 15 or 20 coffins were laid out on the ground, each one labelled with a name. They pointed one of the boxes out to me and said: "That's your son," and then they took the boxes away. They said he had fallen ill and died. But we still have our doubts, because just 10 days earlier, when we had escaped to Mullivaikal, he had come to see us because his sister had been injured by a shell attack, and he was very healthy then. What kind of a disease could he have caught that killed him in 10 days? And why didn't they allow me to see his body?'

We must have sat there for three-quarters of an hour, scribbling down facts about lives that may or may not have already ended. The village official, having wrapped up his meeting, watched us with lukewarm curiosity for a few minutes and then sauntered away. Then the crowd thinned, although a scatter of people remained even after they had spoken to us, as if they were expecting some sort of promise or announcement. My companions and I looked ashamedly at each other, as if we had engaged in a wicked duplicity. What could we even say that would not be either a lie or an admission of powerlessness? I chose to stare down at my notebook's pages, as if I was searching hard for some pattern to the information, trying really to avoid the eyes of those who had stayed back.

'Thank you for giving us this information,' one of my friends said finally. 'We'll do our best to get it to people who can find out what happened to your relatives.'

We hadn't driven far from the school—a couple of hundred metres, perhaps—when we heard a shout behind us. In the rear-view mirror, we saw a bearded, pudgy man in a sarong of blue-green checks running after the van, his hand aloft, beseeching us to stop. We pulled on to the shoulder of the road, and the man got in and sat next to me, quite bereft of breath.

'I heard,' he said in between swallows of air, 'that you're registering people who are still missing?'

'No, no, we aren't,' my friend said in haste. 'We just took some names down. We aren't even sure if we can help in any way.'

The man wasn't fazed. 'That's all right. Let me tell you anyway,' he said. Then he recounted to us how his son, 15 years old and still in school in Iranapalai, was commanded by the Tigers to join their ranks. It was early 2009, the Tigers' cause looked desperate, and the man pleaded with them to show some mercy and let the boy stay with him. 'They threatened us,' he said, and although his son tried to be brave about it, he was crying when they led him away from their house. 'I didn't see him again after that.' We weren't even writing these details down, but he didn't seem to notice, or if he did, he didn't care. He narrated the story staring in turn into each of our faces, as if a clue to his son's whereabouts might be inscribed in the whites of our eyes.

Eventually my friend asked the man for his name and address, telling him: 'We'll call you if we find anything in Colombo.' It was a hollow thing to say, and we knew it.

'Thank you,' he said, with a jagged smile. He slid open the door of the van and hopped out. We could see him in the rear-view mirror, as we drove away, walking slowly back towards his house.

The jumble of names still resides in my notebook. At some point, after we returned to Colombo, I typed them up and emailed them around, to people who were trying to track down the missing of the war. Nothing would come of it, I thought, feeling wretched for being so pessimistic. But I was right; the inquiries went nowhere. Often, I considered calling one of the phone numbers, to ask if a son or a sister had miraculously returned home. Every time, though, I decided against it, reluctant to remind them of their loss or remind myself of my incapacity to help.

As the summer of 2009 set in, the masses of displaced Tamils were pressed further east and then south, around the curve of the Nandikadal Lagoon into Mullivaikal, a village that perched on a splinter of sand between the lagoon and the Bay of Bengal. The original population of refugees—

thought by the UN to number 350,000—had been cleaved into three: the dead; those who had managed to surrender to the army's custody; and those who continued to be on the run, corralled at gunpoint into ever-tighter parcels of land by the Tigers. Nobody knew—nobody still knows—how many people streamed into Mullivaikal. The Sri Lankan government claimed 15,000, all of whom made it out of the final battle alive, whereas the UN estimated 100,000, many thousands of whom perished.

In these last three square kilometres of land controlled by the Tigers, the displaced dug themselves fresh bunkers. They were trapped. From the north, along the way they had come, the army was advancing, firing into the dense colony of people. To the east was the sea. To the west was the width of the Nandikadal Lagoon, impossible to traverse fast enough to avoid being shot by the Tigers. To the south was a slender causeway spanning an inlet of the lagoon; the near end of the causeway was blocked by the Tigers, and the other end ran right into the army-held towns of Vattuvahal and Mullaitivu. The pieces thus arrayed, the war of three decades had boiled down to this compact endgame.

These were the worst days of them all. The May sun screamed down without pity. There was little food or fresh water available, and almost no medicines. A makeshift hospital was established in a secondary-school building, but it was soon shelled; when the doctors moved their meagre staff and equipment to an abandoned primary school, these new premises were shelled as well. The limbless and the dying lay strewn about the stretch of coast. They could have been shipped out, but the Sri Lankan navy prohibited the Red Cross ship from reaching Mullivaikal, fearful that the Tiger cadre or their leaders would use it as a means of escape. There was nothing to do, really, except wait for the end.

Everybody had a Mullivaikal story—either a first-hand one, if they had lived through it, or a second-hand one, told to them by someone who had been there. There were no third-hand accounts. That's how closely the trauma was held within the Tamil community, and how vividly it was narrated.

I listened to dozens of these stories, allowing them to pile up in my mind, layer upon layer, like sediment. They would lose their potency as they accreted, I had thought at first, but in fact they grew more and more powerful, their sheer weight imposing and exhausting. It surprised me how sharply these stories were remembered. The confusion of the fighting was already two years into the past, and I had thought that those dazed days, full of hunger and fear, would have been difficult to recall. But here they were, laid out in sureness, even annotated with dates and times. Time had clarified memory, instead of muddying it.

In Kilinochchi, a still-broken town, a friend had promised to introduce me to two women whose families had been in Mullivaikal. She called the women, assured them that they could trust me, and arranged for us to meet at one of their houses. Then she summoned an autorickshaw driver she knew personally and asked him to ferry me there. 'You can't be too careful,' she muttered.

The autorickshaw bumped and limped painfully over the ruined A9 and then turned off into a road of packed, hard mud. I noticed a decal of the Buddha pasted on to the windshield, and I asked the driver: 'I've only seen that in Colombo. How come you have the Buddha there?'

Yasotharan—or Yaso, as he asked me to call him—shrugged. He was a lanky man with outsized features; even the roll of his shoulders seemed large and theatrical. 'It's all the same now, anyway,' he said enigmatically.

We stopped in the middle of a sparse grove of palm trees, through which dirt paths ran slender and crooked. Nandini lived here, with her two young children, in a shed constructed of mud-and-stone walls, wooden lintels and a tin sheet. A tree grew right out of a hole in the roof, and to its trunk, somebody had affixed a duct pipe; inside the pipe was a wire that filched power from a nearby line. On the metalled shutter of what passed for a window, the letters 'CERF UNOPS'—standing for Central Emergency Response Fund and United Nations Office for Project Services—were stencilled in fat blue letters. Behind the shed, a low, thatched coop housed some chickens, and their gurgles broke every so often through the hot, still morning.

Nandini and Ponnamma watched me with wary eyes as I got out of the autorickshaw, but they seemed to recognize Yaso, because they grew visibly easier as soon as they saw him. 'He's the one, he's the one,' Yaso said, pointing to me, and he pulled up a chair to sit and listen to us talk.

Nandini gave us glasses of sweet, scalding tea. She was a young woman wearing a red nightgown with Rorschach-blot patterns in black snaking across it. She displayed the tokens of her marriage prominently, almost aggressively: the parting of her hair was streaked thick with vermilion, and her golden wedding necklace hung free of her neckline instead of being tucked discreetly into her nightgown. Her husband was still missing. Ponnamma was an older woman, in her mid-50s, her hair more grey than black and her lips more black than pink. On her lap, she clasped a plastic sleeve full of letters, photographs and documents. She rubbed the serrated edges of the plastic repeatedly between her thumb and her forefinger, as if it were a sort of talisman.

Both women came from Tiger families. In 2006, Ponnamma's 26-year-old son travelled to Vavuniya on some union work, where he was nabbed by the Tigers; at least, this is what she thought must have happened, because she never saw him again. Her daughter married a member of the Tiger's intelligence wing, a stocky man with a moustache seemingly grown in mimetic tribute to Prabhakaran's. Nandini's husband, who used the nom de guerre Santhan, worked in the Tigers' political administration unit. He had been with the Tigers since 1990, when he joined up as a 21-year-old, and Nandini fully approved of his profession when she married him in 2001.

'The fighting started to come through the Vanni towards Kilinochchi in the summer of 2008, and we left in October,' Nandini said. Her family, and Ponnamma's, took the well-traversed route east: Viswamadu, Suthanthirapuram, and finally cornered in Mullivaikal in the middle of May. There were, she estimated, at least a hundred thousand people in the area, sandwiched between the lagoon and the sea. 'The shelling was so heavy. A shell fell on the bunker next to ours, and a family of eight was killed instantly.'

'Something like that happened to me,' Ponnamma said. 'There was a bunker near ours, with a family of six, including a baby that had been born just 10 days earlier. They were all killed by a single shell.'

Ponnamma was hit by shell shrapnel. On 16 May—she remembered the date clearly—she exchanged some of her jewellery for five kilograms of rice, vegetables and a couple of coconuts. 'Rice was a thousand rupees per kilogram. A coconut cost 200 rupees.' When her daughter protested at this profligacy, Ponnamma snapped at her: 'Look, we may not live through this, so we might as well eat while we can.' She cooked her rice, diced and boiled her potatoes, and had almost finished stewing her curry when a shell landed nearby and demolished the meal. 'Pieces of the shell hit me. I was hurt and bleeding in two or three places.'

'Where?' I asked.

'On my scalp,' Ponnamma said, and she parted her hair to show me a weal, glossy and crimson. 'Also on my abdomen and on my back,' she added, and she pulled up her blouse to show me a crescent scar just below her left breast. Another scar ran nearly horizontal across her spine, just above her waist. 'My daughter was hurt as well. I took her to the Tigers' clinic, and they gave her an injection and took out a fragment of the shell.' The shrapnel wedged into Ponnamma's abdomen remained there for many months, until she asked a doctor to extricate it after she returned to Kilinochchi.

The bodies were everywhere, scattered like breadcrumbs along the trail from Nandini's bunker to the hospital; you could tell how long they had been dead by the thickness of the flies around them. 'There was one woman who had been injured, and they sent her back from the hospital,' Nandini said. 'She was walking with a bandage around her head, and there was another shell attack, and she was hurt yet again, his time in her back. She collapsed right in front of our bunker, the blood flowing out of her like a fountain. Or maybe she just lay down, I don't know.'

Not exactly lying down, I thought. More a surrender to her fate, an admission of defeat, a white flag waved in the face of death.

'But she was there, in front of our eyes, and Santhan said: "Go keep some water next to her. She looks like she's going to die anyway." Just as I was doing that, she rolled over, and her eyes rolled to the back of her head, and she died. My son was screaming and crying: "Amma, she's a ghost! She's a ghost!" My children were traumatized, so I had to drag the body off to one side.'

Nandini wept at the memory. I wanted to look away, but there was an utter absence of self-consciousness about her tears, as if they were essential accessories to the discussion of those weeks. She continued to talk through her sobs, and her voice became stretched and thin.

Santhan was struck by shrapnel too. He had lost his right

leg many years earlier, when he had stepped on a landmine, and he wore a wooden prosthetic below the knee. One day in Mullivaikal, Nandini saw him hobbling back to their bunker, his arm slung around a fellow Tiger, his stump bleeding and raw. 'In the hurry, he had lost his wooden leg,' Nandini said. 'Later, a Tiger cadre found it and came and gave it to him. It had stopped fitting properly, so he had to tie it on with gauze.'

Santhan maintained a sturdy sense of responsibility towards the civilians in Mullivaikal. He stuffed their bunker full of other people's children, while he himself remained in the open. Without the knowledge of the people around them, the other Tiger leaders were eating heartily, collaring whatever rations were floating around. 'Santhan refused to do this. He said: "We're going to eat exactly what the people are eating." If I somehow got hold of a fish and cooked it, he would take it out of the bunker and give it to somebody else. Then he'd tell me to bring him some rice gruel, and he would drink that. I swear that he didn't eat one solid meal during any of those days. He just wouldn't.'

On the humid morning of 17 May, from across the causeway to Vattuvahal, the army hollered through megaphones to the civilians: 'Give yourselves up. Come to us. We will take care of you.' Early that day, Nandini and Santhan and their children entered a long, sluggish river of people preparing to cross over. Santhan had not wanted to go. He had decided to die there, with the other Tiger leaders, and only because of Nandini's alarmed hysterics did he allow himself to be dragged into the queue. 'He knew he couldn't do anything, finally,' Nandini said. 'The shelling was fearsome, and people were dying all over the place. We kept looking at this and thinking: "This will happen to us too." Even when we were on the causeway, the fighting continued.'

'I heard that the Tigers tried to shoot some of the people crossing over to the army,' I said. 'Is that true?'

Nandini seemed uncertain about how to answer this. 'That was what people said earlier. And that was what I thought then as well. But now, when I think about it, I'm not sure. I don't think they would. They wouldn't, would they?' She was asking not for clarification but for assurance. It simplified her life to know that the Sri Lankan government was the enemy and the Tigers were on her side, and she was reluctant to tamper too much with the clean, bold lines of this division.

For a whole day, Nandini's family stood in the queue at the Mullivaikal end of the bridge, inching forward, dossing down on the ground for the night, until on 18 May, they made their way across. At the other end of the causeway, a former Tiger stood, peering into the faces of the bedraggled men and women as they passed. He stopped Nandini's husband and asked: 'You're Santhan, aren't you?'

'I am,' Santhan said. He was lurching along on crutches, his prosthetic askew. There was no point in denying it.

The soldiers let the family go, and they walked a few kilometres down a path demarcated with stakes planted in the ground, until they reached a large enclosure made out of metal posts and chain links. It looked like a cage. They stayed there throughout the day of the 18th. 'There was nothing to eat or drink, and when some people got restive and asked for water, they were beaten. Some people died in that enclosure, I think.'

Late in the evening, along with other Tigers, Ponnamma's son-in-law had been led out of the cage by some uniformed men. 'His children had small injuries, and he didn't want to leave them, but he had to go,' she said. 'Then a girl came running from the other end of the enclosure, shouting: "There's a bus! The army has loaded them on to a bus!" My daughter took her children and ran, asking to be let on to the bus as well. What could I do? I was injured myself, I couldn't hold her back.' Ponnamma gasped for air as she wept, holding her side as if her body was racked with cramps. 'There was a local parish priest there telling the soldiers: "At least don't split the families up." So they let my daughter and her children on to the bus as well, and the bus left at around 10 p.m.'

At 2 a.m., early on the 19th, a Tamil-speaking army man came into the cage, holding a diary, and clapped Santhan on the shoulder. 'You're Santhan, no?'

Santhan said that he was. Nandini and her children watched apprehensively. None of them had been able to sleep through the night, and they had observed the soldier move through the crowd, shining a light into faces, asking questions, pulling people out. He didn't know what Santhan looked like, Nandini thought. He had only been told: If there is a man of this description, bring him.

'Come with me,' the soldier said. Santhan heaved himself up on to his crutches. Nandini tried to follow, she said, but the soldier told her, not unkindly: 'We'll question him and release him. You sit down now.'

'Don't be stubborn,' Santhan scolded her. 'You have to think of the children. You have to get out of here.'

They put Santhan on a bus, along with an assortment of other mid-level Tigers. At 2.30 a.m. or so on 19 May, the bus rolled away into the night. A few hours later, the sun came up on a Sri Lanka purged of its insurgency for the first time in decades.

3

NANDINI NEVER FOUND out where Santhan was taken, or what happened to him. Ponnamma never saw her daughter, her son-in-law or her grandchildren again.

As a broad rule, the army sent mid-level Tigers and their families—men, women and children—to internment camps that were sealed to the outside world. The Red Cross and the UN were not permitted to visit; indeed, some of these camps were operated in undisclosed locations, so that international agencies could not even demand to assess them. Very few stories emerged about the conditions within, because very few people emerged to tell these stories.

What did the government do with the Tigers who fell into its hands? In most cases, especially with senior Tigers, they were probably put to death, as a matter of policy. In its approach towards the remnants of the Tigers, the state behaved less as victors towards the vanquished than as doctors towards a tumour, seeking to expunge every last malignant cell. But the chemotherapy was surrounded by dense obfuscation. The government always denied that it had ever executed any Tigers, and this stance never wavered, even in the face of circumstantial or eyewitness evidence.

Not surprisingly, mystery and conjecture piled up thick and high. How, for instance, did the foremost Tiger of them all die? The preliminary reports of Prabhakaran's final moments on 18 May placed him in a van, with some of his family and his closest confidants, driving away from a scene of pitched battle. The van was hit by a shell, the news said, but that would have pulverized its passengers entirely. So the story changed when the army released photographs of Prabhakaran's corpse, the top of the head blown so comprehensively away that its contents needed to be held in place by a blue tea towel. Prabhakaran and a few remaining Tigers had fought on, and they had been killed by army fire, their guns still clenched in their hands. Or Prabhakaran and his innermost circle had capitulated and had been brought as captives to the army's top commanders, so that they could have the satisfaction of executing him. Or Prabhakaran had escaped, on a helicopter or a boat that had spirited him away from the coast, and that waxy pallor on the corpse in the photographs was simply the result of bad Photoshop or inadequate make-up on another poor stiff. Even among Tamils who believed that Prabhakaran was no more, how he died was a crucial article of faith, as if a courageous end still somehow validated the decades of misery that came before it.

A small band of other Tigers had tried earlier to surrender. Through intermediaries living overseas, they had negotiated carefully with the army, wanting to be sure that they would be safe once they turned themselves in. Led by two senior leaders, Nadesan and Pulidevan, the Tigers walked across the causeway at Mullivaikal, their families in tow, a white flag hoisted high as per instructions. Once they were in the fold of the army, they were stripped and then shot by machine guns. Nadesan's wife, who was Sinhalese, is believed to have yelled at the soldiers, 'He is trying to surrender and you are shooting him!' before she was killed herself. Photographs emerged of the bodies of Nadesan and Pulidevan, their bellies blackened and punctured by close-range fire.

They were odd, mutated relics, these photos and videos, captured on cell phones by soldiers who were revelling in their victory and wanted souvenirs of it but then used as evidence of war crimes. The images remained the same, but their significance transformed sharply. They became different documents altogether.

The most infamous such photos found their way to Channel 4 in 2013. Prabhakaran's 12-year-old son Balachandran sits quite alone on a bench, in what appears to be an army bunker constructed out of green bags of sand. He wears a pair of shorts but no shirt; instead, somebody has thrown a black-and-blue towel around his shoulders. In one image, he is holding a packet of snacks in his lap; somebody has also given him water to drink, in a plastic orange mug. In the next image, he is dead on the ground, five bullet holes punched so tidily through his torso that the muzzle of the gun must have been jammed right up against his skin.

The morning after Santhan was taken away, Nandini and her children were sent to a camp for the internally displaced, where they stayed for nearly two years.

The government called these camps 'welfare centres.' They were distributed across the north and the east of the island, holding a third of a million Tamils while security forces rooted among them for Tigers who may have slipped in as civilians. The largest, Menik Farm, sprawled over 700 hectares near Vavuniya and was stuffed with more than two hundred thousand people, so that one person often shared a tent with a dozen others. Food, water and sanitation were in sorely short supply. Rumours leaked out about physical and sexual abuse by soldiers, and about interrogations under torture and extrajudicial killings. For the Tamils' own safety, the government claimed, they were not being allowed to go home immediately, because the villages in the conflict zone had to be demined to be made safe for habitation again. But really, no one was allowed to go anywhere at all. The camps were wrapped in barbed-wire fencing, and the army regulated entries and exits, releasing detainees in batches over three and a half years until the last of the camps was emptied in September 2012. Journalists and NGO workers were blocked from accessing these camps; even the UN Secretary General, Ban Ki-moon, got only a short, curated tour of Menik Farm when he asked to meet some of its residents. 'There is a word for places where people are held against their will for years at a time, you know,' an aid worker in Colombo once told me. 'That word is "prison."'

When Nandini returned to Kilinochchi, broke and heartsick, she found no news of Santhan. Of all the people on that bus with him, Nandini said, not one had returned. She was sure of this because she knew their families well. 'My neighbours tell me: "I heard they just shot all those people," meaning the people in the internment camps. My mother blames me for everything. "You found him, you married him. You should have known this would happen to a Tiger."'

Nandini was crying again now, hunched in her chair, seeming monumentally tired, as if she had relived the last three years in the space of five hours. The previous day had been her son's ninth birthday. 'He told me: "If my father was here, he would have bought me so many gifts. You aren't buying me anything. You aren't even able to get me a toffee." She wiped her eyes so fiercely that I worried her long fingernails would rake her eyeballs. 'I can't take the children's suffering at all. He had two spare wooden legs, and they're still here. I can't bear to throw them out. The children tell me: "Keep the legs. He'll come."'

Yaso spoke up. I had forgotten completely that he was sitting behind me, but now he asked Nandini if she had heard anything about an acquaintance of his, a Tiger who had not been seen since the end of the war. Ponnamma thought she recognized the name: Hadn't he managed to get away to

Canada or England? That wasn't him, Nandini said. The conversation started to resemble a grisly version of office gossip: which of Santhan's former colleagues had died, which of them was still missing, which of the Tiger's leaders might possibly have escaped to a foreign country.

'I firmly believe Prabhakaran is still alive,' Nandini said. 'He'll give us a way to live our old lives again.'

'I think so too,' Yaso said. 'Some days, I dream that the struggle will start again.'

'It can't be a dream. It will happen. It has to,' Nandini said. 'After all, how long can we continue living like this?' It took me a full minute to realize that these people, their lives so thoroughly demolished by conflict, were starting to yearn already for a new war.

Ponnamma and Yaso fell into conversation, so I wandered the small lot of land around Nandini's house, making my way finally to her chicken coop, where I slipped my fingers into the holes of the wire-mesh door and peered into the gloom. The air inside was cool and pungent, and the chickens' warbles grew loud with alarm. When I stepped away, I noticed, propped up against the coop's side wall, Santhan's two spare legs. The veneer had chipped off the calf of one of them, revealing blonde wood underneath; the second was speckled with what, on a real limb, would have resembled some form of skin disease. The legs leaned comfortably against each other, not expecting to be used any time soon.

4

YASO DROVE ME back to the Kilinochchi district secretariat, where my friend Ananthy, who had sent me to Nandini and Ponnamma, was employed. 'Did you meet them?' she asked, coming out of her building to meet me. She was wearing a sari of excruciating pink. It seemed to be a day that called for a particular dress code; through the just-ajar door, I caught a glimpse of other men and women, in pink saris or shirts, looking like a bureaucracy of flamingos. 'Come,' Ananthy said, 'let's go to the canteen and have a cup of tea.'

Even in the fat heels that she sometimes wore, Ananthy stood only up to my shoulders, but she walked twice as fast as me. She thrummed forever with energy. Her three daughters were enrolled in a school in Jaffna and lived with her sister there, so Ananthy stayed in a cubbyhole of a room in a women's hostel in Kilinochchi; still, on most days of the week, she finished work and travelled the 60 kilometres north to see her children, spend the night with them, and get on the 6.30 a.m. bus back to Kilinochchi to make it to work on time. Through the day, she snatched moments to write letters, file appeals, and badger the government for news of her husband Elilan, one of the Tigers' chief political operatives, who had surrendered to the army in Mullivaikal and had not been heard of since. Nearly always, Ananthy had with her a bulky handbag, in which she carried a plastic pouch stuffed with newspaper articles, copies of letters she had written, and photographs of Elilan.

In the canteen, she bought us cups of tea and an oblong roll of sweet bread. 'I can't eat anything spicy,' she said. 'I've had ulcers for a year and a half now.'

A stout, dark man, in the regulation pink shirt and with his trousers hitched nearly halfway up his chest, occupied the table next to ours. Ananthy leaned across and whispered: 'He's the one who is an army informant here. He's a Tamil, but he works for them.'

'How do you know?'

Some months ago, she said, she had been called in to a nearby army camp to be interrogated by a colonel. She told a friend and her lawyer that she was going, and that they should sound an alarm if she hadn't called them in three hours. A Tamil-speaking major from Kandy had translated the interrogation, she said. 'Again and again, the colonel asked the same question in different ways. "Are you supporting the Tigers still?" I told him: "Show me where the Tigers are, and I'll go to them right away. But there aren't any." This made him angry, but he couldn't say anything to this, so they let me go in two hours.' Then Ananthy bent further towards me, until our foreheads were almost touching over the table. 'The Kandy major was a nice man, a soft-hearted fellow. He told me: "It was the fatty in your office who told us about you and Elilan. Stay away from him." Then he also said: "Keep searching for your husband. I really hope you find him."'

I rolled my eyes into the corners of their sockets, trying to sneak a long look at the army stooge, who was lapping at his tea. By this time, Ananthy was teasing a colleague at another table, who had just bought himself a late lunch: 'What happened, old man? Your wife isn't cooking for you at home?' Her giggles sounded like hiccoughs of delight.

Ananthy was impossible to dislike, I had thought. Then, one day in Jaffna, I mentioned her to M., and he smirked. He liked to surprise me, to show how much he knew. 'Just

last week, I met somebody in the market, and she came up
in conversation. This man I was talking to said: "If I meet
that wife of Elilan, I'll rape her and then hang her from the
nearest tree."'

The raw violence of the sentiment startled me. 'Why would
he say that?'

Elilan, it turned out, had taken charge of recruiting more
Tamils into the movement during the last years of the war,
sending out squads of Tigers to grab young boys and girls out
of their families. 'This man lost his son in this way,' M. said.
'He shouted at me: "How could Elilan take my son and then
surrender like a coward?"' M. had seen Elilan's teams at work
in the Vanni, in the thick of battle. 'Shells would be falling
all around us, and I would go out to look for sugar for my
daughter. People would be standing in line to buy food. Then
these recruiters would come, and everybody would just flee,
like chickens before a swooping eagle.'

To me, Ananthy always denied, with hot eyes, that Elilan
ever dispatched children into war. At first, she also tried to
convince me that his teams never abducted anyone at all; then
she admitted that it had happened, but she found roundabout
ways of defending the policy of forcible recruitment. 'The
Tamils are just being hypocrites. In 2007 and 2008, every
Tamil was asking for Eelam, not just Prabhakaran. So why
shouldn't families give a member to this cause? If some other
Tiger militant came to the house of one of these families, they
would welcome him in. They would say: "Come, eat lunch
with us." All because he is somebody else's son. But the minute
it is their own son, they'd tell him: "No, no, you focus on your
studies. Don't join the Tigers."'

Elilan's role in the Tigers made Ananthy's life in Kilinochchi
a difficult one. Much of the town held her husband responsible
for the deaths of their children, so Ananthy lived within a fog
of hostility. 'When I had just returned, people would see me,

and they would get so angry, because they thought that Elilan had somehow escaped abroad,' she said. 'I had to convince them that I was looking for him.' Young women who had scrambled to get pregnant in 2008 and 2009, so that the Tigers would spare them, were now raising their babies alone and in destitution. Ananthy once had to face down such a woman, who stopped her on the street and shouted curses at her and Elilan. 'There's a man who works in my office. The Tigers took his son. I don't talk to him much, and he never says anything to me directly. But around me, he will often speak out against the Tigers and criticize them.' She did not miss the irony of the situation. 'My husband fought for the Tamils all his life. But now that he's gone, the Tamils hate me, and these Sinhalese NGO workers are the ones who are trying to help me find him.' Everything was backwards. Ananthy had returned to a Sri Lanka plucked out of some alternate reality.

Ananthy had never had anything but convoluted relationships with the Tigers and with the Sri Lankan state. She was working now for a government that her husband had considered illegitimate and fought against. She herself had hated the Tigers, until she married one of them; once she did, some members of her family stopped speaking to her altogether, because of how the Tigers had ripped apart their lives.

In 1983, when the anti-Tamil riots flared in southern Sri Lanka, Ananthy was 12 years old, wide-eyed enough to drink in every detail of her surroundings and old enough to remember what she saw. The local junior college in Jaffna declared a holiday, because it had to house the people flooding in by boats from the south. One of her older brothers, Sivakumaran, was a student there at the time, so Ananthy went with him to visit the refugees. 'People had been burned. Their limbs had been hacked off.' They lay on makeshift cots, or on the floor, either glassy-eyed or hysterical. Not long thereafter, Sivakumaran joined the Tigers, but he quit after three years. Afraid that the Tigers would come after him to punish his decampment, his mother scraped together the money to send him to New Delhi, where he vanished off the face of the earth.

Ananthy had other siblings: her eldest brother Kumar, two sisters named Santhi and Lingeswari, and a younger brother named Kirikumar. Their father worked as a research chemist in a cement factory near Kankesanthurai, on the northern coast of the Jaffna peninsula, and he taught them all music and karate. Kumar was the first to be seduced by Tamil nationalism. In the early 1970s, he joined the Tamil Youth League, one of the precursors of the Tigers; after he was arrested for some minor infraction, his mother sold her jewellery, raised 13,000 rupees, and sent Kumar to Holland.

'He came back to Sri Lanka in 1999, actually,' she told me. This was on the first afternoon we met, in a little restaurant in Jaffna. She had ridden a sweaty bus up from Kilinochchi, but she bustled in with tremendous drive. I thought of her as an unstoppable force. 'But then he married a Sinhalese. He lives in Colombo now, but we haven't spoken to him since. We've washed our hands of him.'

'Why?' I asked.

She looked at me with her head atilt, as if I had wondered how she knew it was daytime. 'Because he married a Sinhalese. Because of the things the Sinhalese have done.'

But the Tigers did so much worse by Lingeswari, her sister, the one who had taken avidly to her father's karate lessons because, as Ananthy said, 'she always had a lot of male habits.' Beginning in 1983, Lingeswari tried to join the Eelam People's Revolutionary Liberation Front, a group of militants that rivalled the Tigers and that went by the mouthful of alphabets EPRLF. 'They weren't recruiting women at the time, so they'd smack her on the head and send her back home,' Ananthy said. This happened three times, but she was stubborn, so when she went back to the EPRLF camp on a fourth occasion, they let her remain and began training her.

After the EPRLF was banned in 1986—the same year Ananthy's father died—Lingeswari briefly went to India, to study English. Five days after she returned to Jaffna, she bumped into a former EPRLF colleague who was now with the Tigers. He suggested that she join them, but she refused politely, wishing to put her days of violence behind her. That evening, accompanied by a couple of his mates, the Tiger called for her at her house, convinced her to go for a walk with them, steered her into an empty alley, and shot her dead for spurning their offer. 'Then they came home,' Ananthy said, 'and they just told my mother where she could go to collect the body.'

So, some years later, when her youngest brother Kirikumar fell in love with a woman in the Tigers, Ananthy's mother threatened to disown him, and right until her death in 2003, she did not speak to her daughter-in-law once. 'She never forgave the Tigers for what they had done to Lingeswari,' Ananthy said. In these ways, the Tigers had utterly disrupted the constitution of a single family: recruiting one person, killing another out of sheer pique, earning the hatred of a third, and snaring a fourth by marriage. The web of these relationships, these various loyalties and loathings, was densely knotted, the strands looping back and across and under each other until they were impossible to unravel and understand.

Ananthy sent me photographs of Elilan. 'Dear Friend,' her emails would begin, and she would sign off, 'Your Friend.' The photos were never of her and Elilan together, or of Elilan with their daughters. Instead, in one, Elilan kneels next to a fallen Tiger in a stretcher; in another, he is shaking hands with a Buddhist priest, and both of them are flashing strained smiles at the camera. In the third, he stands with an unidentified Sinhalese woman in front of a portrait of Prabhakaran. Elilan is a stocky and moustached man, and in his white shirt and khakis, he resembles a mid-level marketing executive out on a sales call. Ananthy never got around to explaining the contexts in which these photos were taken, so the more frequently I looked at them, the more my imagination started to fill in the stories. The man in the stretcher was a recent recruit and a guerrilla of striking promise, until he had been mowed down by an army sniper. The Buddhist priest headed a peace delegation, but he and Elilan fell into heavy ideological argument and their conversation went nowhere. The Sinhalese woman— and you could tell she was Sinhalese by the way she draped her sari—was an employee of the Sri Lankan government, sent out to Kilinochchi to meet Elilan and rationalize some administrative details. The meeting over, she asks—because she has derived a secret thrill at being in the heart of Tiger territory—if she might have a photo, and Elilan hospitably obliges.

Before she married Elilan, Ananthy had been courted by a Sri Lankan army major named Mendis, under bizarre circumstances. In 1997, Ananthy and seven others had been rounded up and sent to a military camp for a day, to be probed for any generic knowledge about the Tigers that they might possess. This was a routine part of life in Jaffna under the army's rule. Ananthy had been struck with a stick, and some of the others had had their heads thrust into plastic shopping bags filled with petrol, so that the fumes made them retch and addled their brains.

'Then this Mendis came by, and he saw me, and they stopped harassing us and let us go,' Ananthy said. Two weeks later, Mendis arrived at Ananthy's house, in civilian clothing and with a translator, and asked for her mother.

'I want to marry her,' Mendis said. 'She isn't a Tiger. She's a good girl, and I like her.'

'I can't give her to a Sinhalese man,' he was told, 'and I especially cannot give her to a Sinhalese army man.'

Ananthy's mother—who seemed by now to have spent her whole life keeping her children out of the clutches of the Tigers and the army—put her on a boat to Trincomalee, in the east. This was just as well. After a week, Mendis returned in full uniform and put a gun to her mother's head: 'You've hidden her. Tell me where she is.'

'If you want to shoot me, go ahead,' Ananthy believes her mother said. 'But she isn't here.'

In truth, nobody in Ananthy's family knew that she had already fallen in love with Elilan. They had met when he gave a lecture about the armed struggle at the local technical college, where she had been studying for a diploma. They kept their relationship hidden from even their closest friends. In any case, the times were hardly conducive to an epic romance. The army was attacking Jaffna relentlessly, finally seizing the peninsula in 1995. Elilan, along with the rest of the Tigers, fled south into the Vanni. When Ananthy was sent to Trincomalee by her mother, she rejoined Elilan, and a year later, they were married. 'He wrote a letter to my mother, saying: "We're sorry for hiding this from you, but we've been in love, and we're married now,"' Ananthy said. Her mother accepted this, but without grace.

'She liked him, I think. She liked that he didn't drink, and that he was responsible. But she never came to visit us.' Ananthy pulled a face, as if to remark: What an obstinate old woman! 'We moved to Kilinochchi to be closer to her, and we even added a room to our house there, so that she could come to stay with us, but she never did.' Her sister Santhi, however, could not stomach Ananthy being wedded to a Tiger. 'Until our mother died, Santhi did not talk to me at all. She couldn't believe that I had married into the organization that had killed our sister.'

I remarked to Ananthy that this surprised me too. 'How did you make your peace with that?'

I expected her to tell me that love trumped everything, or that it was not, after all, Elilan who pulled the trigger on her sister. These explanations I would have understood, but Ananthy offered neither of them. Instead she reasoned that the armed struggle and the Tamil cause were bigger than Lingeswari's life, and that she eventually came around to recognizing that. This was the leap of faith that Prabhakaran asked Sri Lanka's Tamils to take. The Eelam movement will consume many of your nearest and dearest, he told them, but it will all, once the fighting was over, be entirely worth the sacrifice. Clinging to this belief was the only way in which the violence-ridden universe of the Tigers could make any sense.

One afternoon, when I was in Jaffna, Ananthy phoned me. 'Are you very busy?' she asked.

'No, no, I'm just in my guest house,' I said. Her voice sounded ragged. 'Where are you?'

'In Jaffna, in my sister's house,' she said. This was unusual, because it was the middle of the week, when she should have been at work in Kilinochchi.

I took down the address and caught an autorickshaw there. Ananthy's sister Santhi lived in a small, cluttered house that lay half an hour north and east out of town, within a steel-gated compound fringed by banana trees. No one else was at home. Ananthy's and Santhi's children were in school, and Santhi was out. Ananthy and I sat on a divan in the living room, opposite a television set covered with a sequinned purple cloth. On shelves that had been built into the concrete walls was the regular paraphernalia of a Jaffna childhood: a cricket bat, dolls in cylindrical containers with see-through windows, toy cars with sirens and flashing lights, a carefully curated collection of pebbles, and a tin full of cowrie shells.

That morning, a couple of men from the Terrorist Investigation Department (TID) had come into Ananthy's office and demanded to speak to her in private. 'No,' she had told them, 'we'll talk right here, in front of people.'

Did she know where Elilan was? they had asked her. Had he managed to escape overseas?

'I don't know where he is. You do,' Ananthy had replied defiantly. 'And if you give me his address and phone number, I'll go and join him as soon as I can.'

The TID dropped in upon Ananthy in this manner once a month, without fail, and it upset her every time. Sometimes they visited her at her hostel in Kilinochchi; on a couple of occasions, they came to Santhi's house and questioned her and her children. The TID was playing a heartless game, Ananthy thought. They knew Elilan had disappeared into the custody of the army at Mullivaikal, and they knew Ananthy had been trying to find him. Perhaps they wanted to suss out what progress she had been making, or perhaps they wanted only to rattle her, to keep her unsure and confused.

'Once, I started shouting back at them: "Am I a terrorist? Why are you questioning me like this?"' Ananthy said. Fat tears bubbled out of the corners of her eyes. She rarely cried, and when she did, she paid no attention to her tears. She let them course down her cheeks and drip off her chin, as if they were conducting their business on someone else's face. 'Those two TID men were startled, and they left. But I can't keep doing that, shouting at them when they come to see me.'

Ananthy had been asked many times, by many people, if she was absolutely certain that Elilan had been captured by the army. In early May 2009, when the Tamils were on the run, she had arrived in Mathalan with her three daughters but without Elilan, who was on the move separately, with the

Tigers' top leadership. 'He would come and see us every couple of days, just to show us that he was alive,' she said. 'I asked him once or twice to just not go back, but he didn't like that, so I stopped asking him.' On 8 May, her second daughter's appendix burst, and a Tiger doctor performed an emergency surgery, in an operation theatre that had been constructed out of palmyra trunks and branches, a roof of thatch, a stretcher and a single blazing lamp.

On 15 May, Ananthy and her daughters were in Mullivaikal, sharing a cramped bunker with Elilan's parents, his sister and her family, and his brother and his family. A small fleet of boats was leaving for India, carrying the relatives of some of the Tiger leaders. Ananthy wanted to go, but Elilan did not want to leave; he wanted to send her and the children away, but she refused to leave without him. It was a stalemate, and they stayed on, ducking the shelling and praying for a ceasefire. 'The army was firing phosphorus rounds. They burned your throat and made you dizzy.'

On 16 May, Ananthy said, Elilan talked on a satellite phone to a prominent Tamil politician in India. Turn yourselves in, this politician urged Elilan, because the war is as good as lost now: 'They'll hold you for two years or so, but we'll make sure they release you after that. We'll get you out.' Elilan was not fully assured, Ananthy remembered. 'But we didn't think that it would be this bad, that he would just vanish like this. Otherwise we would have tried harder to escape.'

On 17 May, an hour before dawn, Ananthy and her daughters joined the queue to walk over the causeway and surrender to the army. Elilan stayed back, promising to leave in a few hours and find them. His daughter's surgical scar had become infected, and she was whimpering from the pain. The summer sun was fierce even at 7 a.m., when the crowd slowly started to move. In the water, Ananthy saw the swollen bodies of people who had tried to sprint across the previous day and had been shot, either by the Tigers or by the army. The war was ending not in a final blaze of combat but in abject misery.

Elilan crossed over later that day, having shucked his Tiger uniform for a sarong so that he could pass for a civilian, and he rejoined his family in the vast holding pen for refugees that the army had erected in Mullaitivu. 'My daughter had fallen asleep out of exhaustion by the time he arrived,' Ananthy said. 'He was so upset. He was saying: "We've given so many people and endured so many difficulties, and it has all come to nothing." He knew it was the end. And he told me: "I'm very worried about what will happen to you and the children."' Ananthy's voice was still strong, but by now she was crying— sobbing, really, so that even she had to attend to her tears. She started to dig around inside her handbag for tissues, but the handbag wasn't yielding them up, so she was digging and crying and talking, all at the same time. 'I told him: "You don't worry about us. You make sure you take care of yourself."'

They knew what was going to happen. Early on 18 May, a squad of soldiers, accompanied by a few guerrillas who had defected to the army's side, came into the holding pen to take away the Tigers they could identify. 'I wanted to go with Elilan, but he told me: "You stay here." One of the army guys looked at my ID and said: "Why do you want to get mixed up in all of this?" He must have had a kind heart, because he didn't force us on to the bus with Elilan. Otherwise we would have disappeared too, like so many other families.' Elilan was gone before Ananthy could wake her daughter up to say goodbye to her father.

5

THE SRI LANKAN government put itself into a bind when it swept into its arms thousands of Tiger combatants like Elilan. These men and women, and their children, were not individually nabbed off the street at night. They were picked out by soldiers who worked their way through a list of names, hustled on to military buses in front of witnesses, and transported away. Theoretically, they were all still somewhere in Sri Lanka, held with the full knowledge of the army; theoretically also, the government was required to produce them when asked, and to process their crimes against the state through the judiciary. But the government had no wish to try these guerrillas in court, or it had already executed them, or it had decided to detain them endlessly. So it evolved a mixed strategy of denial, silence and complication, all of which successfully muffled any clues to Elilan's whereabouts. He had stepped off the lip of a chasm into deep nothingness.

Ananthy started writing letters. She was good at that. Once, when she had wanted to get Elilan out of an unsavoury assignment, she had written directly to Prabhakaran, as if she was asking her daughter's teacher to excuse her from gym class. Forever thereafter, Prabhakaran teased Ananthy about her letter-writing habits, saying: 'I had never realized that Elilan has stronger supporters than I have.'

She wrote her first letter two days after Elilan was taken away, addressing it to the Red Cross at Vavuniya. Later, she marked copies of that letter to the Red Cross in Colombo, to the Human Rights Commission of Sri Lanka, and to an Indian office of the United Nations High Commissioner for Refugees. She also sent letters addressed to Mahinda Rajapaksa and Gotabhaya Rajapaksa, to the British embassy, and to the American embassy. 'I didn't send anything to the Indians, though,' she said. 'They could have pressured Sri Lanka to stop the shelling but they didn't. They let us down and slit our throats.'

None of her letters received a response, so she started visiting the offices of these NGOs and of government authorities. At the Human Rights Commission office in Vavuniya, a Sinhalese man was on duty, and he struggled to understand what she had to say. She filed a report somehow and was asked to call back for a registration number.

The next day, when she telephoned him, he said: 'I've lost the report.'

So Ananthy went back to the office and filed a fresh report, and this time she waited in front of his desk until she got her registration number. 'You realize,' he warned, 'that the TID will probably come and ask you questions? I hope you aren't scared.'

'I'm not,' she shot back.

The Kilinochchi police told her that they couldn't take her statement as it stood. 'We won't accept it if you say he surrendered. Why don't you say he disappeared?' they said. But Ananthy refused to do that. In December 2009, when she travelled to Colombo to petition the Human Rights Commission chapter there, an official advised her that the wheels might move faster if Elilan's relatives abroad made a representation. 'But when I asked them, they were scared that they would get into trouble if they ever came back to Sri Lanka,' she said.

A year after the end of the war, two TID officers walked

into Ananthy's office, rousted her out of her seat, and ordered her to accompany them to a nearby military base. There she was taken into a long, dimly lit room to meet Mahinda Hathurusinghe, the commander of the armed forces in the north.

When Hathurusinghe began to accuse Ananthy of still working for the Tigers, she thought she was in for a routine session of intimidation. Then he told her that Elilan had been killed in the fighting, and that he could show her photographs to prove it.

She didn't believe him, she said. She had seen him surrender to the army with her own eyes.

At this, Hathurusinghe grew wild. '[He] said I must stop blaming the army and say instead that it was the LTTE that shot and shelled the people,' Ananthy recorded later in a letter to the Norwegian government. 'He asked me if I had complained to any organization about my husband's disappearance. I told him I had lodged complaints with the Red Cross and Human Rights Commission . . . He told me if I continued to talk about my husband's whereabouts with anyone, he would shoot me and my children.'

This was coercion, simple and ugly. But there were also marginally craftier ruses attempted to keep Ananthy quiet, devised by people who spent their time thinking about these things. Ananthy once received a telephone call from a man who said that he worked for the TID. He spoke in Tamil, in a low, anodyne voice. Elilan was alive and well, the caller told her, and he would be returned to her in a few months if only she stopped speaking out in public about his disappearance and surrender. It was she who was standing in the way of Elilan's release, the caller suggested. Ananthy weighed this, the gilt-edged word of a TID man, and decided that she should, if anything, agitate louder.

Her best chance of finding a sympathetic audience arose in

September 2010, when the Lessons Learned and Reconciliation Commission held public hearings in Kilinochchi. A local government official had already selected a few people to present their testimonies before the commission, but word had spread rapidly about the hearings; by 10 a.m. on a Saturday morning, when the eight members of the commission took their seats in the district secretariat, a couple of hundred people had clustered outside the doors. 'The TID was there, and they weren't allowing anybody in at first,' Ananthy said. 'They checked our bags and turned some of us away. Then they asked all of us to write down our depositions first and hand it over to them. Nobody had pen or paper, and a lot of the people there couldn't write.' Ananthy went home, wrote out her complaint, and returned at 12.30 p.m., when some of the crowd had leaked away.

In the official transcripts of the day's hearings, the conversations run not between the commissioners and the Tamil public but between the commissioners and the translator, who is condensing and patting into shape the testimonies being delivered:

> *[Translator] At Omanthai Army investigation centre her husband was taken on the 4th of May 2009. We were taken to Ananda Coomaraswamy Welfare Centre Detention Camp and we were informed through the ICRC that he was being detained at the Omanthai detention camp. For 6 months from the inception of his detention we couldn't see him . . .*
>
> *Q. Where is he now?*
> *A. They told us that he was going to be released but subsequently he was taken to the . . .*
> *Q. Where is he now?*
> *A. He is at Omanthai.*
> *Q. Omanthai. So ask her to give those particulars.*

A. She says his one leg is amputated.
Q. So ask her to say that also. How was the leg
amputated?
A. He was in the LTTE.
Q. So give all those particulars to her.
A. We have made written appeals on many occasions
but no . . .
Q. Ask her not to be frightened, but to give all those
details.
[Translator] I have told them, sir, all that. I have told
them. Very clearly I have told them, very elaborately
in detail I have told them.

It is clear, from the transcripts, that the commission is being swarmed with the relatives of missing people. Again and again, the chairman or one of the members tells the assembly that the details of those missing must be put into writing and submitted. 'We have reserved a special day where the TID is coming to meet us,' the chairman says to the translator. 'Say that we have summoned the TID to give us particulars about people who are in camps, and we will question the TID and find out what material is available against the persons whom they are complaining about and then try to expedite their release. You tell them.'

Ananthy testified in camera, when the room had been emptied of everybody but herself, the commissioners and the translator. Her session lasted more than half an hour. 'It was the middle of the afternoon, and all these people looked like they were falling asleep. The chairman was actually nodding off!' Twice she bolted out of her seat, beside herself in outrage. 'They asked me such inane question, like: "How close were you to Elilan when he surrendered to the army? Are you sure it was him? How can you be sure it was him?"' After she spoke for 15 minutes, the chairman motioned to the translator to switch off the tape recorder. 'At that point, I lost all confidence,' she said. Ananthy's deposition does not appear in the final version of the official transcript.

The last time I saw Ananthy, before I left Sri Lanka, was when she had come to Colombo for a day. 'I'm here in the Kolpetty area,' she said on the phone. It was a Saturday morning. I hadn't known that she would be in town, and I had been lazing over my breakfast when she called. 'Come over, if you can? I'm sure I'll be made to wait here for hours anyway.' She was visiting the Centre for Human Rights and Development, yet another NGO that probed cases of missing people. In May 2009, the centre's own programme manager had vanished, after he had been abducted by men bearing guns and dressed in army uniforms.

The centre occupied a set of hutch-like rooms on the ground floor of the Ceylon Estates Staff Union building, on one of the many slender Kolpetty streets that lie perfectly parallel to each other, like the teeth of a comb. The ocean lay at the end of every one of these roads, and from the Ceylon Estates Staff Union building, I could just spot the slice of aquamarine wedged between the sky and the land. It looked bracing and inviting, and for a moment I was tempted to dally for another half hour so that I could sit by the sea and be worked over by the wind.

Ananthy wanted some air too, so we stood and talked by the gate of the Ceylon Estates Staff Union building. One of her friends, a doctor, had been recommending that she perhaps see a psychiatrist, to help dissolve some of the trauma that had calcified inside her. 'If I do that, though, they'll dismiss me as a madwoman, and everything I say will be dismissed as lies. So that isn't an option,' she said. 'But it's true, my thoughts are a mess. I'm at a stage where everything that went before the last day of the war, and everything that came after—it's all melting together.'

I misunderstood her. 'Do you mean you're beginning to have doubts about where Elilan went?'

'What? No!' she snapped back. 'I'm sure about that, and I'm sure the army has him.' But she was starting to reflect on the wisdom of her persistence, she said. 'My daughters have stopped watching films entirely, because if they see someone on screen beaten or killed, they'll come crying to me, saying: "The army would have beaten him like this, wouldn't they?" So I'm in a dilemma, because I want to pursue it, but at the same time, all this uncertainty is so awful for them.'

Around her right wrist, Ananthy wore a loop of thin thread that was bleached pale now, but that would have been turmeric yellow six months earlier, when she tied it on during the Tamil festival of Karadaiyan Nombu. The festival remembers the courage of Savitri, whose story is found in one of the byways of the Mahabharata, narrated by a sage when he is asked: 'Has there ever been a woman whose devotion matched my wife's?'

Even as Savitri, a young princess, marries a prince named Satyavan, she knows that he is destined to die in a year. It has been written, and the texts of fate are indelible. On the foretold day of his death, Savitri goes with Satyavan into the forest, and after he dies while he is chopping wood, Yama, the lord of the shades, arrives to claim his soul. Like a female Orpheus, Savitri follows Yama, intent on wresting back her partner from the realm of the dead.

'Turn back, Savitri,' Yama instructs her, 'for your husband is gone.' When she refuses, he offers to give her anything she wants—anything at all, except Satyavan's life. Savitri asks first for her father-in-law's sight and kingdom to be restored to him, and then for her father to have many more children, so Yama grants these boons. But when Savitri continues to trail him doggedly, further and further into the underworld, he promises to fulfil one last wish.

'Give me children as well, then, and let them be the children of Satyavan only,' she asks of the god of death.

Yama is tickled by the cunning of this request. How can he grant it, except by reanimating her husband? 'You shall have it, Savitri. Satyavan shall be returned to you.'

After Yama shimmers away, Savitri cradles her husband's head in her lap until life washes back into him.

'Have I been asleep?' he wonders. 'I dreamed that I had died.'

'Death has come and passed you by,' Savitri replies. She helps him to his feet. 'Come now. We have a long way home.'

It felt like a grave breach of manners to ask Ananthy if she thought Elilan was still alive, so I never did. She must believe that he was, I reasoned; she was working too hard for someone who knew that her cause was already a lost one. But there were times when I thought she was wilfully deluding herself, as if by stretching this period of limbo she could keep one foot in 16 May 2009, when her family was intact and the Eelam movement was still the barest bit alive. Acknowledging Elilan's death would involve acknowledging how convulsively her life and her world had changed, a process laced with so much pain that even this present torment of knowing nothing and fearing the worst was preferable.

6

IN THOSE DAYS, like Ananthy, I too shuttled between two distinct slices of time. I would spend hours with her, or with others who had squeezed through the war alive, and in those moments I inhabited their memories—of the 1983 riots, or of the siege of Jaffna, or of April–May 2009. Then I would find the exit and return to my life in post-war Sri Lanka, in which Ananthy was searching for Elilan, Buddhist radicals were harassing Muslims, and the army tightened its grip over the island.

Gradually, in my head, the boundaries between these slices of time—between wartime and post-war Sri Lanka—melted away. The phrase 'post-war' lost its meaning. What country, after all, had ever passed cleanly from one epoch to another within the space of a day? Outright battle had stopped, but an unbroken arc of violence stretched from the war right into our midst. The present conversed with the past. The Rajapaksas presided over the peace in much the same way that they had presided over the war, with arrogance and force. People still lived in fear, and some of them still died in sudden, unnatural ways. Anger still rippled through the island. The state still pummelled its society to submit before its powers. Having acquired the temperament of a country at war, Sri Lanka had forgotten any other way to live.

Colombo milled fresh rumours of violence daily: who had ordered a hit on whom; who was beaten up in the street or threatened with harm over the phone; what transpired during police detentions. During three months in 2012, the newspapers reported 21 cases of missing people and attempted abductions—one every four days, Tamils and Sinhalese alike vanishing into the void. The word used most often in these reports was 'disappearance,' but in its verb form, an external agency was tacked on to it, which rendered it ungrammatical but also more accurate. 'He was disappeared,' which is to say, 'He was made to disappear.'

Everybody appeared to know that many of these disappearances were the work of either state security forces or the goons of individual politicians. As a matter of further alarm, it wasn't even always possible to distinguish state security forces from the goons of individual politicians. The president and his brother Gotabhaya, as well as a couple of other powerful figures in their government, were each believed to be operating their own personal death squads. The state still ran the unmarked white vans it had so grown to love since the 1990s, using them to stage abductions and teach dissidents lessons. As you walked to the shops one evening, a white van pulled up next to you, its door slid open, men pulled you in, and it sped off. If you were lucky, you were deposited somewhere remote, with only light torture marks or a broken limb.

People had been disappearing in this manner for decades in Sri Lanka, ever since the first Marxist insurrection in 1971. I once met a man who had, in March 1974, been arrested for publishing a little Communist newsletter. 'Arrested,' though, is almost certainly the wrong word: it implies a warrant, a judicial foundation, the start of a familiar process. Instead, officers from the Criminal Investigation Department dropped by at his house, took him away, and kept him for the next two years.

'That long?' I asked him. 'What did they do with you for two years?'

He was a gnome of a man, wearing spectacles so thick that, in magnifying his eyes, they leached them of every expression except bewilderment. 'They were very angry with me,' he said. 'They'd put a ledger on my head and then hit me on the ledger with a stick, so that there were no marks directly on my scalp. They'd insert my penis into an open drawer and then slam it shut. They'd bring me to a house here in Longdon Place'—a particularly ritzy neighbourhood of the city—'and they'd beat me up in that empty house. They'd ask me to talk about dialectical materialism, and when I did, they'd hit me for that.'

'How many times did this happen?' I asked.

'Oh, many, many times,' he said. 'For four hours a day, for days and days on end.' The state was nothing if not assiduous when in its exercise of violence. It was almost as if the violence itself was a duty, owed by Sri Lanka to its people along with elections, clean water and public transport.

These attentions were visited frequently upon journalists: violence as reprisal for writing about violence. 'You need to be careful,' I was warned again and again. For most of my time there, though, my mind inhabited two contradictory spaces: believing indeed that the state could be swiftly brutal towards those prying into its ugly secrets, but believing also, and against all reason, that I was not in danger myself. Perhaps such foolish exceptionalism is the real essence of bravado. Only with the passage of many months, as the incidence of attacks upon journalists started to mount, did I begin to feel jolts of fear. In Colombo, a visa official would take an unusually long time peering at his terminal and my pulse would quicken. In Kilinochchi, I would spot a white van driving past me and my stomach would twist itself into sick knots. If I left the country for a week, I always returned fully expecting to not be let back in, thinking also that this summary denial of entry was in some ways the best of many possible alternatives.

One journalist who was resigned, well in advance, to an unnatural death was Lasantha Wickrematunge, the editor of the *Sunday Leader* and a Sinhalese. Wickrematunge's newspaper was often shrill and gossipy, and not without its own deep prejudices, but it had stood in grand defiance against the Rajapaksa government and its abuses of power. The president once called Wickrematunge to yell furiously at him, promising in a moment of rash honesty that he would be killed if he went on criticizing the government. Gotabhaya Rajapaksa, the defence secretary, sued the *Sunday Leader* for defamation when the newspaper claimed that he had cut corrupt defence deals. Other more anonymous threats reached Wickrematunge as well, breathtaking in their lack of subtlety: arson at the shed that housed the paper's printing press; a funeral wreath delivered to his house; a page of the *Sunday Leader* ripped out and sent to him, with 'If you write you will be killed' smeared in red paint across the newsprint.

On 8 January 2009, at 10.30 a.m., four men on motorcycles blocked Wickrematunge's car on the road. One of them shattered the glass of a window, stuck a gun into the car, and spat bullets into the editor. A man in a car, driving to work, and killed for it. I thought of Neelan Tiruchelvam, bombed to death in his Nissan by the Tigers—such a similar death, except that Wickrematunge seemed to have been killed by the men who protected the country from the Tigers. In the long war, the two sides had grown closer in temper than either would have cared to admit.

Nobody was arrested for Wickrematunge's murder, and everybody knew that nobody would be arrested. 'Everyone is asking how four motorbikes could get in that high-security zone and carry out that attack,' one Colombo journalist told the *Guardian*. 'You can't go out to buy two aspirins without being stopped at a checkpoint. This kind of attack couldn't be done by someone without influence.' Then the journalist said: 'Please don't name me. They'll come for me next.'

The next day, Wickrematunge's wife, Sonali, announced the discovery, on his office computer, of a document labelled 'Final Ed.' It was a 2500-word column to be published in the event of the assassination that Wickrematunge knew would come. Maybe he had written it in advance, intending his voice to sound from beyond the grave. Or, as some people thought, maybe Sonali had written the column under the byline of a dead man—a perfect *J'accuse*, its author far out of reach.

He had been assaulted in the past, the Wickrematunge of the column wrote. 'I have reason to believe the attacks were inspired by the government. When finally I am killed, it will be the government that kills me.' Then he addressed himself directly to Mahinda Rajapaksa, whom he had known, and once even been friendly with, for nearly three decades. Rajapaksa was 'drunk with power,' and he had 'trampled on human rights, nurtured unbridled corruption and squandered public money . . . Indeed, your conduct has been like a small child suddenly let loose in a toyshop. That analogy is perhaps inapt because no child could have caused so much blood to be spilled on this land as you have.'

But Rajapaksa himself would not have commissioned his murder, Wickrematunge thought; instead, he hinted at some shadowy, more malevolent planner: Gotabhaya, the president's lightly moustached, grizzled brother, the one with the smile of a shark and the small black-onyx eyes. Mahinda would fail him, Wickrematunge predicted, only by sitting on his hands in a most unpresidential way:

In the wake of my death I know you will make all the usual sanctimonious noises and call upon the police to hold a swift and thorough inquiry. But like all the inquiries you have ordered in the past, nothing will come of this one, too. For truth be told, we both know who will be behind my death, but dare not call his name. Not just my life, but yours too, depends on it . . . As anguished as I know you will be, I also know that you will have no choice but to protect my killers: you will see to it that the guilty one is never convicted. You have no choice.

Arjuna and I—Arjuna not being his real name—sat at a table in the sun-flooded veranda of the Cricket Club Cafe, in Colombo. Even though it was late in the afternoon, on a weekday, every table around us was occupied, bottles of beer still being diligently emptied and exchanged for full ones.

'How are all these people out drinking on a weekday afternoon?' I asked Arjuna. 'Don't they have places to be, or work to do?'

'You and I are out drinking on a weekday afternoon,' Arjuna retorted. He tapped with a fingernail the Lion Lager bottle sweating on the table between us. 'What's the difference?'

Arjuna knew people. He wasn't in public service himself, but he knew ministers and sundry bureaucrats, and from them he learned of things that went on within the government. He didn't do anything with this knowledge—he wasn't a reporter or a lawyer or an activist—and perhaps that was why he continued to receive it.

That afternoon, the subject of Prageeth Eknaligoda came up. Prageeth, a journalist, had been missing for more than two years, since January 2010, and I had met his wife, Sandhya, who—much like Ananthy—had been hammering on the doors of the government, demanding to know what had happened to her husband.

'He's dead,' Arjuna said.

'Are you sure?'

Arjuna stopped himself from replying. A waiter was gliding towards us to clear away our empty plates. 'You've got to be careful these days,' Arjuna said, when we were alone again. He pointed to my phone, which was on the table, recording our conversation. 'Listen, can we kill this for a second?'

I switched it off. 'How do you know Prageeth is dead?'

'I know Prageeth is dead because a government minister told me he's dead. But also because no one abducts a diabetic and keeps him alive for two years. The insulin costs too much.'

Arjuna chewed his beer. I suddenly felt exhausted. My brain refused to absorb the news of one more death, as if it was just full to its brim and was now shutting down in protest. 'I wonder if Sandhya knows this,' I said.

'She has been told, many times,' Arjuna said. His voice had dropped even further. He had known Prageeth once, been friends with him. 'I don't know if she believes it. Maybe she's in denial, and maybe that is her coping mechanism. It's crazy. But Prageeth is dead. Definitely. He was abducted, and he was killed.'

The government did not let on, of course. Sandhya wrote to the Human Rights Commission of Sri Lanka, to the United Nations, to the attorney general and to the president. She badgered the police, who would say only that an investigation was in slow progress. She filed a habeas corpus motion, but the court took two years and 22 hearings to even order an inquiry to be conducted. After the 21st hearing, when the judge had adjourned the case yet again, she came out of the courtroom and, right there in the corridors of justice, howled and wept with pure anger. 'I'm not crying to get my husband back now,' she said. 'I'm crying because this is what our judiciary has come to.' She procured the personal phone numbers of the country's top ministers, so that she could call them and ask them to intervene personally in Prageeth's case. They hung up on her. She wrote to Shiranthi Rajapaksa, the first lady, appealing to her, wife to wife, and asking for her assistance. Through this all, she was followed, her phone was tapped, and her email was hacked into. She didn't care. There was nothing in her soul that she wasn't already baring to the world.

In November 2011, Sri Lanka's attorney general told the media that Prageeth was living, whole and well, in a foreign country. He provided no further elucidation. This was an odd proclamation to make about a missing man, and an odder way still to assure his wife and children that the government had nothing to do with his disappearance. So Sandhya called a press conference, in which she posed some patently obvious questions.

If people in the government knew this much, why didn't they tell her more?

Why didn't they tell her where precisely Prageeth lived now? Or give her his phone number?

Why didn't they produce more information, so that she could stop her public campaigns of denouncing the government and blaming it for his disappearance?

Droves of reporters attended at the press conference, quite possibly in solidarity, since Prageeth had been one of them. Sandhya had invited representatives from the government as well, but no one came.

I met Sandhya for the first time later that day, in a conference room at the NGO where my friend Romesh de Silva (as I'll call him) worked; Romesh, who had led me to Ananthy, was working on Prageeth's case as well. Sandhya had changed three buses, riding right across the congested heart of Colombo before walking the last couple of kilometres. Even when she was sitting, she seemed kinetic, as if she was bursting out of herself.

'She's manic,' one of Romesh's colleagues said to me later.

'If I live one day out of her life, I'll fall flat on my face. She goes to court every day when Prageeth's case is being heard, sits through proceedings, walks to save money on bus fare, comes home around 9 p.m.—and all this on a bun and countless cups of tea. It's like if she stops, it would be an admission of defeat. She's very different from the woman I knew a year ago. Back then, she'd be crying all the time, and she'd read me poems she wrote to him. Now she's a hardened, but very depressed, warrior.'

Sandhya sat at the table, next to my friend Subha, who knew her and who had agreed to translate between my English and her Sinhalese. Sandhya had a round face, hair curled into a bun, and a sari tied and tucked with pin-neat precision; she would have looked every inch the Sinhalese hausfrau, had it not been for her tight, clenched jaw. She put her hands out in front of her and clasped them together, prepared to talk about Prageeth. This was what she had done nearly every day since January 2011: talk about Prageeth, talk to everyone she could about him, hoping that her loquacity would shame the government into starting a real, credible inquiry, and hoping that her loudness would keep her safe, because it is risky even for a government to reduce the vociferous wife of a disappeared man into sudden silence.

Sandhya met Prageeth in 1989, when she was working on women's development with a Colombo NGO, and when he was a dabbler: in trade union affairs, in journalism, in cartooning. He had promised to help her NGO assemble its own in-house publication, so one day Sandhya was sent over to see him. When she arrived, he was sketching a portrait of the Indian film-maker Satyajit Ray, and even after she entered, he didn't turn around or acknowledge her; he went on working, brow furrowed, for another 10 minutes, until he had finished his drawing. 'That was what I was attracted to first:

his art, his drawings,' Sandhya said. Years later, when they had their first son, they named him Satyajit, in honour of their very first encounter; then they found out that, by remarkable coincidence, their son shared his birthday with Satyajit Ray.

'We became friends, and until 1992, we were really just friends,' Sandhya said. 'I wrote a little also at that time. I wrote poetry, and I wrote this children's story, which he illustrated. We entered it into a competition, and we came second.' They spent all their time together, so it surprised no one when they decided, in the summer of 1992, to get married.

Sandhya had a photograph with her, of the day of her wedding. She is standing with Prageeth outside the registrar's office, dressed in an olive-green sari, smiling blissfully. 'I only got dressed up because my mother wanted a photo,' she said. 'We were both sure that we didn't want a big wedding, because we were both unemployed at the time.' Prageeth, rakishly good-looking, with a trim beard and a third of a grin, stands next to Sandhya. It isn't immediately visible, but sandwiched between their bodies are their hands, entwined tightly in each other's, as if they are frightened to ever let go.

Prageeth found a job as a cartoonist at the state-owned Lake House group, which publishes a host of magazines and newspapers. But just as Satyajit was born, a couple of years later, Prageeth quit.

'How come?' I asked.

'They had told him to design a poster he didn't want to do,' Sandhya said. 'It was a character assassination of some opposition leader. And he didn't want to do any work of that sort.'

Whatever else Sandhya and Prageeth disagreed on, their minds were in perfect union when it came to politics. 'Prageeth was opposed to the war,' she said. 'He was in favour of a federal solution—a federal Sri Lanka. The Tamils had a right to govern themselves, he'd say.' Prageeth distrusted the government. He had seen its vengeful whims at work when some of his friends—Marxists who may or may not have participated in the 1987 insurrection—were killed or disappeared. He had been roughed up himself, once in his village of Matale, when police rounded up an assortment of suspected Marxist revolutionaries and beat them, and then once again during the insurrection, on a road near his house. 'He lived in constant fear, and he never went to the police,' Sandhya said. 'Going to the police meant that you were making a statement against the government, and he didn't want to do that.'

'Where did he work after Lake House?' I asked.

Sandhya pinched the bridge of her nose, between her eyes, to think. She did this so often that I thought she was coping secretly with a headache. 'He was only a freelancer after that,' she said. 'He mainly liked to draw, to do cartoons. But he wrote articles also, because we needed the money.' Sandhya had stopped working full-time; their second son, Harit, had been born in 1997, and the two little boys consumed all her energies at home.

Somebody had shown me a collection of Prageeth's political cartoons, which appeared in several publications, in print as well as online. He was a polemicist, fond of attacking the government in unsubtle ways, and he wrote captions intending them to be aphorisms. 'The parliament helps maintain a Neanderthal darkness,' he wrote under a sketch of a primitive man carrying a stone axe and a ballot box. 'War for peace is seen as the new slogan, but it is really peace towards war,' was another caption, accompanying a cartoon of a politician dressed and built like Mahinda Rajapaksa, one of his hands holding a revolver, his teeth masticating a flower. Prageeth's best images were haunting in themselves; they did not require his hectoring text as further exposition. In an untitled, single-panel drawing, a fountain pen bends in servility towards a Rajapaksa figure, bleeding a single drop of ink from its nib. Rajapaksa looks contemptuously down at the media he has just subdued. The landscape is stark and sere, and a livid sun glares down from the sky.

In his articles, Prageeth hit similar notes of acid—and occasionally hysterical—commentary. 'He was a good spinner,' Arjuna had said, when I asked him for his opinion on Prageeth's journalism. 'See, during that period, the truth in Sri Lanka was so distorted that what you needed to be a good journalist was the ability to spin.' He meant this as a compliment; he meant to say that Prageeth could marshal a sharp opinion out of a bewilderment of facts and half-rumours and aim it squarely at the government. This was useful work.

Then, as the war advanced towards its finish, Prageeth began, with the help of a contact in the military, to put together some investigative stories: about spurious arms transactions, and about the use of chemical weapons against the Tigers and civilians. At the same time, he also published articles about a government minister who beat his wife and kept her prisoner at home, and it may have been these titillating pieces—rather than the ones about the army—that daubed the bullseye on to his back. 'That's how things are in Sri Lankan politics. Everything goes, including personal attacks. Even now, things are personal and political at the same time. There's no sanctity here.' Arjuna stared away into space for a few seconds. 'He was a mild-mannered guy, really. Prageeth, I mean. He was passionate and set in his thoughts, but he was such a gentle soul in person. It's just that he painted everything big. Big portraits, big scenery, big issues, big everything.'

In 2005, right around the time he was becoming more vocal

in his criticisms of the government, Prageeth underwent heart bypass surgery. He had always been a heavy smoker and committed to his drink, and when he was 35, he was diagnosed with diabetes and prescribed two doses of insulin a day. The surgery seemed to lend him new fervour.

'Prageeth was depressed about the way the war was going, but he was also furious,' Sandhya said. 'He was constantly working, and he started attacking Mahinda and his presidency more and more. Some friends of his, who had sources in the government, began to tell him that he was making the people in power angry. He was convinced that he had evidence about these chemical weapons being used. He had seen photos of civilians with horrific injuries.'

In 2007, the phone calls began. They delivered crisp, blunt messages. 'Stop writing or we'll cut your hands off.'

'Did they call him at home?' I asked.

'At home, and also on his cell phone,' Sandhya said. She held her head again, her eyes screwed shut in recollection. 'He never discussed the calls much with us, and of course our sons never knew. He would just come home and tell me: "I got another phone call today." I don't know everything they said to him, although I think they talked often about cutting off his hands.'

'And how often would these calls come?'

'Not often,' Sandhya said. Then it seemed to strike her, as if for the first time, that she didn't truly know. 'Actually, I'm not sure. Since he didn't say much about the calls to me, maybe he received more of them than he let on.'

In August 2009, Prageeth was abducted for the first time.

He had gone to Dambulla for the day, and at 10 p.m. he was on the bus back to Colombo. 'I'll be home in an hour or so,' he told Sandhya. Midnight slipped past, and when Sandhya tried his cell phone, it rang but there was no answer; when she tried again, it had been switched off. Sandhya spent an agonized night dialling Prageeth's phone at intervals, willing it to ring.

'What should I do? Something is definitely wrong,' she told a friend the next morning.

'Let's wait. Let's not worry yet,' he advised her. 'I'll keep trying the number also.'

At 11 a.m., Prageeth answered his phone. He sounded drained and ill. 'Bring me a pair of slippers and come to the bus stop near our house,' he said. So Sandhya put his slippers into a plastic bag and rushed to the bus stop, where Prageeth eventually staggered off a bus, his feet bare, his ID and his wallet and keys in a shopping bag. They went home.

'What do you think happened to me?' Prageeth said.

'I have no idea,' Sandhya replied. 'I cannot even begin to guess.'

Prageeth had gotten off his bus the previous night and was walking home when a white van without a number plate blocked his path. Two men wearing masks hopped out, handcuffed him, and instructed him to lie flat on the floor of the van. Around his eyes, they cinched a big, dirty singlet, of the sort worn by a man above his sarong. They drove for what felt like an hour or more, and throughout this time, the men rained questions upon Prageeth.

'Do you remember who was sitting next to you on the train?'

'What?' Prageeth replied. 'I wasn't travelling by train.'

'Who was that man?'

'I don't know what you're talking about.'

In a rare spell of silence, Prageeth said: 'I have some medicines in my shirt pocket, and I need to take them. Can you give them to me?'

The men refused. 'When you meet our boss, you can have your medicine.'

The van stopped at a deserted building, and the men hustled

Prageeth into a room and handcuffed his arms around a post that rose up to the ceiling. The room was airless and lit by a single high-voltage bulb, and it was bright and hot. Somewhere Prageeth could hear a strange, high-pitched noise—intended to disorient him, he thought.

Through the night, more questions about the train. Who sat next to him? Who was that man? What did they speak about? And yet not a single reference to his articles or his cartoons. Prageeth's perplexity deepened.

In the morning, the boss arrived, a deeper-voiced man, clearly in control. 'It looks like we may have made a mistake. I'll tell them to take you back. Don't tell anybody about all this.'

Prageeth flared into rage. 'How could they have made a mistake? They have my ID!'

Another man responded: harder, more thuggish. 'You have too much of a mouth on you. Be careful of what you say.'

The men untied Prageeth's eyes and shoved him into a bathroom, where he washed his face. He remembered seeing shirts stained with blood lying on the floor. Then he was handcuffed and blindfolded again, returned to the van, and dropped in an unfamiliar suburb of Colombo, far from where he was picked up. They had taken all his personal belongings earlier, and these they now dumped unceremoniously back into his hands; Prageeth had to tear the singlet off his eyes and then ask for a plastic shopping bag from a shop nearby, to hold his things. They never returned his shoes.

'Did he go to the police?' I asked.

'He didn't want to, at first,' Sandhya said. 'But when word got around, many of his friends called him and urged him to file a complaint. So he went and did that. They took that singlet as evidence. But nothing came out of it.'

After this abduction, Arjuna warned him. 'Man, if you keep this stuff up, they're going to kill you.'

'No, don't worry,' Prageeth said. 'I'll be fine. I know how to look after myself.'

'Did he grow more watchful after that?' I asked.

Arjuna shrugged. 'No, I think he was careless. I think he didn't care. The way he saw it, the whole incident was a power trip. He said: "If these men are abducting you and they're the one covering their faces, then who holds the power?" Who's the one who's scared?' I told him that he couldn't think that way, that this was a warning to him. He said: "I understand that. But I need to do what I need to do, what I think is the right thing to do."'

7

WHAT WAS HAPPENING to Prageeth was also happening to many other journalists. Through threats and blows, the state was scraping away at their lives, fraying them thin.

One journalist found that, every time he came out of his house, a helmeted man on a motorcycle was waiting patiently for him; if he wanted to walk to the bus stop, the motorcycle followed, making no effort to hide itself. 'The first time, I panicked. Then after two weeks, it felt normal. I learned to look upon him as a faithful shadow.' Another journalist was abducted and released twice, so when he got a telephone call asking him for his hard disk, he scrambled out of town. For a year, he hid out in villages, in Buddhist temples, in the homes of friends. The first night he was back in Colombo, as he was walking to his house, he saw a man with a gun hiding behind a large water tank. He fled indoors and, not knowing what else to do, dialled the police; then, as he watched from a corner of his window, he saw the man with the gun receive a call on his cell phone. The man departed. Fifteen minutes later, a white van rumbled slowly down the road, as if it was examining its terrain. The journalist left Sri Lanka not long after.

In New York, I met Poddala Jayantha, more grin than man, a journalist who had applied for asylum in the United States and now worked as a janitor on Staten Island. On a June evening in 2009, Jayantha had been bundled into a white van by six men, who covered his eyes, tied his hands behind his back, and snipped off chunks of his hair and beard to stuff into his mouth. Then they proceeded to pulp Jayantha's left ankle with a wooden club, a methodical destruction, as if they were line cooks tenderizing meat for an evening service. Jayantha needed two plates and six bolts screwed into his leg to walk again. The attack occurred in near-total silence, except for one raspy warning: 'Don't write against the government. If you do, you'll be shot dead.'

Had you been warned earlier? I asked Jayantha.

'Oh yes,' he said, with an empty laugh. His skin was speckled with vitiligo; his doctors had told him that stress had aggravated the condition. 'Many times. Once, I remember, I and two other journalists were leaving Lasantha Wickrematunge's funeral, and we were just standing on the road, talking to each other, when all our cell phones rang. At the same instant! And we picked up, and we all got the same message. "If you go on doing what you're doing, we'll have to light candles for your funeral as well."' As if the threats were not dramatic enough, there was this added theatre of the synchronized calls, a bonus piece of proof for emphasis. This is how closely we are watching you, this is how hot our breath is on the backs of your necks.

In the conference room that afternoon, Sandhya was flagging. She looked depressed and worn from rehearsing Prageeth's life, and from rehearsing her own life, which had frozen to a halt the day her husband was abducted one last time. We hadn't talked about that yet, but I was reluctant to press her any more.

Subha, my friend, stepped in. 'Sandhya, maybe we can come to see you at your house on the weekend? And talk about how Prageeth disappeared then?'

Sandhya nodded in dull agreement. She had to catch the bus

back anyway, to be home for her sons, she said. But we could come over in two days. That would be fine.

In that slim window of time, a devastating story about Prageeth surfaced. A two-bit hoodlum, in the custody of the Criminal Investigation Department, had admitted under interrogation that he had, a couple of years previously, been ordered by a politician to dump Prageeth's body into the sea just north of Colombo. How this scrap of information sped from the CID's interrogation chambers into the city's newsrooms was not made clear. The gangster had further said, according to the reports, that his instructions had descended to him from the 'big boss,' Gotabhaya Rajapaksa, and that Prageeth's had been one of many bodies wrapped in rough sacking, trussed to blocks of granite, and tipped into the ocean. It was only later, during a party at the Hilton, that one of his minders had told him that he had just disposed of Prageeth Eknaligoda.

The next day, Subha and I took an autorickshaw south and west out of Colombo, to a suburb where a section of the Southern Expressway, running right down to Galle, was under construction. The air was clogged with dust and commotion, but then we turned into a modest residential neighbourhood and crept up a hillside, counting off the small bungalows until we reached Sandhya's house.

In the living room, I sat under a poster board, on which ranks of greeting cards had been affixed, each wishing Sandhya well and praying for Prageeth. Next to me, on a table, was a framed poster of Prageeth—his face, silhouetted against a bold yellow background, with the caption: '200 Days, Still Nothing.' Behind the poster stood a gigantic fish tank, home only to one big goldfish and two smaller ones. The tank's aerator steadily pushed bubbles to the surface of the water, making a sound all the while like an old man breathing noisily in his sleep.

Sandhya sat down, looking more emotional and overwrought than she had on our first meeting. She twisted her hands around each other, and she perched on the very lip of her chair, as if she wanted to bolt out of the room. She sent an apologetic smile in my direction, and then she turned to Subha and spoke in a torrent of Sinhalese.

Subha looked confused. She replied to Sandhya, and then she turned to me and said: 'She doesn't want to talk about Prageeth any more to you.'

I couldn't fathom this. 'Why? What happened?'

Subha and Sandhya spoke a little more, Subha's smile polite but strained, Sandhya appearing to become increasingly resolute about her decision. 'She says she doesn't see how this will advance her immediate agenda of getting Prageeth out, or getting justice for Prageeth,' Subha said to me. 'I told her that she needs to talk to journalists, to get the word out there about what happened, but she doesn't want to believe that. I think she's just upset today. Her son isn't well. She's having money problems.'

'Could you ask her if I could come back another day? Or maybe even in a month or so?'

'Maybe, maybe,' Sandhya murmured, a little too quickly. She smiled again at me. 'Thank you,' she said in English, with what sounded like firm finality.

In the autorickshaw heading back home, Subha continued to be puzzled. 'She has never done this before,' she said, looking out of the window speaking almost to herself. 'I don't know if she was just feeling particularly hopeless today. Was she indirectly asking for money? I don't think so. She isn't the type.' But I thought I understood. If you have to tell and retell the story of the greatest loss of your life, if your life has started to revolve wholly around that loss, and if each additional narration enhances your pain a little, or if it chips away a little at your conviction that you will find your husband again, you want the pain to be worth it. You want to greedily conserve what meagre peace of mind you possess, because it is all that can protect you when gangsters claim to have flung your husband's corpse into the ocean.

Later, from Romesh de Silva's colleagues, I managed to piece together the events of the evening on which Prageeth had disappeared. The details were scant and foggy, as if the abduction had happened a century ago, as if the memories of the people around him that night had crumbled and abraded as they do over decades instead of over two years.

On 24 January 2010, Prageeth and a few other journalists had met at the house of an editor of Lanka eNews, a website for which Prageeth frequently wrote. (For their protection, one of Romesh's associates told me, she couldn't reveal who these journalists were.) There was some drinking involved that evening, but Prageeth stayed sober, and he left at around 8 p.m. or 8.30 p.m. He may have said that he was going to meet a friend elsewhere, or he may have said that he was just returning home.

'How're you going?' somebody asked him. The presidential election was slightly more than forty-eight hours away. No journalist went anywhere alone in those days, and Prageeth had increasingly begun to feel as if he was being followed.

'Don't worry, I'm sorted,' Prageeth replied. Somebody was picking him up.

Prageeth left, and the group of friends continued to drink for another hour; then they decided that it would be a lark to drop in on an opposition politician for a final round or two. Much deeper into the night, when they had hailed an autorickshaw to take them home, their driver told them: 'Do you know a white van is following us?' They didn't know. They went home and stumbled into bed. The next morning, they heard the news that Prageeth was missing.

Not long after leaving the party, perhaps at a quarter to nine, one of Prageeth's other friends had called him on his cell phone. 'I'm headed towards Koswatta,' Prageeth had said. From the background noise, it had sounded as if he was in a vehicle. 'Koswatta is nowhere near his house, so clearly he was going somewhere else,' Romesh's colleague told me. 'And apparently he sounded normal on this call, so he must have been with somebody he trusted. Although really, in this kind of situation, you can't trust anybody, and you don't know if somebody was forcing him to reply in his regular tone of voice.'

Just as he was about to hang up, however, the friend heard Prageeth say: 'But this isn't the right route.'

Since his first abduction, Sandhya and Prageeth had evolved a custom: she would call him punctually at 9 p.m. every night to ask him how he was coming home, and she would continue to call, every half an hour or every hour, until he was safely back with her. Barely 15 minutes after Prageeth hung up with his friend, Sandhya tried his number. He didn't pick up. She called one of the journalists who had been with him earlier, who told her that Prageeth had left a while ago. She tried Prageeth's phone again and again, into the night. At some late hour, she started to hear an automated message that the phone had been switched off.

In the morning, Sandhya tore down to the police station to file a case. The officer on duty refused to accept her statement and accused her of lying or of overreacting. 'How do you know he's missing? I'm sure he'll come back.' It took her an hour and a half to convince them to register her complaint. By which time Prageeth had already been missing for 12 hours, the first 12 frantic hours of the rest of Sandhya's broken life.

8

FOR MONTHS AND months after the end of the war, the north-eastern shoulder of Sri Lanka, the territory that had been shredded and pitted by the final months of the fighting, was off limits to civilians. The land had to be demined; it had to be cleared of rubble and unspent shells, and human remains. Then the government began slowly to open up this section of the Vanni: the corridor running east from Kilinochchi to Mullaitivu, Puthukkudiyiruppu and Vattuvahal. But access was still restricted, and it wasn't always clear to whom it was restricted. When I heard that buses full of tourists were being permitted into Puthukkudiyiruppu and Vattuvahal, to see the site of the army's glorious triumph, I called a travel agent who arranged such excursions.

'Mmm, it'll be difficult for you,' she said.

'Because I'm not Sri Lankan?'

'Because you're not Sri Lankan, but also because you have a Tamil name, and because you're a journalist,' she said. It was a trifecta. The army checked the IDs of tourists entering these areas, she said. This was in October 2011, when somebody like me would have to get a permit in advance from the Ministry of Defence—a permit that would almost certainly not be granted.

A month later, Romesh called me. 'I'm headed into the Mullaitivu area in a week. Do you want to come?'

'I'm not sure I'm allowed in there,' I said.

'That's all right, we'll try our luck,' he replied. Romesh's work was often depressing, and he was beset by various pressures and watched with a beady, disapproving eye by the government, and yet he never sounded anything but blithe and cheerful. No situation was too dire to be massaged or worked around, he seemed to feel—and if it was, there was nothing you could do about it. 'I'll do the talking. You just sit in the back of the van and don't say anything.'

In Vavuniya, Romesh and I met up with Father Anthony Pandian, a middle-aged Tamil parish priest (Anthony Pandian is not his real name). 'He's our additional passport,' Romesh joked. 'The soldiers usually see his white habit and they let him through.' Fr Pandian, who had a chest like a barrel and a voice so deep it sounded as if it had been dragged up from the bowels of the earth, stroked his beard and grinned.

We crossed Omanthai late in the afternoon on a Monday, 28 November—one day after Heroes' Day, when the Tigers had annually remembered their dead, and two days after Prabhakaran's birthday. The Vanni felt strange and quiet—not noiseless, exactly, because there were still vehicles on the road as always, but filled with a more fundamental, prickling silence. The government had been anxious to stop any observances of Heroes' Day. Temples and churches were prohibited from pealing their bells. Another Hindu festival, which fell coincidentally on the same date and which involved the lighting of small lamps, had been banned. A local middle school, which had planned an environmental drive on Saturday, had been forced to cancel its programme. Any sort of collective action by Tamils—even by Tamil children picking up plastic bags—was considered suspect. 'One of my friends was preaching Sunday Mass at his church somewhere in this area,' Fr Pandian said, 'and apparently only five or eight people turned up, because everybody was so scared to leave their homes.'

We stopped for a few minutes at a church in Kilinochchi, where Fr Pandian needed to talk to a nun. Romesh and I sat in the courtyard, nibbled at by the mosquitoes that had amassed in the thick dusk. In a Tamil newspaper, I read that the army had swarmed over the campus of the University of Jaffna the previous day, intent on nipping any Heroes' Day commemorations in the bud. Even so, in fealty to a tradition of past years, a student, or a group of students, had managed to sneak up to the roof of one of the buildings, light a brace of candles, and hoist up on the flagpole a banner bearing the legend 'Heroes' Day' in Tamil. It wasn't even necessarily that the students wanted to celebrate fallen Tigers, I thought. It was just that, in a climate of repression, any gesture at all of insubordination—any thumb in the government's eye—was appealing and sweet.

The van turned right off the A9 after Kilinochchi, and we began to jounce along the A35, the highway that ran east and south to Mullaitivu. Like a vice, the night snapped quick and hard around us. The van's headlights could pick out only the next crater in the road, or the looming masses of scrub forest, or the barriers erected at army checkpoints. Every time we had to stop, a soldier would poke his head into the window of the passenger seat up front, where Fr Pandian was sitting; then he would survey Romesh and me, sitting in the middle row, upon which Romesh would say something soothing in Sinhalese. Once Fr Pandian had to show his ID card to a soldier, who examined it by flashlight and then waved us on.

We needed two and a half hours to travel the 65 kilometres to the outskirts of Mullaitivu, where we were to stay the night in a guest house owned by the local church. There was no running water or electricity in these parts; the guest house, a low two-room building, stood out only as a dim white smudge against the deeper blackness beyond. A caretaker who lived there had cooked us fish curry and rice, which we ate by the thin light of a candle. Then we sat on the veranda and dosed ourselves, sombrely and deliberately, on whisky, until we were sure that we would, oblivious to the mosquitoes and the heat, slip right off into sleep and not surface until daybreak.

The next morning, we drove towards and then through the town of Mullaitivu, over terrain that I could now see was swampy and malarial. The sides of the road teemed with waterbirds—snowy egrets, grebes, talkative gulls and ducks—and with the husks of destroyed buildings. The roads, such as they were, consisted either of loose gravel or, worse, powdery clay that the night's rain had carved into sharp-edged potholes and knee-high hillocks. Fr Pandian sat in the front passenger seat again, the golden cross on a chain around his neck swinging madly from side to side as the van lurched and wobbled. Ahead of us, there appeared a trio of girls in perfect white uniforms, riding their bicycles to school, their hair pinned back into plaits and lashed into place by bright red ribbons. They were laughing and shouting to each other as they rode. Amidst all the ruin, this was the most heartening sight in the world.

We reached Vattuvahal, the little village on the silvered Nandikadal Lagoon where the Sri Lankan military had crouched and waited, and from where it had shelled Mullivaikal, which was tucked into the vegetation on the opposite bank. This was the spot where Ananthy and hundreds of thousands of other Tamil refugees had arrived from across the water, during the last three days of the war, to give themselves over to the army. At our side of the causeway, a roadblock had been set up: a red-and-white wooden pole on a hinge, broken partly in the middle so that it looked like a splintered toothpick, and weighted by a cinder block tied to its end. No vehicles were allowed on to the causeway, but a row of squatting fishermen had been permitted to let lines and nets into the water. A dozen young uniformed soldiers with guns patrolled the area; as we watched, another truck full of soldiers in blue tracksuits arrived from Mullaitivu and stopped on the bank of the lagoon.

'Can we walk into Mullivaikal from here?' Romesh asked, feigning innocence, of one of the soldiers.

'No, you can't,' the soldier said, cordial and chatty. 'There may still be landmines or weapons lying around, so we're not allowing anybody over there. It isn't safe.' Romesh, ever sceptical, would scoff at this excuse later: 'How can they still be cleaning up those couple of square miles of land two and a half years later? What are they hiding?'

'What about from the other side? If we circle around the lagoon?' Romesh asked.

'No, sorry. It isn't allowed.'

With the help of some wheedling, Romesh obtained for us permission to just stroll over the length of the causeway. Halfway across, I squatted for a few minutes to peer into the water. The lagoon was swollen with rain, and a fisherman next to me was pulling up a net filled with slim, wriggling fish.

'What kind are those?' I asked.

'We call them Japan fish,' he said. This sounded like an interesting name, but he did not appear to be eager for conversation, so I let it drop.

'Which village are you from?'

'Mullivaikal,' he said.

'Have they let you go back to your village? After the war?'

'No. They say they're still clearing out landmines from there, so we can't go home.'

'How far can you go, then?'

He pointed to the other end of the causeway, where we could spot the tin roofs of a canteen that catered to soldiers. 'Until there. I can go and have a cup of tea there. But not further.'

I walked to the canteen, which was deserted. A large signboard had been erected nearby to proclaim to tourists in Sinhalese and English—but not in Tamil—the importance of the Vattuvahal causeway during the army's 'humanitarian operations' in May 2009. The explanation sounded fevered and breathless and repetitive, as if it was being delivered by a person who knew well that his facts were not quite true.

The ruthless terrorist were adamant of holding the innocent civilians as a human shield to influence the local and international pro terrorist organizations to bring a discredit for Sri Lanka Army as it was killing innocent civilians in the NFZ [No Fire Zone]. However, with an excellent command and prudent planning of the army, the brave soldiers of the great Army was able to conduct themselves stealthily across the lagoon from the West and East by dislodging the terrorist, from the shoulders of this Lagoon bank without harming the innocent civilians. This causeway has made a significant feature in the history of Counter Terrorist Operations in the world, by rescuing approximately 100,000 innocent civilians from the clutches of terrorists during the last stages of the Humanitarian Operation. However the frightened civilians were forced at gun point to prevent civilians fleeing from terrorist clutches towards Army controlled area.

We walked back over to Vattuvahal and into a tiny snack shop, right on the water next to the causeway. Romesh knew the owner, a man named Udaya Kumar, who once ran a full-service seafood restaurant at that very location but now sold only tea, sticky buns and Kik Cola. His wife was cooking their lunch on a stove at the back, and smoke filled the shop until my nose ran.

Udaya Kumar sat down with us for a cup of tea. His

restaurant had been destroyed in 2004, when the Indian Ocean tsunami pounded Sri Lanka's east coast, the wave of water sweeping into the lagoon and bearing down with fury upon every man-made structure on its banks. Udaya Kumar ran his tea shop for five years until the army began to advance into Mullaitivu and Vattuvahal; at that point, he and his wife fled across the causeway, hoping to find protection in the heaving population of Tamil refugees in Mullivaikal.

'That's where I lost my hand,' Udaya Kumar said. He had been sitting across the table with his arms crossed over his shallow chest, but now, with a sharp shock, I realized that his hand was missing altogether, and not just tucked behind his left arm as it had appeared. His right wrist ended in a stump criss-crossed in still-shiny scars. 'A shell exploded somewhere near me, and my hand was blown off.'

'Have you heard anything about your son?' Romesh asked.

Udaya Kumar's son had been forcibly drafted into the Tigers in 2008, and although he had escaped three times in nine months, he was always tracked down and pulled back in. They were all together, though, when they surrendered to the army in the late April of 2009. Udaya Kumar and his wife were sent to a welfare centre, from where they were released in 2010. Their son, however, was arrested for being a Tiger, and he was being held still at a detention camp in southern Sri Lanka. At least, this was what the authorities told Udaya Kumar. 'We haven't heard anything else about him at all,' he said, his face creased with grief.

'Where did you go after you were released from the welfare centre?' Fr Pandian asked.

'Where else could we go? We came back to Vattuvahal and started this shop.' This location, on the eastern lip of the island, had brought them nothing but misfortune, but this is where they had returned, now minus a son and a hand, to begin life from scratch a third time. And yet even having lives to renew and being able to go back to their home village were strokes of extravagant luck that had been denied to many, many others. In the wretchedness stakes of post-war Sri Lanka, there was always somebody worse off. Even hitting rock bottom was difficult because it was so thickly carpeted by the dead.

We got back on the road, driving now in a tight curve around Nandikadal Lagoon, heading north towards Puthukkudiyiruppu. The land was a scramble of fields and jungles; it had, at one time, been firmly held by the Tigers, who had been so optimistic of their longevity that they had seeded vast plantations of teak here. Now all of it—literally, acres and acres of land—was one extended army base. I could always spot, amidst the dark green of vegetation, the paler green of the roofs of the military's prefabricated sheds. Every few kilometres, a checkpoint shimmered ahead on the road. I crunched myself into the corner of my seat, hoping that the explanations Fr Pandian and Romesh were providing for our trip satisfied the soldiers enough for them to wave us through without asking for my ID.

At the main intersection of Puthukkudiyiruppu, the van was stopped again, and Romesh got out and went into an army shed to say that we just wanted to have a quick look around. This was where the tourist buses were usually cleared to proceed. Another van bearing seven or eight people had halted behind us, and out of its open windows, I could hear faint snatches of spoken Tamil.

Romesh climbed back in and said we could drive on. 'The van behind us? They didn't get permission to go in. They were a group of Tamils. The soldiers said they had to turn around.'

Puthukkudiyiruppu was a bombed out ghost town. Seven hundred families had once lived here, until the village was inundated by the 350,000 Tamils pressed eastwards by the

Tigers and by the army. Shells had fallen from the skies like scalding rain, and they had decimated nearly every building in sight. The few walls that remained standing were pierced with bullet holes, and weeds had begun to curl around their bases and into the masonry. The army had erected dozens of metal signboards around the village, featuring red skull-and-crossbones emblems, warning of still-buried landmines. Next to a small Hindu shrine was a tumble of brick that had once been the Puthukkudiyiruppu hospital, which had been targeted with meticulous rage by the army's shells. It hadn't been this thoroughly pulverized when he had been here a few months earlier, Romesh remembered. 'Of course, even at that time it was just one or two walls. But they seem to have knocked it down altogether now.'

One of the roads from the main intersection led to a war museum, assembled around the circumference of a marshy lake. In a shiny new information centre, along one long wall, 38 mounted posters described how the north-east was won, with fat black arrows marching over maps to show the progress of the army. The text on the posters was all in Sinhalese; so was the headline running across the top of the wall, reading: 'The way of the victorious Vanni operation.' So was the text in another exhibit, of photographs of arms and vehicles captured from the Tigers. This was a museum where Sinhalese people were encouraged to come to revel in, and to own, a Sinhalese victory. Even as the government gloried in winning a war that brought Tamils back into its fold, it held them at arm's length, kept them out of the project that was the unification of the Sri Lankan state. How could any Tamil—even a Tamil who believed fully in the notion of a whole Sri Lanka—not chafe at being doubly excluded from this museum, first by physical barriers and then by the barriers of language?

Outdoors, on the bank of the lake and in a large shed, were the spoils of war. Machine guns, rocket launchers, pistols and shoulder-borne anti-tank weapons, along with their ammunition, were arranged tidily on tables and shelves draped with black tarpaulin, all having been seized from the Tigers and now rusting rapidly away in the salt-flecked air. The weapons were crude and jury-rigged, slapped together by the Tigers out of spare parts in a metal shop. For all their international networks of arms and money, the Tigers' foremost genius had still lain in their ability to improvise, to convert little into more, to move base at the slightest hint of danger, to wage a war with nimble hands and quicksilver feet. Only when they acquired the heavier accoutrements of a military and fell into the regimented, leaden patterns of a traditional military did they make themselves vulnerable and easy to run to earth.

A lone soldier, stationed at the entrance of the shed, had grinned at Fr Pandian and me when we entered. There were no other tourists on the day, and the soldier had looked bored and hungry for conversation. He followed us into the armoury of relics and, as we walked around, said in Sinhalese, almost admiringly: 'They built all of these themselves. Can you believe it?'

'It's remarkable,' Fr Pandian replied.

They exchanged some further pleasantries in Sinhalese, but before the soldier had returned to his chair, I made the mistake of calling out a stray observation to Fr Pandian in Tamil. The soldier's face was suddenly scrubbed clean of its smile, replaced by a mixture of anger and embarrassment. When we left, I thanked him in English. He glanced away and refused to respond.

More captured equipment by the lake: small ships, patterned in white-and-black camouflage and used by the Sea Tigers in their sorties around the eastern and northern coastlines; tinier one-man vessels made of metal, described by a signboard, in Sinhalese and English, as 'Terrorist's Suicide Boats'; the fibreglass shells of speedboats, gutted of their engines. The boats sat on the long wheeled carts that had brought them there, in the velvet green shade of palmyra trees. They seemed utterly out of place, like cars in the ocean or camels in the snow.

I walked along a dirt path that had been marked out with boulders, hugging the far bank of the lake, until I came to a bridge with wooden planks and iron-piping handrails. The bridge led to the centre of the lake, where in December 2009 a victory monument had been installed upon an artificial islet. You could see what it was even from a distance: upon a square base, a mound of rocks cemented together, out of which rose a pedestal with the head and torso of a helmeted soldier, cast in bronze. In his left hand, he clutched a flagpole bearing the Sri Lankan flag. In his right, he held an AK-47 with a dove perched upon it; peace was won with the gun, and Sri Lanka would never let anybody forget it. The dove looked as if it might take flight at any second, its wings unfurled, but the soldier's grip upon his AK-47 was firm and unyielding.

The afternoon was clear and warm, and the sun bounced off the soldier's helmet, the light so fierce that it blinded me for a moment as I walked over the bridge to squint up at the sculpture. From the bank of the lake, the soldier had appeared to be cheering in jubilation and triumph. Closer up, though, his face was a contorted rictus, his eyes wide and joyless, and nothing seemed to be coming out of his mouth except an empty scream.

ACKNOWLEDGEMENTS

A sad reality about Sri Lanka today is that it is unwise for me to thank, by name, everybody who has helped in the writing of this book. Criticising the government is risky business, and abetting such criticism can invite dangerous attention from the state. More than a hundred people with whom I spoke requested that I keep them anonymous or leave them out of the book altogether. Dozens of others supported me and shared their company, and I leave their names out of these acknowledgements too, out of worry for their safety. Many others are already mentioned in these pages by name, and I must thank them once again for their time and patience.

This book wouldn't have gotten started without Ayeshea Perera and her family, who were my first hosts in Sri Lanka. Ayeshea has provided unstinting friendship and encouragement, and through her, I made many other friends. Sanjaya, Deanne, Sully, Dayan, Thilanka, Subha, Prasad, Venuri, Dinidu, Kanishka, Ravi—thank you for your immense warmth, your hospitality, and your company on Barefoot quiz nights. Aney Bung!

My profound gratitude to Nazreen and Dominic Sansoni for putting a roof over my head and for being generous with advice; to Sithie Tiruchelvam, for feeding me often and for her memories; to Samyuktha Varma and Martina Mascarenhas for high spirits and late-night shenanigans; to Soumya Balasubramanya and Kumari for hosting me so often; to Gananath Obeyesekere, for his wisdom.

Thanks to a vast host of people in India and Sri Lanka who brokered introductions or shared contacts: Kamini Mahadevan; M. Kannan; S.C. Chandrahasan; Kannan

Arunasalam; Suba Sivakumaran; Sumathy Sivamohan; Mahesh Pathirathna; Menaka Balendra; Darshan Ambalavanar; Carlos Mena; Gayathri Fernando; Asiff Hussein; Sirinimal Lakdusinghe; Anura Manatunga; P.K. Balachandran; Ambika Satkunanathan; Mirak Raheem; S. Sivagurunathan; Morgan Meis and Stefany Anne Goldberg; Ahilan Kadirgamar; Sunila Galappatti; Anton Jeyanathan; Jeyanthy Siva; Ram Balasubramaniyam; B.D.K. Saldin; Sunil Wijesiriwardene; Nirmal Dewasiri; Indi Samarajiva; Pradeep Jeganathan; Jeyasankar Sivagnanam; Shehan Karunatilaka.

In Canada: Meena Nallainathan; Namu Ponnambalam; David Poopalapillai; P. Kasinathan; Cheran Rudramoorthy; Kumaran Nadesan; Kanaga Manoharan; the wonderfully named George Ckrhushchev; Aranee Muruganathan.

My thanks to the OMI International Arts Center, for allowing me to be a resident for two weeks in the fall of 2013—two glorious weeks in which I found various ways to avoid writing and gaze at the Catskills instead. Also to my employers at the *National* in Abu Dhabi, for giving me the time I needed to research this book.

My gratitude to the manuscript's first readers, for taking the trouble to send me their thoughts and their encouragement: Padmaparna Ghosh; Ayeshea Perera; Jonathan Shainin; Ravi Venkatesh; Amarnath Amarasingam.

Nandini Mehta and Chiki Sarkar of Penguin Books India were staunch and early believers in my ideas, and their edits helped immeasurably. Nothing would have happened without Shruti Debi, whose vision and acuity became my constant touchstones, and who saw far earlier than I did what this book could become.

Most importantly, I could have done no writing at all without the constant, unquestioning support from my parents, and from Harini and Padma. Thank you for tolerating my silences, my moods and my obsessions. This is your book as much as it is mine.